0.174

The Complete Numbers Cycle

Gordon Massman's 0.174: The Complete Numbers Cycle is an intricate exposure of the self. In this 20 years' culmination of work, he has dared to make the invisible visible. Perhaps on some level a perverse project, 0.174 lays open in depth-confession, in laboratory precision Massman's innermost fantasies, obsessions, urges, and fears which might, he hopes, provide at least a splintered reflection into one's own humanity. In either case—whether private or universal—here opens an increasingly cathartic examination of Massman's particular psychology observed as acutely and honestly as he is capable. In so doing he has treated what mainstream society generally considers vulgar or unsavory, as valuable and often beautiful. It is his hope that some who attempt this book will agree that all human thought and feeling is worthy of song. Often satirical in tone, this book represents the nekyia, the down, inward going, of an epic tale that is life itself.

0.174

The Complete Numbers Cycle

Gordon Massman

The New York Quarterly Foundation, Inc.
New York, New York

NYQ Books™ is an imprint of The New York Quarterly Foundation, Inc.

The New York Quarterly Foundation, Inc.
P. O. Box 2015
Old Chelsea Station
New York, NY 10113

www.nyqbooks.org

Copyright © 2011 by Gordon Massman

All rights reserved. No part of this book may be used or reproduced in any manner whatsoever without written permission of the author. This book is a work of fiction. Any references to historical events, real people or real locales are used fictitiously. Other names, characters, places, and incidents are products of the author's imagination, and any resemblance to actual events or locales or persons, living or dead, is entirely coincidental.

First Edition

Set in New Baskerville

Layout and Design by Raymond P. Hammond
Cover Design and Artwork, "Fear of Anaesthesia" ©2009, by Noah Saterstrom | www.noahsaterstrom.com

Library of Congress Control Number: 2011921532

ISBN: 978-1-935520-44-3

0.174

The Complete Numbers Cycle

Acknowledgments

Another Chicago Magazine, Antioch Review, Artful Dodge, Black Dirt, Blue Monk, Borderlands, Caketrain, Carleton Arts Review, Chelsea, Columbia Poetry Review, Confrontation, Connecticut Poetry Review, Contemporary Voice 2, Cortland Review, Court Green, Cutbank, The Fiddlehead, Fire, Flyway, Georgia Review, Green Mountain Review, Karamu, Harpweaver, Left Curve, Greensboro Review, Harvard Review, Hiram Poetry Review, Iron, Left Curve, Libido, The Literary Review, Many Mountains Moving, The Malahat Review, New York Quarterly, Old Crow Review, Paperplates, Paperbag, Pavement Saw, Penny Dreadful, Pleiades, Poetrybay, Porcupine, Prairie Journal, Prism International, Quarter After Eight, Rampike, Rattle, Response, Tarpaulin Sky, Third Coast, Toronto Quarterly, Windless Orchard, Willow Springs, Windsor Review, Yellow Silk

Special thanks to the editors of Tarpaulin Sky Press, Pavement Saw Press, Six Gallery Press, and Spork Chapbooks where many of these poems appeared in book form.

for William H. Lyons,
psychoanalyst,
who saved me from the flames.

The splinter in the eye is the best magnifying glass.
—*Theodor Odorno*

If the book we are reading does not wake us, as with a fist hammering on our skull, why then do we read it? Good God, we would also be happy if we had no books, and such books as make us happy we could, if need be, write ourselves. But what we must have are those books which come upon us like ill-fortune, and distress us deeply, like the death of one we love better than ourselves, like suicide. A book must be an ice-axe to break the sea frozen inside us.
—*Franz Kafka*

1

I would like to go into the office next to mine
—it belongs to Dean, a kind, sweet man—
and just sit and cry. I would like to sit and
cry, sit and cry without inhibition, shoulders
shuddering, big tears rolling down my
hands. I would like to wander into his office
with its filing cabinets, sticky notes, and
bulletin board, sit in his client chair, and cry
for nothing and for everything. "Love," I
might mutter, "mountains," "children,"
dissimilar words pulled from a larger and
deeper phrase whose meaning I lost long
ago. How nice it would be to crumble before a man, without shame or guilt, to curl
into a sculpture of pain and hopelessness
and fall apart. As simple as a blossom
widening before sun, a man aware of his
humanity. I would like to go into Dean's
office for he is a kind, sweet man, no
longer a boy nor yet an adult opportunist and, solvent of bone, muscle and
curvature of skin disassemble in a chair
in the center of the day, to say in that
soundless abyss underlying words: understanding is emptiness, vision is puncturing,
and loss a bubble expanding in our hands.

2

To lay a sheet of light over a sheet of dark
over a sheet of light over a sheet of dark
like a pastry formed of filo dough, light,dark,
light,dark,light,dark until the whole personality
is included, sadness over joy over love over shame,
to lay sheet over sheet of flaky delicacy
so easily hurt and devoured, yet so delicious.
And there you are gorgeous and valuable and
acquiescent and whole whose feet stand you up,
and smile snaps you level, and hope pulls your
great frightened mass of aliveness through the world,
and fear shoves you back, and obstinacy leans
you forward into the claws of the wind, and
beauty sears your eyes into the fire of desire
("Holy shit!" he mutters about a stunner in
his vision), and grief sits you down on your ass
like a boulder, and jubilation flings your blood
into the circles of the air, and greed grabs need
and rips out throats, and joy electrifies toes
into dance, and rage explodes your breast
like a mushroom cloud in reverse, and agape
flattens you into an inner-planetary hug, and lust
returns you into a bullet splitting air,
and tenderness hurls you over-the-falls,
and love,love,love alternately reconstructs you
stronger and cracks your bones one by one—
the cartilage in your nose, the match
sticks of your fingers and toes, the bell house
of your skull, the chalk of your thigh bones,
the brittle timber of your ribs, and packed sand
of your hips—all crushed like a ruby-throated
thrush under the enormous closing pressure
of the valentine fist. So go easy, be kind
to the oozing baklava, the popover, the puff-
pastry stuffed with blueberry, blackberry, almond,
or pecan; the spinach and feta strudel
wrapped in buttered gauze; the deep-dish
pie steaming from the oven, bubbling, tantalizing,
gold around the edges with a yielding heart....

3

Gently, but authoritatively,
he swipes her with the blunt arc of his paw,
gurgles, then rolls onto her,
his mane tumbling to one side, like wheat.
She growls, pushes him as if away
with only one surge of her boundless will,
then opens to admit his vibrating bridge,
which he lowers into her, like a wish,
and, in honest witness of the sun,
the Baobab trees and the nation of cranes,
in the cradle of the sweet-grass,
the ticking bugs, and the shooting fronds,
in the center of a golden field,
their fur softened in the heat, like beds,
they free the beams inside their breasts
through slits they rip with passion-claws
in each other's skin. The bright beams flow,
the blood-red rush of evening's flood
slammed off their living walls and
shot into the stars, until, spent, they
lie splayed, like calla lilies, leg-petals
fallen open, on their backs, mouths
slack, dozing in the dying sun. Human
beings, muscled, belligerent, elemental,
arms and chest capable of applying
an enormous number of pounds of pressure
per square inch, territorial, and dense—
tendons extending to the ends of their fingers
powering the grip—
don't try to come between one and his mate.
It would be to stick one's hand in a mill.
Even the most meek, upon feeling piqued,
finds his thumb in a fist or his forefinger
on the eyelash trigger of a gun.
What happens when a woman splits her thighs
to let her man in, climbs up his balls,
is something more than nerves and flesh,
or the ignition of hot blood.
I see it with my side vision in your feet
in the rush of copulation—
strong, blunt, underestimated, ecstatically
arched, stiff, V-ing toward the sky
as if you were pulling some primitive law

through the sap of your toes: the statute
of ownership and the interlock of knowledge.
We know each other, and therein
form beliefs. We, all of us, are so
adorable: the furniture of the eyes
(brows, lashes, curves), the tenderness
of the lips, the sweet groove along
the contour of the spine, nipples
and areolas, the rounded curves
of the sex, the soft halos of hair,
the beauty of the Achilles phrase
tapering to the slender heel,
but just beneath the surface
of the skin, like an inserted metal plate,
lies the hard muscle, the tight net
of selfishness, jealousy, desire,
the fear of hollowness, in-
satiability, hunger, pride, the howling
for completion, greed, insecurity,
possessiveness, the need to nurture,
the need to fold in, knowledge,
knowledge, knowledge which once inhaled
creates us.
It is playful, but deadly serious,
the having of a mate,
and the males have very sharp knuckles.

4

Afterward, he wondered about the enormous and complex
connectedness, the intertwining of tendrils delving
deep into the ground, the DNA spiral of love and histories
plunging into dark loam their inextricable root systems
of dependencies and desires. He thought of the apparent
simplicity of cows, sweet, brown-and-white spotted Holsteins
who mount each other in open fields, multiply, and low;
who shake their necks and wander off into valleys
stupid and indifferent. He stared at his chock full
bookshelves, the multi-colored spines of novels and non-
fiction, the encyclopedias and dictionaries, the OED, the tome
titled "Dissection of the Vertebrates" and wanted to hide.
The blinds rattled from a mountain breeze as he lay
with her—cactus needle, aspen leaf, and cottonwood spume
fragrances filling their dusk-rich room. How huge, he pondered,
are our heads, like great glass globes scrimshawed with
complex geographies and delicate intricacies. They bang
against one another on ordinary strolls through public streets,
cracking at times, like fault lines. Pride straining
the faint capacity of weak necks. Afterward, he gloried
in the rich confusion of being human, the intermixtures
of love and reticence, the textured knowledges, the almost
infinite possibilities. His eyes rolled, like sparkling
marbles, wobbling to the source. He felt so blessed he wanted to
prick his finger to see the dark blood. He wanted to suck
his toes to feel the pillow tongue. "Contours," he thought,
the word "contours," "curves," "sensuality," "bones," "tendons,"
"knees," "words." The unfathomable alphabet of longing, the
refusal to stop wanting. This is life. Wanting is life. His
penis felt cold surrounded by air, by the room, the breeze
drawing across it, like water. He thought of the agony of his parents
in Texas, in Corpus Christi— "Body of Christ." How his father,
paranoid, guilty, and ashamed bruised his mother, knocked her
onto cold bathroom tiles; how he pops his pills. So beautiful
and tragic. He felt like a fish quivering on a hook. He
thought of beautiful diners at outdoor cafes, under the shadow
of mountains, sipping coffees, flicking sandaled toes, and
speculating on the attributes of future lovers. How gentle
the bed sheets felt on his face—floral and new—as he lay
with his palm tucked under her thigh and his toenails brushing her
foot bones. What landslides fall within the skin, what acts
of confusion. Clear, his love for her, unquestionable—that is
not the issue—but life, like rock, pulls down. "What did you say?" he

blurted, but she had said nothing. He thought that if he
could retrace his life back to the fork, back through
the tree-and-leaf-crowded path to the critical point,
and progress anew…but that would be false and suicidal.
He would lose the one woman he loves. How packed hard
the earth is. "Oh" he thought, "what a plethora." Where
are the cows lumbering on simple femurs to the lovely slaughter?
He looked at his watch and it was 7:15. Afterward, he felt
the dark dilation that normally accompanies him, the flooding largeness,
the pool of ecstasy and blurred boundaries. Populations of
women and men bled into his pores, like trickling fjords,
like finger lakes, and settled in his heart, as he bled
through them. Lost borders. Stretched head. Melted. But
focused, too, and sharp as steel. The contradictions. The
conundrums. If skin had pockets he could have slid notes in
to calm himself after the water rushed away. The baby wriggling
in its crib. The mother's throat. The easy sleep. Afterward…
after what?…fusion?…union?…coitus? After breaking apart
he thought of the swerve on ice, the soundless slide,
life turning sidewise on its axis. He thought not about
loss of control but the inexorable fact of motion. And once again
cows appeared in his dreams—heavy, docile, dumb, and—
oh, what does he know of cow, cow love, cow sadness, cow joy,
cow complexity? They lumber head down, chests sagging, bones
sticking out, like scaffolding, burdened perhaps with the failure
of the world. Dispel this myth, man, of omniscience. All
he knows is that he loves the woman, that she fills him, that
he's loved by her, that he was born sticky and wild through
his mother's loins, that life seems like a black-ice skid
sometimes when he shuts his eyes. All he knows is what's
in the concavity. Afterward, all his variables in unison sang
of the clear, hard realities: the lamp, the desk, the
chair, the bath tub, time's fine blows on the sun-thickened
window sill. Of those he sang,
and of life's spectacular uncertainties.

5

I want to pour children, like a pitcher of water,
through the hallways of my company: waifs, urchins,
gamins, orphans, brats, prima donnas, toddlers in
diapers, darlings of the upper-class; to roll them outward,
like a basket of eggs, from which individually
they would burst, whole and adorable. What a
mountain breeze that would be. What an exhalation.
To see them shrieking through the halls: the bow-legged
babies, the mischievous grade-schoolers, the lawless
pre-adolescents hole-punching the memo pads, defacing
the fax machine, dancing with in-boxes on their heads.
Primitive energy in this stale old hospital, like
the pulse of jungle drums. There in Matthew's office
Frederick pounds dumpling fists, wads Scotch
tape, coos fresh policy from his pouch of sweet
breath, and poops the Presidential chair. And little Sally
dirt-smeared, direct, and dictatorial pontificates
from Spencer's air. From outside our structure would appear
a bastion of multi-national efficiency, but inside
Justin would be yanking Debbie's hair, Chloe dumping
client files, and a barnyard of pigs, chickens, goats,
and hogs frolicking on the plains. Yes, I want to
reconstitute my office because I am sick of this
stiff-back sitting, this wrecking of spontaneity,
this snuffing of the soul. We were elected to be
their mentors, not their subduers. Let them miss the
urinals by a country mile, let them glop the rubber
cement. It's not a matter of disrespect, but of
keeping unpetrified. And I'm not an insurrectionist.
I want to loose a puddle of children from my palms, like
a genie who's scooped fertile mud: an ooze of hearts
jumping, a tadpole-like whipping through the
meticulous rooms. Sharpen pencils to the nub, bawl
for mother in a blast of honesty. We have failed
with our bright red pop cans, our cell phones,
our steroidal meat. We have served up hell in the
guise of success. Are you ashamed or is your pride
too steep? Have you been so inculcated that you can't
find the seams? Did you father's fist seal your brain,
and your mother's screams? Can you rebuild the citadel?
I want to release them, like a spasm of sea lice,
en masse, agglomerated, bricked-together, who are
abandoned by divorce, dragged screaming by the wrists,

criticized, beaten, taught lessons, sexually abused,
exploited, desolidified, in horrible times flipped in
the air, caught on saber blades, and occasionally loved;
to see them burst through the doors, explode into joy,
bubble the atmosphere, oh, seed the labyrinths! Until then
I will ache for the crack in the core which lets them in.

6

See me slice down the face of a wave, like
paring knife and potato, strips and curlicues
stiffening, then raining across the tube; a
thundergod. This is no metaphor. I am surfing
Port Aransas, Texas, on Sunday, wetsuited,
February, cold offshore breeze. A rare jewel
of a day in what is usually split pea soup.
Doesn't a teenage boy have the right to a little
fun without a parent chasing him, like a pig?
The waves feel powerful, like Behemoth humps
rising out a floor and rolling forward in rage.
Do you know how freeing it feels to control such
power? My "friend," that anti-Semitic thug,
freaked on weed, drowned here last summer,
choking, like a cat. Good for the Jewish sea!
Over my back the horizon rises into a bowl
of blue sky, nothing but seamless shades
of azure, cerulean, blue-green, baby blue,
sapphire, aquamarine, and crystal beads of water
blurring my eyes. The immensity out there.
I sit on the continent of my WeberPerformer,
Rodin's "The Thinker" with legs immersed in
water, flunking school. I'm nothing for books.
See my Jams and black skin flash against the sun,
myself a fin on a finned thing. What it would be
like, I wonder, to slip it to a girl
at night on a sand dune; to slip it
to Sheri Long, for instance, that dripping
babe, or Dianne Wyneken? Watch me carve
this wave. No, no. It's just a serpent
sliding under me. This one, then. Oops,
another snake. A sea-vat of snakes. Let one
raise its cobra-head and I'll show you how
to ride it down its cold belly to the tail,
and kick out before it kills. That's
what I can do. Oh, to fuck Dianne Wyneken.
Oh, my gonads! What a bodily lurch to be
alive, sproutings everywhere, like a thorn
tree. I want to slice open my breast
and sing. I sometimes imagine the bleeding
crimson line as I razor down the center
of my chest, pull apart the walls, and
release what's there—a flock of birds and

dicks. I'm all feel. Blue are my hands,
blue my lips. Let's bring it in on one
last big wave, like the one on the album cover
monstrous and feathering, and probably roaring,
like a firestorm. Yes! Yes! Here it comes!
Free. Free. The prison door trembles
to fling open, at last.

7

And when I pulled a ribbon fish from the deep—
my God, it looked like a lethal umbilicus—
my father shrieked, "Look out, a shitsky!"
and he ripped the rod from my wrist so I would not get
sliced by its teeth. It shimmied and flicked,
brilliant snake, like a strip of razor wire,
flinging blood and silvery waterdrops everywhere.
But the pliers came, needle-nose, and down crushed
the foot over its flattened length, and my father
ripped out its guts with the treble hook and flung
it back into the blue-green deep. Stunning beast,
primeval, head full of teeth, instinctively darted
down like a sunbeam, before dying. On the deck
its blue-red throat, slime, clots of gore, a slash mark
were all that remained. The boat rocked in the sloughs,
like a cradle, and a pelican stared indifferent as a rock
as the clouds sailed by. And then later under the hammer
sky, I shrimped my hook, waited, my lips parched and
un-soda-popped (we drank them dry), my baseball cap shielding
my Jew eyes, I hauled up a dogfish, spiny, dangerous,
useless, tough; it bloated, croaked, dared me to touch
its urchin spines. He came again, this time gloved,
ripped the pole from my hands and, grabbing the line
three feet above the fish, like a sling with a stone
tied to the end, bashed it against the side of the boat.
Swung and bashed, swung and bashed, the dark weight
hooked in the throat-bones hanging on to this hellish
ride. But soon its tail began to explode, like plastic
strips, flying apart, pieces spiraling through
the air, gray and pink, sticking in its own black
blood to the prow, and then, its sides frayed and
split, spikes and needles spewing outward, like exploding glass,
its body slammed into a pulp, until finally it slid off
the hook into the grave of its birthplace. All that
remained of this Shylock fish: blast marks, black spots,
whip burns, where it hit and hit the side of our
ship. I stood like an emperor in his Colosseum
and watched. Sea wind parted my locks, sea gulls
swooped, and little pools of water soaked
my feet. It's not profound to say the great ocean
swallows its dead, like a mother, sealing the
wounds they make sliding in. After the pink and blue
ripple, the violence, the splatter of guts, a mirror

closed over the wound and the back-sloughs shone,
quiet as glitter. There is a craft skimming over
cold water, an Evinrude, pieces of raw flesh and
cutbait, an aerator sparse with shrimp bits, tackle
boxes, rods, reels, bloody hands, gaff and fish net,
boatsides nicked and cut, curved, like swan wings,
and a boy and his dad gliding over radiance toward home.

8

Oh Popsy-baby, let me have myself straight from the
palm-open of your heart, delivered like a pearl on
an oyster tongue, let me have my surfer hair to flip
sidewise like a cock-butt, let me have my indolence—
I'm 13 big ones and an individualist. Don't flush
the toilet on my head. Oh Daddyboy give me my blood
sticky & red to fling into my flesh like a string,
my blood/your blood without unleashing that red scream,
"Grow Up!" Daddyhead stop working so much and catch
my ball screwily flung into your mitt. What's so great
about a cigarette machine in a beer joint, that cold
green steel and quarter spill, filthy, slick? The
little money sack? Oh Daddyfuck put your bristly
mouth-beard over my snail-lips and give me mouth-to-mouth
in the parking lot, my head slunk back 'cause I'm yer
come mixed with mumby-egg. Draw me a map, let me
scrap with a handful of dollarfilth and a rustbike,
free like an emancipite in the seawind, hair blowing
in a whipfest and tan laying on, 'cause you don't care
if your boy's himself in his sandy blown town, with
An Attitude, you've applied artificial resuscitation
and his lungs 'r pumpin' in his cellophane membrane,
you betcher life, your son by God full of Bar Mitzvah,
hamantaschen, and himself. Oh daddybum don't blow
brains out like yuv yapped about off & on again, rather
lunge and tackle me shoulderpadded with the tucked-
in pig. I'm going fast, like a tinderfire
enveloped in ageflame: acne, facehair, full bush,
headed for goneness but for a burnmark on the
pinefloor. See the firepit of my loins. See
my branches flame. Then I'll be the lotus opener
and you'll be petrified in rage, old prunepit, canyon-
pile, dungstone. Old fathermine. Don't do it.
Don't pop those cockpills all night in their pill bins,
so coffinesque—diazepam & sleep hammer—nor cuddle
EST like a shock-junkie, no, go, for me, into the scare
house on the hill of your psyche, find the killers,
cry, shatter teeth, fling on the lights and make them
fly—bats—cloud of fears into the sun-strike bleeding
dry and white, so that you & I might, Daddypot & boy-
tyke, dance our feet stinging on this dazzling rind. Please.

9

In the penis colony the men lounge in overstuffed
chairs near the hot buffet talking statistics
and percentages. The ceiling cathedrals and
the sounds are carpeted. Pipes of pin-stripes
stove their legs, socked and gartered in Bergdorf's,
and a signet ring corsets every third piggy. In
the penis colony the chef stuffs an apple between
guilt's snout, bakes it pink and blade-succulent, and
serves it in a glaze of shame sauce. All goes down
easy through the gullet of rage. "What say we have
a game," one suggests, all cheer, the mansion rocks,
and they pull out a gorgeous one from the stock
room: sexy-wet, fresh, full blush, cotton blouse,
untouched, adorable. Her little lungs heave.
"A blonde!" one looking like Mr. Monopoly Tycoon
shouts, and in a swarm the sport ensues. One
tenderly, upon his knees, proposes matrimony, hee!
hee! hee!, another lays down, as if over mud, his
glistening coat, deeply bows, and another pours
her a pink champagne while the face-blacked one
posing as the butler bolts the door. Then, one
plucks at her: a hair, a brow, a titty-tit-tit,
and getting very hot, all chime in. A welt of blood
back-floods and surges through the stump as one rips
off her apricot ear, three or four firmly plant
shoes and tear out an arm—have you ever seen
that gristle and bone rainbow in the baked chicken
leg?—and fall to, eating, one gouges out a gold-
flecked eye and pops it, like an egg, and several
wishing on a side, split her in two by the legs.
And the ritual begins: out come the knives. The
President gets the liver, the Vice President the
spleen, the Treasurer the stomach, the Secretary
her pancreas, the Sergeant-At-Arms both kidneys, and
to the members, the loyal members go the intestines
(both king and queen), the uterus, the appendix,
the fallopian tubes, the eggs, the bladder, the sails
of the lungs, the brain, the lips, the slab of the
tongue, the esophagus, and all the scraps, a feast
beyond the believable, while outside under the
sweltering glow, along the skeleton of the city,
glide the oblivious commuters in glossy steel
bubbles. Afterward they scrape clean the
counter. Her heart they throw to Fi-Fi the poodle.

10

I've taken flight like a flashing colorbird,
quick-winged, darting for the greening foothills,
over the speartops and the greenblades, whirring
like some kind of tissue machine, sweetly
into the Blue-Blue; scarlet-streaked, emerald-
swathed, golden-topped I am; Tinkerbellbird
hovering into the honey tube, beak-dipping,
streaking for red trumpets, and climbing, fruit-
fueled—cantaloupe, nectarine, blackberry,
apricot—light-like, flitting on slumberjoy,
flush with iridescence. Within my atmosphere swirl
the computer, the MasterCard bill, the antiseptic
tube, Fresca and her contemporaries, and the
shrapnel shell turning nebula-esque about
my chest—hefty things stuffed with wheels
& gears, which I, birdily, could scarcely lift. Mama
stardusts up with me, like a wake, Daddy sparkles,
and babies Milky Way as I flash & flit—birdboy,
hummerman. You'll know I've been through by
the trembling bluebells, the shivering feeders,
and the bulleted aspen leaves. No waxwinged
Icarus—dilettante!, experimental boy!—woozy with
arrogance elevatored to his dripdrip, I hover, spin,
wheel, catapult backward (split-tailed), bow, and
burrow into the honeypile, like the court jester
booming on rocket fuel—now that I couldn't care
less, now that life's nowhere, now that earth's
exposed itself as a helmetful of…HA!…now that
I know The Secret—which I'm not revealing—though
it involves the fact that Dreams mean nothing,
money is immaterial, science is a bit of flat-
ulence, the family is a cup of fog, and your
favorite tree—the one spray-painted green on
your brain—isn't. I wrap my arms around "so what,
big deal" like a hippo-big soap bubble, and
suddenly I'm shooting nimbus-ward, skydrilling,
midair halting, tail feathers ashovel. Slim Pickens
slapped the sides of The Bomb with his hat as
he rode it down, his life gone mad—a symbol of
The Recognition—and I roll, soul-blown, free
of relevance, fuck it all—it's okay, it's
unbelievably fine, it's not important anymore,
or even real—nevermind what—we all abandon Daddy
in our own way—bye-bye. And this particular
day I'm vibra-happy, punch-silly, and ecto-stunning,
and I'm borne on air, effortlessly, in full skeleton.

11

If I could stick my tongue through the fat portion
of my palm, completely through so that it waggles on
the other side, like a worm or a soft sword; there
I would find God: an ordinary tongue, an ordinary
hand, but an extraordinary moment—a tongue penetrating
the soft lips of a hand which water-close around it
when withdrawn. God would be there—I am certain—
where the flesh gave way to the wetness, where the
little opening parted for the rooting tip, magically.
This fertile garden in the palm of a hand is where
the true sanctuaries on earth reside; where priest,
deity, and prayer converge in one act of privacy. The
tongue is sweet, like an apricot; the hand salty,
like a sea; and the tissue and blood within the hand
are thick, sticky and pushing, like a wall. I think
of joists and hinges, bolts and headnuts, but here
there is no grinding, gouging, nor dust of saw. It
is almost sex. There are sacred places—grottoes—
where self collides with self sans robes and hymnals—
where the red mouth of a dog breathes in dusk, and
the jewel of a wildcat's eye flares. Try it in your
tattered clothes, in your destitution-cell, with ash
smeared on elbows, and love gone mad. If I could
stick my tongue through the fat of my hand—there's
a blue crab clamped to my heart, a blue crab is
clamped to my heart, something leapt on me at birth
which was blue and hard and it clamped to my heart,
my heart wears the lid of a blue crab shell, the
first three beings I laid eyes on were my mother, my
father, and a broad blue crab—if I could stick my
tongue through the fat of my hand, like a sun-
slash through sky, without anyone noticing, in the
solitude of my room, God would appear, like a sea
floor after the moon draws up the gown into its
globe. There's a knife and there's the robe and
there's the secret soon beneath the robe. The hand
splits and the palm becomes lips, eye, vagina, and
the entering tongue self-love flooding. We all
crumble a little inside. If I—if you—could pass
material through itself, your fists might unrage,
letting milk pour in. Raise your hand to your lips,
finesse your tongue, in your mind slide it through.

12

Like a field of soy beans the pets keep renewing themselves—
those who desire cat, dog, bird, turtle, fish, reptile
harvest, like itinerants in a sweltering blaze. And the little
ones squeal and whine and cheep and cuddle, like teacups
full of Hersheys and mallows, and totter like fur balls, or crane
prehistoric necks through reticulated shells, scimitar beaks
shredding the lettuce, and pieces of poop squiggle out their
butts onto the rug, or squirt into the tank like bits of All
Bran, and the children giggle as hamster travels in its plastic
ball across the floor like a performing bear, and tails wiggle,
and teeth tear, and fishbone claws rip, and bellies slither,
and one infant lizard clings to a wall like Spiderman, and
all the Christmas babies peek from their boxes through big
fluffy ribbon and chew at the bow round their neck, and
leap their whole sack of guts into the air like jubilant
soldiers, and all of them—tortoise shell or brindle or tabby
or piebald or miniature or standard or shorthair or silver-
point—nudge their bowls, crunch, tear down through wet
pink tubes tasty strings of God, while the old bearded,
sagging, ragged, arthritic, glaucomatous, stroked out, senile,
toothless ones alive beyond their biblical ladder, arithmetically
computed in human years, explode on stairs, stiffen by
walls, weave through rooms, retrieve in dreams, copulate
in visions, bloat in bedrooms, fall off ledges, and lie
horrifically in corners with their limbs stuck out like road-
killed deer. Babies leap on the spot they once warmed with
their gray engorged bellies, rehabilitate the acres of air
they once invigorated. Claws of the dying curled under like
ram's bones drag along pavements behind red leashes.
See them die sweetly, adoringly, with snouts in our hands, or
desiccated heads pathetic as cobwebs. For every two
bushels of the deceased or dying a wall of newborns rushes
forward packed with spiky face of spider monkey, scaly
face of iguana, slender face of salamander, rottweiler, Angora,
Chihuahua, angelfish, tarantula, cockatoo, Siamese, bluntnose
milkshake, bottlebrush of ferret, French lop-ear, anemone,
squid, angel-fish, the entire fluffcloud of the puppy kingdom,
and every couch-shredding, flesh-pricking, god-slashing, eye-
slitting cuteness of feline architecture in this contemptuous
world. The wall rushes forth like a veined ocean muscle,
spilling animals into our gaping caves the instant Old
Faithful's heart breaks like a dam of unqualified adoration in
his manger-bed. And your mother dies like a sheen upon the

sea, and your father bursts like a goat spleen, and the surgeon cracks the sternum of your therapist, and locusts eat the cerebellum of the anthropologist, and sixty-eight blip off the radar screen, and Guinevere is raped, strangled, and rolled into a garbage bin, and the channel glasses over the ferry boat, and your grandparents' fingers turn to rot-iron in the sod, and each of us tilts our head toward the great blistering ball while the surging wave of a wall cleanses the surface of the earth and delivers the waiting whelps into our hands.

13

I pluck our baby from your womb and stick it under the skin of my midriff. I, male, am pregnant! I do what woman does. I nurture the child in my warm fluid while its heart crashes against my palm. I groan and eat and witness the miraculous upheavals as the world rushes and recedes in significance. I steal the babe and slip it in the mesa above my penis under the hairswirl and abs in my little pocket of perfection. If you are bereft I am full, no longer a busker's black balloon sculpted into a pirate's sword on the mall. I have curves and globes and the Bulge and the beautiful blue womb. I cry. I flare with rage. I bathe in the sumptuous tub of my soul free of the disgusting violence flesh wreaks upon flesh in the abattoir of the world. I am thief, yes, and plunderer— but am cucumber and glycerin too. I let you—artist and artist's pad—sketch me plumped under brocaded down. My feet are clean and pink, like yeast. How sick I am of the motherfuckers, the pile drivers breaking and crushing lives, the annihilators, the snap-and-eaters, meathunger. I slip our zygote under my gown and wait for the nurturing impulse to slam—here in my wrists and larynx. We are in bed, our feet sticking out the sides like porpoises! Peace of the room's quietude flows into my nostrils, and through. I am content. I am fulfilled. I am terrified. I rip the waist of my pants to make them fit, and my breasts grow tender, yes. I snatch the baby in my beak—nest robber—and slip it in, and this is a sudden and unforgivable violent act, my last. I see my amniotically dripping hand. I see my hate. I see envy's tongue retract, emancipatorily. I see you weep. I see the pink tissues turn brown. I see you crumple, like a soggy stick. I see darkness resmear your face. I see the loss, an empty pocketbook. I see the wail bubble your lips. I see my bigness increase. Being human—soul and teeth—I am capable of embracing rich dichotomies but being male and for my funneling flame, I deprive you of everything.

14

I like the feel of cutting fruit—the pine-like
crispness of an apple; the way juice from a Bosc
pear sluices along the knife blade; the kiwi; ba-
nana; cassava; mango; or cutting unorthodoxly
across orange section, like one shattering
windows; the way apricot rises and gives birth
along cold steel—I am an animal—the manipulation
of the knife in my fingers, the way the handle
presses along my palm, like a baby mouse or the
materialization of my mother's voice. See the
grapefruit rind split open like a cry and weep
its milky tears on the slender flash and divide
fully, its two round halves to the cutting wood;
the watermelon; the fig with its bag of seeds.
I could kill. I could bare the beauty of human
flesh to the moon, liquid red swirled with sil-
ver light, white of bone shot with blue. What
kind of monster might I be? The grape peel bursts
and yields its filament veins to pure air, del-
icate green flesh clear as amniotica. And the
explosions of taste, human milk shot from tough
nipples into the mouths of babes, their heads
receiving, pliable little legs dangling over
cliffs of air. I love the feel of cutting fruit, like
fingerblood, plum red, oozing through an accident.
There are the bodies of men and women lacerated
by car steel, bleeding beautifully, hanging from
fresh-torn hooks, like dead chickens,. There are
the opal bruises and the blackened eyes which
are rainbow blue and green touched with gold,
and iridescent. There are the colors of danger and
disaster and ultimate demise. The juices pop and
arc onto July 4th grass, fat and green, as Stars
& Stripes Forever outwardly spill. We are all
imperilled by our disease of wounds and wounding.
There. The tomato pours forth a flood like a
ruptured nose, and the raisin stops the flow. Moth-
er, mother, when they wheeled you to the ICU
tangled in four heart-plunged tubes, you were sluic-
ing blood, fine long threads which looped in air
and recirculated back through one leg, and I was
your little boy again in sun-parched shoes crying,
"Mama, Mama,"—human fruit, both of us. The ac-

cident plows. We look up. We have broad chests. The father waits. The mother knows. The children sing. The baby rests. Under my hand, along the knife blade, the fruit of the world trembles and gushes forth its seeds and meat and sugars and hair and pools and sheets and pattern and core, a plentiful shell—a precious cave—which empties beautifully and thickens my fingers, like a necessary disaster.

15

Cut the tip of my finger slicing turkey
the day before your heart surgery, Mom, my
memorial to knives and blood. Took four months
to heal and even then, tender, like a shuddering
bell. Mom and son, Jewish, hooked, a couple
of losers. The surgeon cracked you through,
sewed you up, now you're fine save for the
two long worms crawling chest and thigh. Now,
I've broken up with my sweetie pie, my
finger's fine, you're paddling the wading
pool, the sun's banging, and the sky's
some cerulean eye scooping us both, a shovel.
No girl's going to rise up—your prediction—
and slaughter me with a butcher knife, because
there's no girl, 'cept you, mom, with your
bristly beard. I give up. I masturbate to
your red toe nails. Not that I wanted you
to die but a little liberation theology from the
grave wouldn't hurt—did you know, PS, I was
the only family member to cry. Besides, you
bleed money and I want mine. I'm forty-five.
Our lives are joined by their garbage—you've
got Dad and I've got you. You refuse to die.
Look at the little wooly lamb from behind,
so cute, like the back of my head. Don't
swing me round for not even God understands
my face. Now, healed—my finger, your prolapsed
valve—the earth burned clean we walk upon,
I search the personals ads for a new victim:
fit, blonde, blue eyes, looking for romance.
Even monsters try. How ugly all this is
oozing from my brain, like pus. I'm ashamed.
But there it is. You have maybe ten years and
I about thirty-five and by god geraniums in
hot garages have done better, thus far. I press
planets in my eyes. I'm glad you didn't die
and that dad's, I hear, now holding your hand
(the guilt must be piled), but I'm going to
stick the claw end of my hammer into your
eye, somehow, and remove you, like a nail, though
it be my last bursting, boiling, emancipatory piece
of effort this side of the God Blow. That's all.

16

It is the epoch of corporate inhumanity, officious shits
darting about office-places laying off people in the name
of efficiency, big corporations with knock-out logos
presided over by men. The eye glazes over. There are
snaking members stretching into the pouches of distant
women—all powerful appendages—octopus men driving
hard bargains; starvation in the guise of gluttony—glut-
tony in the eyes of starvation. Dumpsters grow empty
while the anthropologists of garbage multiply—a greasy
wrapper, a half-filled cup. Blood in the veins flows
like lava, dignity or not, life's red rush feeds the brain
under skull's cap, hears from the boss, "Lousy luck…sorry…
had no choice." A gull dies in thick oil. There it is,
a perfect film: character, conflict, denouement. The
drain swirls down a person's life. I wretch home in
my hobbling car, another sorry story told, to the boy
of the dream shattered or gone, my abandoned offspring,
angry on guitar. It is a swell period, a humdinger, a
polished chrome time in the profit bowl, in the tech-
nology pit, digitals streaming across the eye, the
Cyclopean screen switched on, like a screaming mouth
tight and wide. I want to pick up a piece of string, a
dirty warm thing, map of a past, drenched in child's
dry spittle, clutch it, roll it in my fingers, feel its
bumpy progress, savor the tiny history inscribed therein:
sensory, primal, basic as a sow grunting in mud or
clods flying from a horse's flight, jam it in my pocket,
like a piece of life unbroken by dehumanizing circuitry.
It is the epoch of betrayal, force-down decisions, karate
blows to the spine. Now it is time to chant, "All is
lost, all is nothing," at the terminal, at the work
station, at the virtual world, "All is lost, all is nothing,"
through the coffee steam, "All is beyond, all is over,"
like a flock of cranes gliding home, "All is—"
whatever word you wish to insert for devastation.
Time to give your heart's flesh to its eater, to shave your
head, to cup river water in your palms, time to abandon
control in the fragmentation. Time to lie in bed and
let the world devour you, like a cone. And so my
love, my no longer mine, I lie under the hail of our
flying apart, pieces of you hail and whistle down slicing
the tops of my ears and my thighs, and thickening the sky
like a cloud of birds. Under this I lie. I prepare to die,
and I die backward into the resurrection of the open hand.

17

My father and Irving, who would ultimately drown,
and "Uncle Shep," who wasn't my uncle—all three who
would be awake and casting by 5:00—snored sonorously
in their primitive beds side-by-side on the screened
porch of the "Mouse House" in Port Aransas, Texas,
on a hot summer night. They were men in undershirts
with wives and businesses and children and hair-whorls
turning gray toward middle life, men with salt-stiffened
sneakers and banged-up skin leaning toward red, God-
defying mortals beyond the mid-point. Snoring, as I
crept home with two black swollen eyes, two shiners
punched black by thugs on the beach within earshot
of "The Music Machine" by the pavilion's east-facing wall.
Unconscious and dragged into the surf by a friend to
waken me and off I slunk to the bed beside my dad, who
started at my arrival, but sunk back, an unnoticeable
sleep-hump. Sea towns are rough. Teenagers are mean.
What did I know of loathing in the soul and blood-lust
or the sheer cutting power of human knuckles? Next
morning a "buddy" kicked sand in my face and I still
envied him. The sea was diamonds, the waves were fine,
the warmth was motherly, but the water stung and no
matter how small an ocean seems, it's huge, which is
what Irving discovered one day with his life. I don't
remember what they caught or the legendary fish fry
or the following days at school skulking about the halls
with black eyes or my sister's surprise or my pain or
my classes or the cafeteria-shame or my girlfriend's
sadness, just the first blunt blow to my face arriving
from nowhere and falling to the sand and covering
my face and being kicked and the word "Jew!" snapping
the air and the surf soaking my clothes. Nothing
more. A little brain tattoo. It wasn't The Holocaust, just
a little beating in Port Aransas of human flesh which
recovered and continued functioning, what you might call
a minor inconvenience. I found no solace in my parents,
but then who or what comforted them in their suffering?

18

Without consciously knowing it I depended on my Daddy
to go to work each morning and return each night with food
on the table. I came home from screwing up at school
each day—slouch, hot shot, practical flunkey with a smarmy
face—to pork chops or prime rib and peas or potatoes and
ice cream or tapioca pudding—I expected this as my
birthright and unspoken due. And he did: slipped on his
pants, uncardboarded his shirt, slurped coffee, two eggs,
toast and every day went to the office, some sleazy vending
machine affair full of weevils, machine guts, syrup bottles,
money filth, and steel furniture, King Daddy of the Milky
Ways. I can't imagine wasting life in such a hell, but, for the
yelling every night at mother, he seemed to love it, left each
morning, chest thrust, as if he were the heavy-weight
champion of the world, and, in fact, he was a pugilist. And
the corn boiled and the burgers fried and the ketchup ran
and the sundaes tickled and Daddy came and went day
after day, like a blurry shuffling of cards through a deck,
nothing but a whir in the air as he whispered by, and I ate
and ate, grew and wanted, and he was no god, but a brutal,
unanalyzed, repressed man medicated to the nines, but
I didn't care because I expected, like a butcher expecting
blade and block to cleave the neck, like a workman expecting
excavator and gasoline to move the earth, which is what, I
guess, life is: blood of the slaughtered sluicing in streams
and the earth puckering under gasoline. My daddy whom
I love but don't like was one of these finally nubbed to
family theft and common misery. And the other three
mantises of the clan—mother, daughter, I—by the fact of
our aliveness and constant need pitilessly watched him, a
perpetual motion machine, speed until he became a smoothed,
muttering piece of insanity. What did I care so long as
cells divided, flesh grew, brain multiplied, jaw clenched
on someone's butt—I had my furnace to feed and it raged
into sex and beer and drugs and cars and Burger Kings and
disregard and little pieces of attitude, peel-outs on Saturday
nights, the jammed-open Holley burning the clutch into a fusion
of junk—daddy at work, daddy at home, daddy pumping down
pills with his head full of cheeping open-billed throated and the thud
of an ax blade meeting the block through an anonymous neck.

19

What was dinner time but a ship in a gale, the
table sliding fore-to-aft, the cables straining, the
liquids sloshing from cups, rocking side to side
and front to back, mother, father, daughter, son
the points of a cross over Formica, nightly, a gale
sending breakers to shatter the beams of the
ark, winds to rip down sails, swells....my father
caught me in mid-air leap across the table to knife
my sister, I saw her dead in my head, shouted
me down, and snatched the knife, my mother
snarled "more money" at my father who blew fire
into her hair, my sister shriveled into her shoulders,
like a scrawny bird, it was dinner in America
behind nice walls—meat, bread, butter, white
rice, Del Monte peas—unanalyzed, undivorced,
and unaborted; repression and her hostilities. My
grades were poor. I hated eggs. My mother
bitched. My father raged. I hated my sister. She
tortured me. The steak was tough. Too fucking
bad. Shut up or I'll give you something to cry
about. Go to hell. Monster! Bum! Dinner time and
the meal was us, we ate each other's livers out
when every White working male could afford a
strip of real estate and a body by Fisher, it was a
drum we made of the kitchen table whose reverberations
felt all night we shocked into motion by six o'clock.
It was a drum, an ark, a stage whose lights
clicked out, whose actors tattooed cigarette smoke
on boozy air, their makeup cracked; it was
the unintentional tragedy of blind optimism, the
middle dawn of TV—Sullivan, Caesar, Skelton,
Benny, California, Conoco—pumping into the family
brain primroses and promises it couldn't keep, it
was illusion outstripping reality across the
dinner table of the world compounded by the
usual human fragilities and the resultant dementia.
Yet, at my table one of us, at least, could split and
float above himself, a conscious balloon watching
the comical evisceration, mother, father, sister,
brother, braving the waves, securing the cups,
swallowing and forgiving, blaming and embracing,

who could see, bumping against the top left
corner of the room, the slow destruction of four
souls, the gradual erosion of joy or love or self-esteem,
or the just plain blessing of feeling right, and the
individual struggles in the boiling sea not to burble
under, and the occasional off-handed victories,
watching with his balloon face this happening to him,
too, while something unbreakable, immovable,
iron-solid inside cried, "but it is us, by God, it is us."

20

There might have been a hurricane and I might
have been in the waves straddling my Hobie
and waves might have hammered shedding spiny
spume and the waves might have sucked and
lumbered and the sky might have hemorrhaged and
the wind might have head-ripped and the rattlers might
have curled on roof-tops and the crabs might have
dug under and the men-o-war might have risen and
fallen on wild horses and the sting rays might have
saucered and my parents might have raged and
my parents might have screamed to me from
the cliffside beside the pink mansion and my parents
might have spewed acid and my parents might have
struck and the mullet might have submarined in gray
schools and the sky might have blotted and I might
have left white hand-prints in the sheen and I
might have hung up in the lip and I might have
dropped down the face of a gray elephant and I
might have stood on my world of foam and I might
have flown, flown and my parents might have
disowned and my parents might have died and a saw-
blade might have ripped my mother's stomach and
a knife blade might have slit my father's side and
there might have been a hurricane and I might have
been young and I might have snapped my Hobie under
my arm and driven it to the sea and I might have
straddled it in the wind-hammered gray dangling my legs
in a bowl of sharks and I might have drowned or
been devoured by any number of things and I might
have heard my father's voice straining into the
wind like a crooked-flying bird and I might have
heard and I might not have acquiesced but
paddled further into the mist where the elephants
herd and the zephyrs whistle in the delicate ear
bones and I might not have ever come back to the
solid brick house to the thick cool room to the neat
clipped grass to the clean round car to the rose red
mouth to the sparkling new curb and my father's voice
originating at the cliff might have plopped finally like a
stone in the sea a thousand feet short of my hearing.

21

I down the water hard, slam dunk it, really,
I'm in a hurry, skateboarding, sandlot ball,
little cellophane chest heart-heaving, little hands,
mother gaping—all my life I've been drinking
it, black rippled crystal in round glass, invisibly
saturating myself with its many psychedelic
permutations: Nehi, Coke, Jello, Popsicle,
lemonade, filling my cells, lining my bowels,
hydrating my eyes, and leaking it out me in
yellow arching streams through my urethra—
human fountain—collected it in plastic jugs as
Alaska's Fox Spring disgorged it up frozen
tubes, cupped and drank it from my palm raw
off mountain veins, boiled and cooled it in
the woods, from my own arms licked rain,
and of course the million spigots, fountains,
and hoses. Scientists say, in nineteen-ninety
six, that they are searching for life on Mars
by searching for water; the poles, they say;
the electrolytes that fuel the battery of life.
Such dependency begs a torture—subjugate an
enemy by depriving water, control the water,
poison the water, provide only enough water
to keep them begging, destroy with water—
rubies for the haves and ashes for the nots, such
a tidy box. And it burbles from the ground
and sheets down air's windowpane—aquifers,
lightning, limestone, manna clouds—and we
aerate it and chlorinate it and defilthify it in
unimaginable processing plants nestled between
foothills or flat along highways blooming water
flowers or stretching alongside outskirting
rye fields for the billion billion mouths and
biological systems to imbibe, suck, and knock
down endlessly without God, mind, light or
eye—its consummate invisibility—like love or
parents or family or friends which evaporate in
the blazing sun or torture of unconsciousness.

22

Fucking the Virgin Mary: she's my greatest conquest:
for her I am tender and wonderfully seductive—sincere,
boyish, open, and terminally listening, letting my
doe eye lashes work magic, convincing her that I am
harmless by playing the sensitive poet, psychoanalyzed
and enlightened. I tell her that I above all understand,
and sliding my hand over hers, that her deepest fears
are safe with me. No cheap Courvoisier seduction, I
move systematically into her soul or rather convince
her to open its door to let me curl there by playing
the sufferer, the youth abused by a brutal dad into a
wound requiring salve. This is achieved without
words, without hammer or nail, I employ her superior
intuition. She could never know that her cunt lies in
my cross-hairs, undulating, preparing to let me in,
partly because I repress from myself the full extent of
my dishonesty—the self-deceived is the finest
criminal. You would think that she would be clothed
in fluted white, but here on my couch she is wearing
muted red with black pumps and her leg skin is
creamy brown. I love her. I crave to slide my penis
between her breasts, such firm, heavy breasts. God
convinced her eternity exists on a shaft of air,
frictionless in a sea of emptiness, that the most
powerful man on earth sprung from the unbesmirched
womb. I have a bridge in London to sell! My gift
is pleasure, ecstasy, messiness, fluids, sucking, biting,
life's vicissitudes, connectedness, imperfection. I
acknowledge ego. Now I slip my hand under her
dress, now I feel her hair's wiry-ness, now she leans
down to kiss, now I glide one finger in, now her
tongue thickly comes, now a shoulder strap falls
down, now her bra is undone, now I tip one breast
from underneath, now she repositions herself on my
inexhaustible couch for my mouth, now I fasten, now
my pants are down and some flood surges against
thick tall walls within hearing, now her eyes are closed,
she breaks, and "gentle" quivers across my lobe, now—
you know the indescribable, miraculous slipperiness of
teenage lubricants, they net down the inner thighs and
can guide even the most oblivious in—now the blood
bursts under her broken skin. Oh Mary, Mary.

23

I tell the stranger sitting beside me on the plane which is
slanting in for a landing that I am going to rescue my
son from a psychiatric ward where his mother placed
him for experimenting with drugs and truancy, and the
stranger, a young woman, Born-Again, says, grasping my
hand and pressing her forehead against my arm, "May I
pray for him?" and proceeds to chant a most beautiful
prayer. She prayed as passengers filed by our side and
deplaned. The craft landed eventlessly and the visit with
my son was gut-wrenching and difficult. I brought him
home with me and, amazingly, he still lives! What we
cannot measure well we deify; Jesus is an immeasurable
commodity. My friend, long inexplicably depressed—
self-critical internal monologist, self-hating—worships
the serotonin reuptake pharmaceutical Zoloft, restores
balance daily, like a bath, to the immeasurable chemistry
of his brain. The twenty-four-hour-long self-regenerating
monologist dies, he says, at sunrise by the Marshall in the
pill—fast, deadly shooter. "I'll be on it for the rest of my
life," he adds. The great mysteries, the ones that over-awe—
Michelangelo's Chapel, Les Miserables, the Pyramids, the
microscopic gaps at human synapses: caverns we
fill with God to the brim, and over. How wonderful to
have glue to hold the whole together, clear, amber glue—
like bread—good, heavy bread to paste inside hunger.

24

So I'm watching Oprah interviewing teenage sex addicts—
we called them "nymphos" years ago—and their mothers—
and there's crying, accusation, hostile body language,
the works—all the daughters are beautiful, stacked, nicely
nosed, slender, and craved male attention, and admitted to
exhibitionist sex, adulterous sex, group sex, interracial
sex, monogamous sex, drug sex, and sex on the Internet.
None of them took money for it. One, looking into her
mother's eyes, said she could hook her father into fucking
her if she wanted, that he had made overtures. Oprah
was shocked. She spoke morality, birth control, re-
sponsibility, consequences, besmirchment, regret, ruination.
The girls sat unmoved. Then there were ads for Downy,
Advil, Tums, and Folgers. I peddled on my recumbent
Lifecycle machine contributing my whir to the whole,
humming club. Oprah, concerned for the fragile structure
of the universe, continued, the TV bolted to the upper
right hand corner of the room beside the fan, both tilted
toward the clientele. All that innocent flesh there on the
screen, and I began to envision smooth, vaginal flesh—having
some of my own—lubricants, silky hair, the pure erectile
tissue of these girls, like unbaked dough before becoming
pies; I thought of the positions to deepen the man's
entry, their buttocks firm as pears digging into the bed
or parted for the rear entry; I thought of confusion and
retribution and rage and craving, the pull through girlhood
to be woman, the woman pulling herself out prematurely;
I thought of the lewdness of it and the ecstasy, the stir
in the gut of naughtiness. Sweat popped out. I took a
swig. Oprah is not without her coups-de-gras. I wondered if,
at their tenderness—I was eighteen when I first got laid—
if they climaxed—I didn't and find it even now problematic—
if they well-pleasured—if climaxes hit them hard like
they do uninhibited women. I wondered if it was all
rebellion and how powerful rebellion-love could be. It
set me spinning. Oprah, as I say, is not without her grand
finale. From the back row of the audience she produced—
presto!—a mother and her late-teen daughter, a former
teenage sex addict, formerly on this show, now diagnosed
with AIDS, a disaster and an object lesson. I pedaled on.

"Don't let your daughters do this," the mother pleaded,
"stand by them—do anything to stop them," and in the
distorted, elongated sounds before disintegration, cried,
 "She's been robbed of her childhood." Breakdown.
The guests looked on. The mothers appeared to soften
with tenderness—they had all evicted their girls—negative
sisterly influences, disgust, etc., but the daughters, leaning
heavily away, looked unscathed and further resolved with rage.

25

My wife and I debate this: sex is the dominant preoccupation of our species; sexual conquest, dominance overpower flesh and soul of everyone in their public and "cultured" iterations; an unconvincing veneer of civility covers consuming carnal conflagration without which human would be desiccated extinct jaw-pieces. My wife says no, I insist yes, witness swaggering adolescents plying themselves full of drink to face colliding necessities–awkwardness and lust; witness adultery; witness the wailing manifesto of singles culture; sample the monomaniacal content of popular lyrics and television. Behind every door blooms a climax. My wife says mine is the position of the adult child of sexual abuse—the "insatiable hole" mentality—that lovemaking is ecstasy, yes, but that human is a complicated striver, pursuing partnership, peace, security, love, nobly and with dignity. I tell her addiction is neither dignified nor ennobling. She says I am projecting; I say, not now. She says we are not animals; I see the opportunistic kill crouched inside human flesh. She spirals pasta onto fork; I down sangria. I know women, she retorts, whose lives do not revolve around man and his sacred little member, who are content to attend events unescorted and in Platonic situations, who while receptive to romantic possibilities are not desperate; I say brutal experience has cauterized these pathetic bitter exceptions, that females conquer males they want, wield equal aggression and ruthlessness, that woman is a match-head ablaze no less than man, the two burning with equal ferocity. We are both by now uncomfortable, sucking the room of energy, blotting light with protruding hostility. She accuses me of sexualizing the world, of predator-rationalization, of having piled past conquests in misogynist psychosis, and suddenly I am aware of my pulled-down pants, my buttocks, my feet, hairless lips and jellyfish hands. I swig cold water. I focus vague sublimated images: *drawn curtains, silver wallpaper, legs dangling off bed, penis thrust into air. She has rich black hair. Red nails. I am scared. I am six. My penis a shell-less snail atop a smooth round stone, a beautiful morsel,* and just as horror cracks open my blood the image

blurs as though mist-coated and I remember not whether she fondled me, my mother. I utter the terms primal directive, hard-wired, DNA. I do not know, I confess, and want to stop the conversation naked in bed, me stiff-arm palming her mouth, she in the female dominant position, breasts swinging narcotically through the air.

26

The right side of me cries, "fuck you!" to my left side
which continues, gloved and masked, packing explosives
into the drilled hole to blow the safe. My left half
flails at him, crumpling off his steely surfaces like a fly.
My right side slits his eyes, uncoils the fuse, hides, flicks
his Bic, Kaboom! Paper bills fly like a shot bird's
plumes. I reprimand, I scream—a siren—we take a leak,
one of our few collaborative acts, others being
defecating, and occasionally, eating. My right side
refuses to shave, smokes stogies, and participates
in disreputable scams, though he can be a dandy
in colognes and cashmeres—indeed, a fake. I have
put my faith in psychoanalysis, honesty, face-offs
with demons, restraint; he is all libido. We are like
a solid steel ball twisted in half, two flat walls which
once were fused. I thrash him and he giggles. He
thrashes me and I hurt like skin. I can burn. Now
he mutters, "fuck off," and drags me into infidelity
against our wife. We enter her bedroom and bang
into action, throwing off clothes and sheets in the
pink afternoon. I scream like a crocodile's victim
rolling under swamp water, up and over, gasping
for air. He groans and pants as he fucks her from behind,
and she, also betrothed, opens her vulva, like a fruit.
This time it was urgent and she didn't come. We lie
in bed, stare at the ceiling, giggle, until he stiffens
again into iron and slowly she crawls on top and
comes hard, like a ship. I cry. I refuse the mirror
in which he shines. I am limp. We stride home, mail
in hand, to the pungency of our dinner and wife. Abed,
we profess our love for her. Asleep our dreams clash.
Now I am holding hands with my right side in a chair,
and the world through our distinct and warring eyes
flows in with undisrupted beauty, pleasure, meaning,
hue—a rare blending—and we are at inestimable peace.

27

I don't want to appear sentimental, but I've got to tell you
there's something about food that breaks my heart, something
about spoons and forks, pastas and beans, something about
the eating which wrenches the human being of me, the way
the biology craves food, the way it spirals on a fork, the way
it fills a cup and glides down tubes, the way it cools, the way
it steams windows and nourishes, the way it gives flesh to
bone, muscle to flesh, strength to lift. I am not religious but
when I sit before food at dusk—rice or enchiladas or greens
or polenta—I suffer a little for the cave between groin and chest,
the ghost, the hungry gift, the grotto of acids, fluids, blood,
enzymes, song, love, and greed, the stream of magma; how
we pull all day, hammer and grit, care, strain, sing, distribute,
need, navigate cars, featureless, like in-the-shell walnut meat,
compose, and hope. Our mouths wrap around sandwiches,
mayonnaise, lunchmeat, cheese, tomatoes, our fingers hold
the spoon of soup, like weight and counterweight, soft balances.
Brain knows, stored in some back cabinet, the crucialness
of food, knows the embedded panic button in the blood,
synonymous with the President's red phone, knows the
proximity of deprivation and fear, the threat of callousness;
but somehow the refrigerator is always full, as if replenished
inexhaustibly through the rear. Security! Forgetfulness! How
easy to reach for the tin of fish while plotting your next
slaughter on the market. Driveways, kids, and lawn chairs.
What breaks my heart I can't quite conceive—something to do
with tissue, thickness, continuousness, sponginess, ambition,
desire, pupils, the stretched-open hand, loneliness, children,
innocence, violence. Something to do with pendulums, opposites—
steel and down, fire and ice, night and light, rage and peace,
honesty and lies—but children most of all—adult and child.
Money covers food, food covers life, failure covers money—
paper, paper, scissors, knife. Something like that. Something
to do with grazing cattle, flipping tails, tufts of grass, blowing
leaves, cars whizzing by on interstates, the smell of dung and
prosperity, and the pendulum swooping back. I don't know. I
don't know. I keep envisioning the homeless with their placards
of distress at intersections beside traffic lights, dark humps in
ratty hats and parkas—Vietnam vets, schizophrenics, drug addicts,
blank stares, refuse, bodies like yours and mine, framed in bone,
wrapped by nerves; stomachs, lungs, livers, brains, parents,
kids, triumphs, failures, saliva, and tongues. That's not exactly it,
but the denial of it, the inoculation of work, the furious pre-

occupation of brain in the world, the arrogance of success,
the skin over sensitivity, the self-congratulatory soul on the
surface of the world in the plush of plentitude, the overpaid
aristocracy of President, Senator, Ambassador, Head of State,
fatuous, on-the-take, duplicitous, transparent. The earth delivers,
keeps, inch-by-inch, pushing from its undepletable source an
ever-exchanging, imperceptibly giving off—like the tips of flames
or the ends of comet tails—nutritive thrill of potatoes, lettuces,
legumes, seaweeds, citruses, grasses, plankton, and wheat which
hogs, cows, sheep, and fowl, and unbelievable fishes, munch, gulp,
cross-cut, and rip to become food on our plates, simple piles of
food; it's not the brilliant nor the complex nor the cunning, nor the
lucky, nor the incessant yammerer at his desk, but the nobility of
food, the beauty of it, the pulsing hand, and the inalienable right to eat.

28

It's time for the humans to lie with the animals, for
the Dubuque-ian actuary on his tree-lined boulevard to
curl with the Dik-Dik, to enter her soft, white fur
with his swollen shaft on the jungle floor padded by
wheat grass; for the Washingtonian Chef de Cuisine to
slide off his pants in the Venezuelan sun and intermix
with the Cotton Rat, sucking its tail in his mouth,
like a string; for the Houstonian sewer & drain man to
wash his hands in Inner Asian sand and break his
semen bag in the red, open flesh of the Lynx Caracal.
It's time, I say, to destroy the human race by forcing
the Walla-Wallan personal injury attorney to spread her
thighs around the Howler Monkey, illuminating a whole
Guatemalan rainforest with her cries—time to dilute,
decimate, and reshape, time to intermingle the un-
speakable—to sodomize—to disassemble the ramparts
of fury and hate, and aggression wild as a chaparral.
Intel and Internet! Cell phones! The muscle-bound
cardboard Superman! Child abductors and gang hell! It is
time to reconstruct the species by crawling into the
animals—the apes, the fishes, the cloven-hoofed race,
the egg layers, and the sky-winged gods; the Tapir,
the Wild Ass, the Harbor Seal, the Caribou, the Tuco-
Tuco and the Antelope. We have desecrated the universe
with our homicides and flick-tubes, transforming the
beautiful back caves of skulls into garbage dumps.
Though it means condemning to oblivion the works
of Sergei Rachmaninoff, Theodore Roethke, Michelangelo,
it is time to plow under the whole rotted superstructure.
Perhaps they will sweeten the soil, neutralize the viral
coils of Gilmore, Bundy, Dahmer, Speck, and the
innumerable rapists, killers, terrorists, pederasts,
torturers, fire-starters, and demagogues—starvers
all; perhaps they will fertilize the fields—Ludwig Beethoven,
Mahatma Gandhi, Leonardo Da Vinci, Sojourner Truth—
deliver blossoms into the sun. This is not poetry I admit, but
my indictment of the human race; reminiscent of apocalyptic mass
suicide, reminiscent of Kaczynski and his packages. You
may think me mad. It is time, I say, to cease birthing human
babies so sweet and innocent in tiny shoes and thimble mittens,
born on a wave of misrepresentation, and to go into the honest
ones, thick of fur, noble, pure-hearted, wise, unwasteful, straight-
forward, and dominated. Perhaps they will teach us humility.

29

A bursting sun unrolls its morning flood through me.
Dipped in gold I scrawl love across this page. Suddenly
I am neither oblique nor mad, just a man in love with
his partner—meals together, talks, tandem sleeping,
the give and take of communion—the glint of gold over
everything. Lake in sun. Mirror. Water hovering
above cup's lip, like a cake of water. Today I will cook
oatmeal and wheat bran together, steaming, served
with milk, drink coffee opposite my lover whose hair
will be tangled still, from sleep, skin aglow before make-up—
we will discuss family finances and who will go to the bank
today about our loan, we will discuss my forthcoming
flight to Texas for my daughter's graduation, and her
graduation gift, we will mention the power of the
Red River and the North Dakotan flood, and perhaps
the Gingrich-Dole three-hundred thousand dollar loan,
the poverty of politics and politicians. The table, oiled
and rubbed from last night's company, will be drenched
in gold pouring in from the door. Our dead cells will
flake off us invisibly, will go about their dying, like a
secret comet's tail, beautiful to themselves, sparkling
off the core. Again the sun. It is a common day of exhaust
fumes and tempers, poverty and desperation, wealth
and arrogance, the usual explosive combinations, but
I am at peace, rising in brick oven-ness, loaf upon loaf
in my glowing soul, and know not why. Is just is. I
think of those images I have seen in photographs of
smelterers pouring molten steel into massive urns, how it
showers and splinters when it spills, and the steaming
veins and rivers flowing into molds—the men are poor
and powerful, but full of pride, so it appears, and the
steel they guide makes something strong. I feel like what
they've made before it dries, still gold and red and brim-
ming. If I am a beam shaped like an "I" to dangle from
cranes above a bridge, that's okay; if I am the cage of
a car, likewise. I am but a piece of things and my love a
part. Today the counter aspill with grains glows gold
under the window pane, each grain a boulder throwing a
huge flame of shadow and I, without warning, awake from
slumber's crumbling, am a heavy bowl, swaying and spilling.

30

I've stopped thinking about naked women so much.
Something fundamental inside me is shifting. I used
to think continuously of them, and when married
seized my wife through a dream to awaken inside
her—often. Now light beams break through holes in
my mind, like rotted cloth. They were a comfort and
distraction, naked women looming before my eyes,
sharpened me one way while dulling me another,
such that I cut myself on my own whetted flesh. Oaf!
What is happening? Is my brain migrating north
from the center where it was small but lethal, for
now I seem utterly listing, diffuse? Am I crawling
into my mind? I think of moles in their long gestation
underground, finally emerging into light. I think
of their blinking amazement. I am equally amazed
and dampened. I know not what to think about! I
loathe politics. Philosophy's too immense. I haven't
the lunacy to speculate on the cosmos. Naked
women have been my specialty; now they're
evaporating. There's just a colony of holes before
my eyes and dazzling light. I want to pull them
back, my naked ones—their navels, midriffs, toes,
breath—like an amputee wants his arm. What do
you do when your subject's gone? I was gourmand,
connoisseur, master chef. My world's blank. I can't
think of a proper topic to fill you with. At what
point does a flower cease craving resplendence—
those bromeliads, calla lilies, magnolias—salting
the ground with brown petals? Is this a withering?
Am I a withering? Am I bleeding testosterone through
some psychic wound? Liquid yellow, gold? Am I
becoming woman? Am I dying—or chrysalis-like, being
delivered, finally, into something beautiful, the world
opening above my spine into a new profession of
love and transparency? I'm in transition. I'll wait
and see. All I know is my third wife's employer's ba-
by has captivated me—her baby smile, her spongy
cheeks, the way she grasps my finger, knee level,
and totters, chest out, like a queen. We go
shopping. All I know is unrelated disasters on the world's
other side wrench me. All I know is I'm not all fuck
and fantasy and man to naked women, braggart and
internally superior to my swarming rivals, and women

have transubstantiated into people. All I know is light
has crashed through some tunnel which dissolved, like
a wafer in its searing. Remember the little boy who
jumped in the milk and his crust of flour broke away
as he flew? All I know is something frightening and
sad is new and the word "screw" has broken into a
million pieces around my soul and bone structure.
When they loom now they are nude and embarrassed.

31

Tightly, they backed the Ryder in, early morning, moving day, bouncing
it over the curb in the morning sunpour, and sliding it close as a
shave to a robin roosting on her eggs. She did not move. They
lowered the ramp. They hacked. They coughed. The dolly echoed
in the truck-drum as they banged it free. Stalwart she sat. She did not budge.
Have you ever seen a robin seal the nest with her breast? She looks
like water with a face poured in it. Instinct glued her to her nest. And
in the green expanse of grass across the street hopped her mate,
fussing, watching, alert as wire, thwarted from swooping to his low
condominium exposed by trimming, helpless. Wheels along the anti-slip
ramp clattered and squealed under the sideboard's load, the workmen
joked, their bodies popped like soda cans beneath the mass of the
redwood burl, they cackled and spit squirming the cadaver of a mattress
in, they drank and refreshed beside the steel walls thundering to the
touch. Fury fused her there in her crumple-bun of feathers, bead
eyes staring, proud as fire, and starving, I think, as her mate kept
trying without avail to angle in. We could have batted him with our
hands. And there lies a parable. We unwrap our things in our new
domicile—dishes, glasses, here's that basket!—from old want ads,
the funnies, front-page news—and place them in cabinets. Try if
you can to take it, my house, my wife, my instinctual plan flooded
with blood, I'll cut you in two and blow you away. Shave my
house close with your sinister van under moonlight and pry in, I'll
slit you with a blade. My feet hold me up, veined, nubbed, tendoned,
tough—do you imagine me a lump of dough when security's
threatened?—standing naked in my robe a coat of mail flows beneath
my flesh and above my bones. You may kill me and rape my
wife, plunder my property, prevail, but not without there being
blood and gore eight feet up walls. We rumbled and scraped
and shattered and banged, cyclopean, Colossus-like, god-statured, and
she sat and sat on her fragile blue architecture in plain view an arm's
length away with her mate screaming, and I am positive that were I
evil she would have battled my huge hand reaching in. I returned
days later in my whispering auto to the site of the slaughter to retrieve
odds and ends—pillows, blankets, the comforter—all was tranquil;
they were still there, this time he on the eggs and his mate on the
eaves, watchful, vigilant, preparing to drop down. And this is where
I left them, forever, to pile the few remaining things on my bed.

32

Watching professional ice hockey on TV, the semi-finals, Detroit
vs. Colorado—brutal, clean, elemental, fast, steel on ice, ripping—
the kind of thing I like to track, like a leopard in grass the
microscopic movements of its prey, like to pretend I'm tiger in
the blades calculating, watching, fangs tasting blood, like to
imagine I'm on my couch sublime, amber-eyed, sleek, and wise.
Never mind the commercials for beer or automobiles, those
false interludes, those insignificant blips between magnificence,
no bigger than grains, never mind mini-pauses in the beast
which flows. I'm a beautiful animal, efficient, quick, my brain
transmits down the length of my skin, this Saturday night wide
with silk flashes of heat, my mate in the grotto nearby soft
and ready on the inside. That's hockey, a tail of star-dust
following a puck-like-a-comet to the score-zone, wham!
I'm all cat and blood-in-the-heart of the players when suddenly
a dead squid wrapped in blue ribbon fills the screen, a wet,
veined, whole, big squid wrapped in ribbon dead on the ice
someone snuck in probably under his shirt and hurled there,
a proud ocean squid, glistening, maybe still full of eggs
or fertilizer, maybe wise. I know almost zero about squid,
but I thought of soft, grey-mauve sacks, of suction cups,
of syncopated pulsing through water, of ink clouds, of eyes
half-buried in slippery skin. I thought of the indignity of not
being eaten, instead being thrown into a stadium of screaming
fans after a propitious score, the scoreboard flashing WIN!
WIN!, eyes glassed over and tentacles lashed, the indignity of
ending up in an arena and then the trash, the waste. I stood
in my human flesh—bald tufts of hair, soft dick, clawless
hands—just rose off my butt, not panther, ocelot, cougar, nor
lynx, and, remote control limp in hand, looked at this jarring
sacrilege. What happened next is hard to explain. Forty-
eight years of advertisements flew through my brain: gleaming
teeth, shiny legs, silky hair, quenched thirst, needless speed,
satiation, dominance, self-righteousness, the whole sewer-
marketplace. I cannot say what I mean. Body parts appeared
before my eyes—lips, napes, knees, hips, tit-cleavage, flat
midriffs, like an oar-shattered lake, all swirled into a
grotesque human ball laced with TV's stupid predicaments,
situations, blowings away, exonerations, manipulations,
mechanical tittering, skits, extravaganzas, and routines.
And small explosions occurred on the surface of my

skin, eruptions through which broad shafts of light ripped, stutterings and decompositions, burnings and disintegrations, breakdowns of the internal circuit board of me, profoundly, as if I were a melting lid around an inextinguishable eye—clear, refusing—shooting rays of vision out all sides of me, like a planet or transmission, a magician in the universe, and I shut off, forever, a piece of my race.

33

Well, I heard that this death row inmate has allowed science to slice his lethally injected corpse into single millimeter strips, every organ scanned, muscle upon muscle, his body filleted into innumerable sheets thin as Kleenex, for the examiners, a CAT scan of his entire disinherited body. Rape won't appear, homicide won't dash between the molecules. We won't find child trauma crouching behind garages, crying. But meat will glisten, like freshly sliced veal, a Hubble scan of grain and ganglia, calcium and tissue, the ultimate visible man. You could make a board game of this, a card game of concentration, what strip follows strip, what strip yearns for strip, you could award money for being close on an anatomical-geographical map: the Country of Pulmonaria, The Cardiac Republic, The Reproductive Coast, your strip draped over your arm, like fresh pasta. The man died for his sins—rape, dismemberment—but lives inside the instruments. Well, it just caught my eye, something I heard from a friend in passing, embedded in a wider conversation about competitiveness, superiority, dominance, etc.,the criminal lurking in my mind after escaping her lips. Grotesquerie curls in the routines. If time were a ground-to-sky wave pushing forward, while you in your circumscribed space were down-shifting into first, elsewhere some technological saw was subdividing a man whom they froze solid first. Now I am a literary agent in the basement of my home with a bone-white phone, a flickering computer, pens like bottle rockets in a cup, crammed book shelves, and, dare I admit it, a stuffed Beagle pup. I rub my eyes. I feel the thickness of my hands. I see my thighs aswirl with hair sweeping to my knees, and knee caps like helmets. I sit in a chair, or wander up the hundred 2 x 4 boards builders years ago hammered into stairs, to feel the sun, my fingers through my hair. And you my love are…somewhere…browsing, eating, day-dreaming, most likely working, drawn around yourself, like a bedsheet full of treasure and tied at the top, one beautiful piece. It's not enough to declare, "and round and round she whirls in space," referring to Earth, like a colossus unfolding, head in the sky, a stock response. We must return to this: a criminal who willed his heft to science, the science itself, electronic saws, weird obsessions, the immortality-drive, rape and dismemberment, the mackerel thrashing of too-tight lives, the infinite capacity of the human mind to escape prison walls and mundanity, the beauty of minutiae and the machinery to enter it, God, galoshes and slickers within which to slip as we examine the blood-sherbert which was man.

34

She hacks the base of his arm, hacks and hacks with her
gleaming cleaver, pieces of flesh fly, like wood-chips, blood
pudding forms, but the arm, all muscle and will, proves
stubborn and thick, nothing like what she thought it would
be, a simple cut-through with a heavy blade to be done with
it. She was never a butcher, just a cold repressor. This
chopping off of limbs is much harder than stuffing
unpleasant feelings, they being non-corporeal. She raises
high her red-streaked blade and slams it down upon his
meat; muscle writhes, worm-like, contracts and gives, still
alive; no bone yet, that calcium shaft, just shoulder meat,
bull thick, endless, wearing her out as she hacks and hacks,
the hatchet extending her crooked arm overhead and flinging
cadmiums: clumps and strings on its downward path. Sweat
drips from her pits, her blouse is wet, stains spread, but
she is intent, even while wrist-cramping and panting
and uttering hellish vituperations, "fucker," "shit," "mine,"
"usurper," "violator," "penetrator," "male," curses hauled
from some unexamined pain-pool, and she being so pretty;
lily and sweet. The boy oblivious in his crib sings
tunes, mobile overhead, an ABC Play Station affixed;
the boy giggles, as, in another room, she strives to dis-
member the father's reach from him, her treasure-trove,
her bud-lipped. Persistence widens the inexpert, inevitable
V—remember diagrams in the girl scout book?—forming
in his shoulder; it groaned, a slit-throat sound, grave-like.
Not understanding, not drugged either, a complicitor, he
doesn't resist, the pain dull as she strikes bone, as if
vibrating a tooth's root to his shins, and not a handful of
shoulder. It takes two fools to ruin beauty. Amazed his
bone is rainbow color, amazing its opalescence, and
amazing to watch good-naturedly her grizzly chopping,
indeed, somnambulistically, to assist. Why not stop her?
Why not grab the boy and bolt? Why not seize her jugular,
this little lethal shrew, his wife? He ceased loving her,
anyway, the instant she delivered, yes. Now one blow
snaps the last underside bone-sliver, his arm hangs invertedly
and she saws with some new serrated instrument the triceps
through, and comes orgiastically—mutters, "daddy," "yours,"
"nobody," "mum," as from the shoulder his arm plops
against the floor, like a naked branch, comes, indeed,
in fact, vagina lolling and rippling ecstasy through
blood and brain, as, from her life and son, this betrothed
one, subterfuging killer, finally acknowledging her dominance
and his mutilated, dead limb on the floor, runs.

35

Half-gnawed, raw black walnuts zing from branches,
a perfect hail, thud the parched ground, hundreds
splitting air: it's squirrels! squirrels! in the canopies
robbing us of nuts, nut pies, nutty oatmeal, baklava—
industrialists against winter, building stores in the
potted plants and soil under petunias, great bulging
cheeks of earth. I look and they plop at my feet,
under rodent barking and copulating, the trees shaking
with nerves. Well, after the first year of emptiness
I stopped expecting my trees to yield nuts for me—
in June I spy green nodes under leaves between
forking wood, and in July walk on a carpet of half-
eaten balls. Each bears the signature of squirrel plow
marks. Isn't that, as well, a symbol for love, leisure,
pain, exuberance, life itself—everything is half-eaten.
Yesterday on powdery, rocky, and sodden trails
I hiked nine miles through mountainous woods
stepping on deer tracks, horse hoof prints, and
human footprints obliterating them who will obliterate
mine piecemeal over time, in chips, knocking off
heel marks, toe pushes, clean lines. Perhaps a mis-
shappen piece of one step will survive years but then
the wind will take it. I am not whole in my skin—the
little nut of me—but whole in the stomach and gut
of the world, flung wide. Even at birth, purple and
new, I was but a piece she found to push through.
My feeling for you fragments, gives food, vanishes,
rains down, glistens, like flecks in fields of rich
ground, resurrects, nourishes with life what's all
around, fuses and detonates, separated by ripping
fingers of air. You may not close your hand
around it, solid and undisbursed, yourself disparate
but unhurt, until, finally, from above, you are
eaten into wholeness by the very God you love.

36

Fish scales filling the air, like sleet, and fish guts
under his high rubber boots on the cold, wet
concrete floor of the wooden hut by the wharf
where the fishermen drifted in on green sheets
of sea and emptied their bins of silvery gems;
scarlet-gilled, blue, pink, and red shimmering
jewels shot through his knife-wheel, the heads
white, and pink meat in cellophane sacks heavy
as lead the vacationers in Towne Cars and Coup
De Ville's carted home in ice chests to wives
and kids and the cat—tan, bald, freckled heads
and backs of hands, marked as beautiful as
the fish themselves before they were hooked
and hauled in under sun fists, flicking glinting
drops and convulsing on the fiberglass floors
of hostile crafts on the green-blue, salt laden sea—
the fish-scaler looking like James Dean in a
knife-blur, those golden locks shimmering with
flakes, flakes on his lips and brow, the knife
when ceased, a scimitar, razor sharp, the
butcher of fish, their down-curved mouths
looking dour, like gamblers peeling off hundreds
under pallid lamps dangling over felt tables,
and chewing down cigars—the hut of horrors
and beauty hovered by pelicans and gulls
looking for a swill, a little wriggling tail, and
feeding off spleens and roe sacks slid down
the wharf far enough to be safe for a quick
swoop-and-lift, the big yellow feet tucked
and trailing, like ballast, under greywhite
down to the tops of masts or severed pilings
stuck in water, like amputated fists covered
with barnacles and seaweed slime—and the
Oyster House where father slurped down
the uncooked eyes of whole lives from their
own slick body-cups full of Tabasco sauce
and salt, chased by soda crackers, he a Buddha
of sorts, slithering them down his slithering
throat opposite his shock-haired, young Jewish
wife when I was eight, nine, ten, and rich
with cousins, "the hoard," pouring through
this small intercoastal town, like a scoop of minnows
wreaking havoc, important as mayors, to

the open air theater, the crashing rubber-rafting
shore, the pails of sand clams beautiful as
money, the market for jaw breakers and
gum, and the little hut on the wharf where
cousin Harriet mooned in love over the beautiful
blonde fish-scaler, like a single bladed windmill
or processor blurrily whisking freshly caught soft
cold animals to their ultimate biblical doom.

37

For an aphrodisiac Japanese glamour-boys clandestinely drizzle over delicacies an elixir extracted from the base of shark fins—slam sharks on hooks, decapitate their fins, and slide them back into the alien sea, rudderless, to spin downward into mud, buried alive, like crippled submarines. See them whip uselessly their strong bodies, live pop-bottle necks stuck straight in sucking silt: shark + beauty - fins = hideousness. While above, in the glint of Creme de Menthe and the distant, irrelevant scream of an ambulance, an elegantly shod woman internalizes a shark fin between her thighs; it wedges darkly, churning blood around the edges, cuts the air pressing her pubis into apple halves, while the man shark-hungry shoves his bone in-between. Below sharks devour The Broken One, teeming, burying teeth, yanking free meat-chunks, whipping bodies, slashing their donor of ambergris, their brother. The lady clenches her fists in the chocolate dark, the one live piece of shark vibrating now under the man's pelvis and shaft, the tray shoved aside, food half eaten, the shark's fin wildly alive, smooth, black plate, silky rough, broad-based, knees crooked, toes pointing to the sky bringing in God, like a tuner, into the V with the small shark fin at the base under the man's spine, while below in the froth nothing remains but a slaughter of bones, soggy meat, a blood cloud, an incident involving powerful navigators and the decapitated. Satisfied, she falls into the pulverized walls of her scrambled brain, like a heroin addict, her fin retracted to a soft, unobtrusive ball, and the man falls open into the hilarity and joy of indisputable domination.

38

The spook on my lap. The weird on my lap.
When I reach down to touch it my hand
comes up bloody. Two eye-slits, like a cat,
warm, breathing. Wants to be stroked, but
oft-times resents it with sharp teeth and
claws. Is thick, furry, loyal, sweet when wants
to be, but vicious when it shall. It sleeps. It
frolics. It prances. It leaps. It loves soft lace.
It loves balls with bells. It loves engorged
blood. It rarely leaves save to slake or relieve
itself. Otherwise it curls collapsed, adoring,
replete. It is my moon-pool, acurl; my baby,
helpless and, therefore, enraged. God made
it thus. God made it small, almost crawling,
humorously arrogant. With a pink mouth.
A gaping mouth in the center of its face,
with a rough or smooth tongue, depending,
full of love and hate, of opposites. Cold, hot.
Dark, light. God, emptiness. Has a throat
but don't touch it! Strangulation is its phobia.
Start with the entire surface of its face full
in your palm and slide all the way down
and feel it purr, your best chance against
malice, keeping a safe distance against
inherent defensiveness. The spook in my
lap, boy becoming man, lies on its back
upside down, soft as a trap, from which the
unsuspecting hand may come up bloody.

39

Each molecule of sea water is a number, randomly
connected into other numbers in all shapes and attitudes,
combining, colliding, merging, and fusing, the sea
a googolplex of numbers, intermixed, overlapped,
forming an undulating organism, rising and falling,
swelling, swaying. Many a human has drowned in
numbers, inhaling 10s and 7s, their last appendage
a raised hand sliding under. The combination of numbers
form sea colors: aquamarine, green, copper, brown—
colors that weave one's breath into bursting, birds
loosed upon the air which are themselves numbers,
3 birds, 46 birds, 328 bursting birds, 2476 birds forming
a cloud whose molecules are numbers. Nitrogen,
hydrogen, oxygen numerals forming the sweet face
of a colt, a colossus, or cow floating, and metastasizing.
One cat sleeps on my lap, 2 squirrels quarrel in the
trees, 3 pans hang from metal hooks, 4 trucks wheeze
down the street. The tongues, lips, and teeth of
children at Eisenhower Elementary School form in
unison the sounds of numbers. Count to 10. Bob
can do it! Wendy can do it! Jason can do it, too!
Numbers bouncing off the walls, doubling back,
and filling classroom, save a few which slip through
cracked windows, like ecstatic criminals. I love you.
You plus me equals love. 1+1=2 or 3 or 5, who
plus 3 generations equals 71. Fourteen people of
mixed gender wait on the curb in the year '97 or
was it '61? Mine is tied with a four-in-hand. Seven
steps; a landing, 7 steps, a landing; 7 steps, a landing;
every other one 45 a degree turn left to a door on
each of 18 floors, counts the man with OCD. There
will be a minimum of 6 and a maximum of 16 chemo-
therapy treatments beginning every 3rd Monday
and lasting 3 hours each. She died at 63 after working
40 years. The system on which I compose these lines
has 32 megabytes of RAM, a 4.3 gigabyte hard
drive, a 1.44 diskette drive, a 56 K fax modem, 4
megabytes of video memory, a 3-D virtual memory,
an AC-3 camcorder, a 600 x 300 DRI printer with
a 100 page sheet feeder, a 7 resistant fax, and a
266 MHZ Pentium processor chip. On the tip of
my last going under finger, thrust high: 1 angel flickers.

40

When the gut growled at the bank book; when
the enzymes cleared their ghastly throat; when
the esophagus roared something terrifying at
the empty pocket; when the intestines cried foul
at the scoreboard; when the white corpuscles
whistled to the shadows for assassins, and the
red corpuscles got out the chains and switch-
blades; when the occipital pulled out its hammer
and tongs and glared at the food pantry; when
the left ventricle valve phoned homicide after
reading the bottom line; when the cornea sodomized
the optic nerve and had blurry descendants, like
fertility-mud; when the bladder screamed
damn! damn!; when the lower python looked
for sludge to fill its gut and threatened with
soundless asphyxiation; when the urethra looked
for steak in the Kenmore, pumped out hairballs
in a fit and took up the skull and crossbones;
when Amazon tongue rolled up like a useless
carpet after the Chief had long since passed
into his world never to return, and shot detumescent
bile jets into the cracks of its parched banks; when
the pancreas broke the glass and grabbed the ax
and with help from the spleen hauled the hose
to the safety deposit box full of worthless words;
yes, when the spinal column glaring one
last time at the empty jars and ended rolls of
Saran Wrap lying side by side, like dead soldiers
in a ditch, threatened to rip itself out whole
and crawl like a scorpion all night on my face;
I wept out into the world and looked for work.

41

I say to myself I am beautiful. I say come
sit by the fire next to me and I sit. I say
you have lovely hands, skin, and hold one
softly in mine. I say your eyes are like comets.
Night's coffee floods over us, night's blood.
I say in the firelight your hair looks like streaks
of wind flowing through and around trees
in white moonlight, like flight over Weeping
Rock. The flames flicker. Silence clambers
up our feet. I say I have only recently known
though we have long been friends—there
have been times I have actually hated you—
known your powers of loveliness, your root
and pulse sweet as sugar cane, have only
just understood. I say if I could only taste
and I put my hand to my mouth. Mmm,
I say, like bread, like life. I am afraid, I say,
so shielded, so laid in layers of protection,
muffled—yet, like a friend you tease me out.
I say I adore you as much as I have any one
or thing in my forty-eight years, and the
cricket of silence crawls up our leg. Come,
I say, let me touch those teardrop muscles
running along your sides, let me taste your
thumb, and slowly I unbutton my flannel
shirt. Come, I say, let me feel, you are so
wonderful, the sheet of your hard-soft
tummy under my palm, and my unhitched
pants pop open. Yes, I say, and the fire
flickers. I say you have been suppressed
in a solid lead box. I say I value your
innocence, your honesty, your sorrow, your
life, slide my pants over the globe of my
ass on the white couch in the ten o'clock
half-light, and make love to one beautiful.

42

I love those people who burn out their brains all day, and all night in dreams, on impossibilities, manically, in a panicky truth-quest, whose Buddhism is limited to toilet sitting, who gnaw their cuticles like lovelorn teens to the blood glue, who are constantly shaking a leg in a blast-off haze, who run crazily through streets towered by edifices on their way to anywhere so long as it's bright and blinding and blaze, who shuffle book pages noses flat against words, whose transmissions blackly smoke and stink with the burn of steel upon steel, whose revelations slam their eyes backward, like spirit possession; revelations on God vs. nothingness, being vs. blasphemy, madness vs. gluttony, or the simple cleavage of the universe. I love they who sleep taking earth's temperature with feet sunk in mud pies and who awake pulling out lives, like plums stuck on toes, and who devour each with purple running the funnel of their love; like those with a dozen Dalai Lamas and three fat sows racing through their blood, like mad geniuses wailing high anthems and waving their patriotic flag—a pair of tattered underwear; love they who, while yapping Nietzsche and Kierkegaard, jumped on Ethiopian dark, subconsciously unravel lips of their Dixie Cup, wax flaking in a phosphorescent snow, they of the mania in dyslexic socks and sole-flapping shoes, who can't impress girls nor the stallion studs from tripping on their tongues and blurting dumb words, who spill across the land, like a throw of tadpoles whipping furiously and driving into silt, the world a blurry, white sphere above their heads which one night they will burst through into clear, blue sky. I love these misfits whose sharpeners shower stars, and over whose lives convention and normality roll and leave shattered.

43

Am I more like steel or fruit inside? If you drilled deep through me would I finally break your bit or ooze pear-meat and weep like a godless Jesus of Nazareth? I want to know. Drill me to the core. Screw out big chunks of me in your deep steel grooves and spit me free, you with your blindness and vulnerability. Make me spasm and curl with your all-nighters and narcomania my teenage son. Find my vanadium or peach-pear-plum blood. You have drilled through my flesh, it flew apart like a burn, and several inches into the beams in my bones, but I'm still steadily beating. Push hard on your tool. Drill through my collar past my lungs into my heart pushing with all your weight, feet off the ground, grinding out meat; find what's there. Get to my mettle. Drop out. Coke up. Fuck the syringe. Find your own gore in vehicular winter. Am I cold? Am I mechanical? Can I walk through closed windows? If you peel back my surfaces do I glisten? This is your mission. Let me see from a distance the crack pusher's wing fold over your shoulder and usher you forward, your two backs fusing. Let me witness dissolution. It is the father's privilege. To strip off my sirloin like meat off a prey to find what's lying inside my cage. Let me see graphically what your brain isn't getting: high school teacher's spittle, orange lunch room chile, that geeky conventional gangly camaraderie, auditorium pep rallies, an appropriate foreign language, stupidity, time, time, time.

44

I strip the raised vein out my forearm by lifting it
whole with the blade of a knife and with it make a
ball of yarn I call my son. Like spaghetti spun on
a fork, thick and high and standing on its own wide
base, I give him eyes, a name. Allan I say, Allan.
The ball glistens red like tomato sauce. Say "Daddy,"
I command and feed him apricots. Say "Master."
The wrapped vein self-perpetuates and renews
by squirting and sucking in a ceaseless repetition of
sleep and food. Say, "I am your nemesis or life dup-
licate. I am your acolyte fashioned to echo your
productivity. I will assume the presidency." I
do not miss the vein that became my son though
it left a tunnel in my flesh for he is me watery and
splashing my stupendous trail. God love him.
God give him meat. Give him feet to incinerate.
I spin my child like a plate of vermicelli and he
quivers, smiles, accumulates—but then he hates,
the procedure awry, me, the plate, the fork, the
sea contained within the vein like a stiff steel pipe
of hell, he digs, he spits, he smolders, he flies, and
eyes two slit exposures of spite attempts to die.

45

She pours her belly and heavy thighs along my side,
my TV, and breathes in me, mouth-to-mouth and sighs
with every cell she wants me, wants me, proves she
has a body full of juicy meat and fluids the way it, en-
gorged, molds and folds and weighs me down, a sack
of soft and silky guts packed into a fiery form, nipples
and toes and lip-prints, my Motorola with the gorgeous
peak between her legs, and how she crawls over me
and slips me in and pops me out to tease, to tease
and drags her slick to my mouth for me to lick and
suck clean, my glamorous screen, I stick my finger
in and release a tun of human love, just we two in
a darkened room. Never have I been so lit upon my
tip as when she flipped and hiked her hips, her great
soft split open like fruit for me to slip my shaft into.
We are promised each to each next June, she chaste
in brocaded lace and I in scarlet cummerbund, my
cable ready, pre-programmed, 26 whose glass and
hard plastic flesh blow me away with unrestrained
insanity. And now she lowers her hips on me and I,
stiff, shatter her tube and microchips, plow through
her circuit board, like a wrecking ship, and mash
her electrical crucifix, and voices, pitches, slaughters,
and salves spill over me—warm ooze—and we are no
longer two but one merged piece of fused technology.

46

Son has tripped the light fantastic into temporality
shooting the crack and horsing about in burglarized
houses, a veritable pine Pinocchio in oblivion-land
eight balling and cataclysmically sprouting alien prongs.
He hallucinates among the rats and stars in the
corrugated bed of a pick up truck, uproariously
bouncing, like a Metallica riff. He has not brushed
his blades in weeks and his face erupts like Vesuvius.
Oh, the beautiful rage of teens stinging them off laws
like racquetballs. Mine has a feather of chest-cavity
hair, sprigs in nose, and a black dusting round his
wrists. What a joke to be a boy—gangly, hot
octopus lying over the mind, like a human palm,
shocking and sticking. You just hyperventilate.
See? Mine applies his mania to conning fools;
he can detach his middle finger and lay it bloodless
in the hand of man. He can weave a ball of hemp
instantaneously into a jumping god, and smile the
smile of UNICEF. Change flies from warm skin
into his cup. He's ordinary stuff like we only inchoate.
The strictures blunt their arrows on his chest. Sun
drowns son into a dot, then nothing, beyond texts,
body soap, and medicine, where on flaming sands,
prince of stones, he ponders the darkling emptiness,
where he may char into a black nest of bones.

47

Left eye, right eye; left eye, right eye; see the world jump; left eye sees a beautiful man; right eye a man being dragged by the arms; left eye a man with youthful locks; right eye a man with head blown off; left eye a man sitting at a table; right eye a man with ground beef between his shoulders; left eye a man bringing on the soup; right eye gore stringing out a neck; left eye a man backing down the drive; right eye a man swinging between two soldiers; left eye a man choosing a grapefruit; right eye tanks powering through smoke; left eye a coin between two fingers; right eye a hole between two wings; left eye ecstasy; right eye God; left eye two grandparents, a child and a dad; right eye two legs, a torso, and air; left eye capitalism and fascism mashed together, right eye a man shorn off at the deltoids; left eye a church steeple climbing the sky, right eye a church with its nipples blown out; left eye a wife; right eye a widow; left eye a dog strutting with its master, right eye a dog slurping blood pie, (I imagine it burrowing into my face, swallowing the meat). Left eye a smile ceased at the larynx, right eye a smile gaping with sky; left eye, right eye, left eye, right eye, the world jumping across my nose, when I open them together: an alphabet soup of horror and love.

48

After binging on Dreyer's butter pecan in a period of
weight gain I went upstairs and almost forced myself
to throw up. I gazed into the toilet like Narcissus. I
imagined slamming two fingers down my throat till
a Vesuvius roared. I felt the weeping of my stomach,
and my accusatory belt. I wanted to kill the monster in
me, the cowardice, the unceasing executioner. Downstairs I heard the John Wayne movie: the charging
bugles, the beating of horse hooves, the swirling commotion of rifle fire and expiration, all muted by a series
of walls and corners, and in my soft cube, wondered.
I knew that finally I was tortured not enough to perforate the tissue of my gut, that I was still a bit of a
hibiscus, that I would rejoin unpunctured my partner
in the film. This brief lavatory interlude was brought
to you by Glamor Magazine, self hatred, pitiful parenting, powerlessness, and a rare form of male bulimia.

49

Once again the bombing planes roar over somewhere and I in my peanut butter and jelly room, in my decaf latte domicile know nothing, a coalition of citizens sanctimonious as bishops having examined evidence of the atrocities are thrashing a fascist in the bushes like a naughty child, inflicting lacerations and contusions with an intent to teach the nasty bastard lessons in humanity. I watch it in the blazing peacock eye over blackened redfish and new potatoes, the acetylene blue rocket bloom puncturing the night in a Baryshnikov ballet of beauty and technology, ultimately a gorgeous dazzling pageant any nightsky would boast of, my head so full of images I veritably tip toward vertical walls: Chevrolets, Nissans, Cadillacs, Acuras, headache and indigestion pills interspersed with the unbelievable depiction of blood-splashed glass shards, fire-ball demonstrations, and manicured commentators cut off at the chests with arms on the table. What the fuck do I know? A genocidal monster across the world on the prowl needs a whipping and Raytheon's equipped to mete it out; better minds than mine are the tacticians and architects, steeped in geopolitical history, ornately enveloped, in the most sequestered of rooms. I am a popcorn gnasher in my clapboard house in a sea of duplicates uncircumsised if you will in the subtleties of diplomacy. I trust my guys, pom-pomming in my living room, protected by two oceans, three keys, and the mightiest military in the cosmos. What I love most frankly are reruns of Rosanne, Frasier, Golden Girls, Northern Exposure, and the latest predicaments of Ally McBeal. You know what I mean? Were I opposed to this piece of seriousness, which I'm not, I could hurl myself before the needle of an F15, Joe Q. Citizen skewered by a hot machine, or conversely were I hawkish, which I'm not, I could grab my teenage bum son by the tongue spike and kick his ass into the Marines, but I'm too confused in my lead-lidded work-distracted world to act, trapped in the cross-hatching opposing million vectors blackening my field to a bloodless vision. Is that the nature of war: the ones at home, hemorrhoidal, sitting their saggy asses on the toilet perplexed; the ones obeying top brass hauling theirs into the molten fray? Look, I haven't a clue. I grew up on the candy green lawns of Columbusland in the fifties, cheated the Viet Nam draft with a 4F asthma deficiency, stayed glued to school, and shot out the other end in a navy blazer and white collar shirt, thank you profusely, my view of history narrowed to the acquisition of the next dollar bill, the only war I'm trained to fight, interpenetrate, negotiate, die for, and win.

50

I have decided I will do this: I will eat my father.
I will cook him to tar and spoon the goo; I will
melt his shoulder bones into his buttocks and
watch his eyes boil like eggs. I own the kettle—
cast iron—and the site, a barn alive with mice and
bats, abandoned, dilapidated. I will stab him
severally, split his wishbone, and boil him till his
brain snakes through. Then the fun! I will eat
every atom of him over years until I have swal-
lowed, digested, and eliminated my father. I will
spice my meals with cranium filings. He will
reappear in the water supply as the rationale
for Perrier! After that who cares! Let them fry
me. Let them waste ink and trees. Let others,
righteous to the pips, over oatmeal, snap off
their lips long balloons of diatribe, the loyal
pets of their shoe-tassels waiting. I will have
achieved my goal, liberated to song, no longer
man but soul. Prosecute the doll of my body,
bloodhound me down, convict me like an SS
man, let the pellet fizz. You cannot kill God nor
an empty robe. When in death my neck sinks
down know that what passed through it in grainy
chunks, savoringly masticated, inspirited me,
peeled back filth to liquid gold, made me beautiful.

51

Double double toil and trouble the cow jumped
over the moon and up they tumbled down the
hill and what a sweet boy am I, oh my, and what
a sweet boy am I. What would love be but a bucket
of nails if not for a bushel of hammers? he cried,
the hankie outflung as if he sang from the corner
of the edge of the hive. I love her, I love her,
and SuperGlue can glue up the pieces so that I
am a pretty round egg, again, so that I am a pretty
round egg. So let me pucker and fuck her and
fuck her, and paint my lips blueberry blue, for
she is a dream and a sofa and chair and several
large hook buttons, she is my pantry, my tantra,
my dancer, my pater su casa sublime, all blonde
and beatific, blue-green-rust-brown eyed,
smelling quite frankly of chives. I must not not
have her, must not post-dispossess her, must
mix her with lettuce and ham, oh my mother, my
dyspeptic father, may hell bite you like a fly for
I am her I, her eye, and her aye, the better to see
you with my girl, the better to smell you up close,
the better to eat you, the better to treat you, the
better to dissolve you the Host, my God, my
Mary, my Nefertiti, my most whom I drape in
pearls, and cover in yolk, and bathe in a bathtub
of milk, my myrrh, my liverwurst, my frankincense
pie who went squealing all the way home with
a basket of cherries, with a basket of berries,
with a basket of hands, heads, and thighs, who
jumped in my lap with my shaft at half mast
which rose like a bone through the rye higher
and higher to the height of a man eating jam.

52

Bumpkee, bumpkee, bumpkee boop! Mama's baby
had a poop. I'll take you down to the livery stable
and fill your anus with horse goop, cause Mama's
baby mustn't poop when dinner's cookin' and
Daddy's ravin', so better watch out, better not cry,
Mama baby's got an eye, two eyes, a double swaddle to stick a knitting hook straight through for reformation of little babies into men or lipstick-caked
black mascara-ed little babes, bumpkee, bumpkee, bumpkee boop, Mama's baby had a poop, and Daddy's
raggin' and Mama's cookin' and we need a little
dope to push us happy, ne ecstatic, I've got a box,
a baby box, to cram little devils in who can't control their little rope with the big brown hole at the
top. Boop, boop, boop, boo! Who are you but a
candle I birthed in the alley behind the DQ at three
AM throwing up my soul beside a box of cracked
wafer cones, hell! Mama loves her little baby, Mama
loves baby little, Mama loves, Mama baby, suck
her thumb in a corner, yes!, ah yes! HITBANG!,
with the spider, and curds and whey, little Miss
Muffet and a nail of powder marked "OBLIVION".

53

I had an affair, yes an affair with an electrical chord,
fed it up my ass, plugged it in, Bang! Stripped off
an inch of insulation like a citrus rind and fried my
balls. Never has love felt so fine. Never so naked as
this socket and copper-wattage. I love it. I love
she with megavolt vibes threaded through my anus
and biting, biting like an old sharp dog, up in the
dark frying attic electrifying my colon, oh babe, let
me have it attached to the wall like a bulb, a flare,
three-pronged, AC, the angel's pitchfork, I shall
stand barefoot in water. Bless my addiction, O
god, rooted to the floor, cold, surrounded by flow-
ers, a whiskey sour, and this, this brown stripped
rubber chord with power pumping through its
soul. It slams the resurrection into hopelessness.

54

These are the grotesqueries: long fake fingernails painted purple glued on the end of bitten fingers used to enter minute streams of data into a PC; a bent and contorted rubber man giving himself a blow job on a chintz bedspread at mid-day behind heavy curtains to a whirring traffic sound in a moderate-sized Midwestern town reeking of sanitized industrial smells and environmental mediocrity, sucking like a pig his red dong, snorting and slurping until the gun fires hot flan into his rasping mouth; two average boobs "anesthetized upon a table" swelling like birthday balloons as the Master slips silicon heavy pouches into slits wide as orgasm-grins, the kind that closes you like a briefcase and slams a Charlie horse into your thighs, two massive mounds rising from ash topped with bright red hard proud maraschino cherries; a half dozen frosted orange vials lining the medicine chest like circus milk bottles daring to be bowled over, one for nerves, one for insomnia, one for anxiety, one for bipolarism, one for rage, and one for love—a puppet theater with a silver curtain behind which reside Princess Penelope, Queen Prunella, Poh-Poh the Clown, Hrothgar the dragon and the dastardly Count Badunov each with their respective handmaidens, henchmen, and courtesans, all attired in peaked white caps and the family crest across which is written the prescription for victory; splatting a human brain against the broad part of a bat, particularly if the scalp is Black and the bat has four running legs attached to and pinwheeled by a common hip, whose politics ends with the word "premicist," if you get my drift, in Bama, Tejas, or Mississip, the bat electrical taped for grip and discolored with consistently smacked grand slams against opponents under floodlights to cheering stands, flashbulbs blinding the victor with grandiosity and capturing on silver the beautiful slaughter; O the grotesqueries are these: shoving the middle finger to the ham-knuckle up the anus of a cat, the cat a frozen sculpture of horror, in the guest room beside the closet and wall-socket into which is jammed a light bulb a lamp a black rubber chord and a two fingered hand; the armless drummer grinning under moustache in a smoky dome full of booze, babes, Cobras, and panthers, one strumpet who from a distant pew coats his body with lust as the cymbals clash, the snares and traps intensify a rap so hot nothing connects the sticks to his stump but blurry air or a heat-mirage whose dust flies round a fool diving in; sinking surgical gloves through fascia and muscle, ligatures and sheath and striking pure granite, like boulders sunk in silt, granite arteries, granite gut, granite lungs, granite pump, rock upon rock in soft mud, immovable, great hereditary tumors embedded and petrified into heavy, cold, dead, blunt, blind, unemotional stone.

55

He wanted to seduce her; she was ready as a Gobi.
She could no more drop her ocean of love, suck and
lick, than eat potting soil. He wanted her panting
and she'd rather curl foetally in a mental ward.
Exasperation overtook him, floodlike, leaving bitter-
ness at existence; she refused his advances, repulsed
by what all males want, furious at vivid images of
future lovemaking fueled by past experiences—
but smiled deceptively (she performing fellatio, he
cunnilingus; she lashed to posters, he teasing; she
playing sado-masochism, presenting herself—all men
are sleaze). He was ravenous and she so ripe he
could taste her plum, but she flinched to her basal
ganglia, rage-imprinted. He perceived the futility
though her beauty stunned; the ostracism though she
electrified. The wrapping does not reveal the prize,
he mused; she is barely alive, yet he who is burning
appears almost dead, what irony. But then he
grasped the key to love's mystery: something about
powerlessness, something about iron, it all coalesced
into clarity, like a night sky of stars after putting
on glasses. Tragic that she can not release, he
thought, masturbating, crashing against her storm
wall like surf. Finally months later after cracking
the door less than a sliver and she worsening
and probably permanently clotted, he backed off,
resigned to failure—primitive failure and animal
frustration—slowly shutting off the spigot of ropy
desire. Now, the ball hemato-blasting a new day,
he is out there again, alone, nicked and blotchy
furred looking for action on Neurosis Boulevard.

56

And this little piggy squealed "no,no,no,no," all the way home. And then all the toes were accounted for: the big, the middle, the nondescript, nondescript's neighbor to the East, the itty-bitty which made baby laugh like a nautilus. And then the toes blinked out like a disappearing photograph, and baby went on a miniature vacation to Puerto Vallarta where a lion almost devoured him like a fortune cookie, but he escaped and wind rattled the blinds like dangling bones, and he whimpered and whispered a prayer-precursor to the Divine Death Overture, something about soft protrusions and blue rain. And baby Carroll decided he was having none of it and shattered two panes in the living room belonging to Daddy and his entourage one of whom played the Ace of Spades and raked in the kitty while on the artery a flying mechanical scream engulfed horizontal human moans in a white steel cube smudged with a red intersection and far, far away two events happened simultaneously: an imaginary Holstein jumped over an idiot moon keeping constant vigil on the continuous catastrophe, and in the silo accompanied by secret platoons of yellow arthropods Jack finally found Jill's gooey ooze representing nucleic acid's undeniable invincibility.

57

Sewed two cat heads onto my chest for breasts, black, whiskered, one chartreuse, one amber-eyed, mouths fixed in terror-grimace (decapitated them alive, naturally); fixed a pig snout into my crotch for cock, raw, red, jagged, but eternally erect; coconut shell pieces for kneecaps. hairy but tough and sexy; cassava skins for butt enhancement, smooth, pettable, delicious, pale; slivered banana peel for hair, long curvy strips with a lilt like a soccer star; the cat stomachs doubled as moccasins and the pig gut made a fine scrotum wrapped round two whole hazelnuts, hanging. Needed a new heart and decided the ripe red plum, so pried my cavity with a surgeon's vise and stuffed it in, veiny, glutted, sugary-sweet, dripping deep red streaks mosquitoes could swill on sweltering moonless afternoons; a scooped-out lemon rind for bladder and blown out egg shell for chin, the kind I smeared Paas over on Easter and called it art, beaming like a watt; bathed in compost to the crown, stuck on pheasant and buzzard feathers to ready myself for she for whom I am cooking shrimp Mozambique with coconut milk, cayenne pepper, and Rachmaninoff, she who by my creole-smooth telephone voice accepted my invitation sight unseen—the Personals, you know— and who I am positive will be wearing for playful aperitif thong panties with the window I've seen in nudey magazines. Decided from ear lobes, to dangle one live goldfish each by needle holes punched through gossamer fins, a touch, an accessory as Paloma Picasso would declare, with a smattering of close-to-surface-blood wrist cologne. I have such a beautiful clean-angled house, roomy, high-ceilinged, everything squared, spacious, shiny, flat, lacquered, and wide, and I inside, part ichthyologically glittering, part vegetatively glammed, mythological, nightmarish, a creature no woman could refuse.

58

When the bullets zinged off institutional walls into the con queso pot or hotdog bin; when the plastics exploded in the parking garage sending truck pieces whizzing like satellites, when the size 38D breast swallowed a .9mm slug down the back of its esophagus and out the other side wide as an elephant's trunk; when the teeter totter, the tether ball, and concrete box sprung mangled pomegranates of human blood matted with hair and rainbow entrails; when the wife's face stuck to the pillow with the smoking black hole and the bedsheet underneath; when 8 ft. up every faux drywall dripped ruby red struggle marks, and below one such edifice slumped two soaked bundles, father and son, with sticky notes straightpinned to each: "revenge"; when among the copper and turquoise river-rush and blunt nosed fish in white-gold sun-needles and moon-dark threads, current-rolled like a broken Ken, the environmentalist's head; when howitzers inside the wild horses' chests blew them into hamburger in a New Mexican field, banquet for birds; when a shovel discovered a pretty Herzegovinian mound to be a fresh blister of skulls; when a razor sharp stretch of Jasper, Texas, asphalt tore off chunks of blue-black skin and apocalyptic gore dragged by rope behind a confederate truck, like hanging living spitwads on a rural classroom ceiling, or plastering storm-strewn newspaper on a chain link fence; when what terrified the crows from a Wyoming corn field banquet was a bludgeoned and naked homosexual; and finally, when in the janitor's bathroom the cackling police officers plunged the toilet of a Haitian prisoner's anus with the handle of a plumber's helper I slid into her slippery flesh and she arched up to deepen the thrust and we both tore out heavy clay scoops of air with our sharp cry and moaning throat simultaneously as if two Earths collided, spewed upward and intermixed forming a new harmonious planet.

59

First I prepare the face with a warm wash rag by soaping off every grain of make-up, not one speck of lipstick, eyeliner, mascara, pancake base; then Witch Hazel-saturated cotton balls deep in eye creases, ear canals, folds and seams until they blacken like baseballs; I have already washed the hair, squeezed it free, toweled it dry, blown it with air, brushed it to sheen (I prefer raven black), and tied it off to expose the neck. Here vulnerability drips like rose petal tears and my tongue pulls to lick the white alabaster and gold tones, but I restrain my animal lust, treat her with utmost dignity. Next, I wash fingers free of Revlon, soil, and earthly dust till soft pouches of blood under cuticles shine like plums oozing yet contained in transparent skin. I swab between the fingers, brush the nails, and delicately rub in circular fashion along the grooves of print whorls. I have already slipped off in suds the wedding ring and placed it like a crown upon a pure linen towel alongside her gold Seiko and heirloom hair brush. Similarly, I have cleansed her teeth, submerging the floss under the gum, flicking free food bits and plaque such that blood strives to ooze small red pearls which with tissue I swipe from inside her soft crevasse until like sap they shut off at the insignificant irritation tap. Then I remove blouse and bra and employ alcohol to swab the areolas, each individual hair round the lunar flow, under the globes where salt lines appear pushing them up and over with hands guaranteeing sterility, and again I repress the centrifugally pulling suck of my open lips in exchange for the parabola of decency which few human males possess in the presence of inert nude femininity. Then I pull down the panties as if popping from the oven a done cherry tart, slip them past ankles folding them acceptably like some kind of soft crab, but this time I trade the fire of alcohol for soapy terrycloth, running it up carefully after folding it round with a gentle release her coarse springy hair, like oiling the blueblack steel of a Remington gunbarrel, then pat it dry till all beads dissolve and the engorged red vulva glows like cataract covered with fern. Slowly with spatula palms under buttocks I turn her and into her pores push impregnated frankincense, ambergris, and myrrh until her globes resemble moonlit isinglass, almost platinum, almost gold. And now, omitting here detail of the few remaining ceremonials, she is ready: pure nakedness, pure the aforementioned vulnerability, pure magnificence, every arm hair sparkling, every vein standing, every plate and shield saddle-soap softened. Efficiently, I take exactly what I need from the tray—nothing more, nothing less—having already, between the bath and the instruments switched on a CD (I have always enjoyed the passion of Rachmaninoff), and in the gray, her body still posteriorly positioned, with a votive candle haloing her head facing northeast, I begin to partake.

60

And the two romantic lovers having recently discovered each other's overwhelming characteristics—the universe's most gloriously pinnacled—praised God in perspiration-coupling, the bed a buckboard wagon, their bodies jamming, the sun-becoming-moon-becoming-sun, surrounded by wrappers of convenience store sandwiches and Hershey's Kisses, the floor sticky as a Cinexplex, praised God the continents on whose extremities they stood like upright Hoovers rotated them together, interpenetratedly, he a Pegasus, she a bronze athletic Rebecca of solid blood-veins, they a bolt of industrial twine, heavy and significant. "We are megaphonic," he exclaimed (she hair-trigger orgasmic between the thighs, and he her master architect), "we are invulnerable," from some pyscho-megalo emerald precipice zagging through the roof of heaven, bare-chested overgazing the world. Marriage being superfluous under such pressure—superfluous and laughable—they will strap on various girdles—rubber or otherwise—to prevent volcano offspring, his very squigglers whipping against their flesh-prison like galloping horses against the flaming barn—mane-melting urgency, my man, in such mock multiplication. Our baby shall be an exponential multiple of our magnificence. And so they panted and heaved and doubled over and splayed and stuck up like a mizzen mast and drank down like a cataract while fools labored and sucked up yapping and strategizing like doomed lieutenants. Let us be plain: flesh is everything. Magnolia flesh, orchid flesh, elephant ear flesh, human flesh engorged with liquids, overflowing, pooling the universe, Jesus being the pale mantra of the desiccated. And so our heroes straight-pinned their floating oil-dot eyes, depth charged their ear drums, devoured their O's, but spared their tongues needed for innumerable flicking and occasional forking. One of them ritualistically shot their mom with a keyboard-powered Lexmark cartridge, she slumped over ritualistically dead. But let's not swerve. Now the cilia of their womb, like the guts of an over-sanctified fig, rot, slimy to touch, send out a stench. The vagina of the floor opens wide its jaw and gulps down in waves like a snake its prey their welded together bones, their eggs and minnows into its esophageal pit, mould topside in their bed, filth and viral writhe. Let it be said that iron drove their love, implacable iron blocks tamped their blood and hardened around handles Superman God gripped, swung, and hurled into the euphoric universe, slamming them inextricable, and let "a raging hunger nailed them to a depthless kiss" be their epitaph.

61

The glorious night, the sumptuous night, the night of turkey stuffing and eating, of fat drippings, of soft meat pulled apart in strong hands, baked and hot, the longed for night engorged with champagne, strawberries, and walnuts, and white iced cake, the risen night, enmounded, slippery with oil, globed in halves, hemispherical, packed with butterfingers; the blind fish night, the nosing mullet night, the night of blunt bumping, scary and inexplicable, the night of dark foreskulls and double-twisted bones, the night of torn lamb's meat soft as smooth pullet, starring the print-whorls; the night of tuxedos, chrysanthemums, and seances and hammering whales' backs; the death night, the coffin night, the night of burning nails, the night of the baby in the sarcophagi, curled and tight; the night of flamingoes and reeking pelicans standing on the open eyes, the night of blue horses flying overhead; it is the night for executing witches with knives and gasoline and eating their charred esophagi; the night of condiments; the night of breakage in a too powerful fusion, of lace and luster bombs, of broken packages and escaping tadpoles, the delectable pie-night, scallop crusted, thumb and elbow crusted, blue juice-bubbling; the night of forests and switches, forests and loam beds, the dream-twitterers tucked under leaf comforters, the night of fairies, dwarfs, and flitterers, chins upon the bed's edge, repositioning pump strings, in camouflage-fatigues, earth smeared faces, loaded with missile trajectories; the night of boa constrictors, cold and draping, of crawling vines and white crinolines, the night of slimy smears on pure materials at the midriff level and the hemline, of slugs, earthworms, and millipedes slithering in, turning up clay like a screwplough; the night of multi-pledgings consisting of three fingers, four knees, and two spines rocking upon the calcium moon clothed in blood clothed in veins clothed in sails wedged in the shape of self in air, explicit, delimited, yet exponentially grand like the firmament on a wizard's hat; the night of lip licking lusciousness no frog shall shit upon nor lizard stink until the fiery knife blazes a glistening slice off the ground like the bleeding flesh off a cantaloupe rind.

62

He departed without food for he did not need
food. The third day he was strong as the second
and the fourth tolerably erect followed by the
fifth of solid walking across hot sand, staff in
hand, and then the seventh, goat skin dangling
dust-dry, feet blistered, tongue eating air, licking
God, the eighth, the ninth, a transcendence, a
blessing, he did not glow but needed no sustenance like common biologies, floated above the
flame, chosen, focused with resolve, walked to
a Promised Land methodically supernaturally
but a man just a man replete with belief, tenth,
fifteenth, slept under dippers, drinking thought,
philosophy, ignorance, innocence, thirty days,
thirty-nine days without sex or food, without
love or lye, without Jesus or Mary, a young
man with Michelangelo toes, a loin cloth, a rag,
wandering, wandering, steady as she goes, like
a prow plowing grain, no one worshiped him,
none prayed to him, nor did he pray, stunned of
prayer by rage and death, on the fortieth he did
not die nor weep nor sing nor stay but ate the
sudden blackness of locusts hilariously clacking.

63

The whole fish skeleton fine as angel hair, as asbestos thread, the transparent rib-fan, the spine, the pinkish head, the jaws and razor teeth, flounder-oval, delicate, a coin of pins and needle, floats before my eyes in grainy light like a negative in air, wispy clean, unblemished, without sand or bill, specimin perfect. Why? This morning. The blinds closed. A milky hovering snowy light. These are not my bones. My heavy bones. My mammoth skull. My mastodon pelvis. My ulna and radius. My patella and swords. My femur and coccyx. My phalanges and metatarsals. This little trout. This millipede. When I die the world will know bones. With no poems stuck to them, with no sexual flesh between. No red and blue sherbert. No pudding afloat in bowls. The world shall know pure massive calcium monument, testamental, absolute. Bones that loved. Bones of masturbation. Bones of no deadly god. Bones that flamed a wall of fire. White clean bones uncremated up no flue but lying bare in glitter soil, eye holes huge as cannon bore. Flagpole without flag. Patriotism without grit. Bones of cat, skunk, or rat; possum or mutt, furious, fixed grimace of fear or hate, decomposed, bits of fur, are beautiful wadded experiments, paper drafts, noble as plaster, paste, or rubber cement to these Ajax, Apollo, Prometheus, and Hercules crumbling towers. Well, fuck it. Nobility blows. Just the bones of cowardice, capitulation, squeamishness, crucifix, mollusk bones, bones of squid, bones of jellyfish and octopus. These were mine and yours and yours. Programmed. Scriptural. Heroic countersquirt. This ichthyonosaur floating before my nose, neon pulsing, psychedelic, iconographic Christ piper-prophet fossilized upon the mind to guide us from our unction like a flame. Rising from these lines I trip over the Sistine chapel of a fly.

64

The bird cries its way out its cage on chromium wings,
wings polished as car bumpers primary and secondary
feathers welded fanned beating by gasoline powered
engines hole torn in wire phoenix-arrowed char marks
found liquid gold at the vanishing point amber and red
but the bars are bent inward from outside the canon
shot from the wild expanse of freedom rich colors dark
savors flesh depths fringes and knotted thread brown
envelopes rage pistoned the thrush fury fumacity steel
axillar wrist speculum cylindrical boring through card-
board hair like a rocketgod pulsing machine pumping
rod nuzzles its cuddle bone cracks seed mashes canta-
loupe between cable driven bone mates the ragged hag-
angel of the emerald/ruby/blue and obsidian black
ball eider and crown the oven gaping a maw the gown
the ancient claws the sinewy metal of constricted riv-
ers the phlegm of fire clotted in the breast the sweet
familiar blessed by Tedium Satan's grist flattened to a
placid lust on a hammered sea, and there there among
the grating colliding grinding gears the ribs blown in-
ward to the tight reunion fusion of bloodsplatter and
Rorschach's smear the body bending out the wire shot
by desperation and fear, spun high in infinite blue on
its luminous fan by epiphany and dawn and bending
the wire right blew back into its pink and perfect prison.

65

I reach into the liquid ball of fire, gloves snapped on, surgical mask, aluminum of utensils, nurses, nurse's aid, iodine for the patient, frosted green skivvies, wipe wipe, sponge the vein, intensified light, technology's finest, magnified mirrors, reach into the ball of flame, showering, shimmering, thick as sea mud, elemental vitality, original sphere, rhino and bull, crocodile and cow, pull out the sun's heart, extract, excavate, sucking live hole, rotate, cut, animal gut, lift it raining sulphurous pelts, scalpel, artery, intoxicated, drunk, myocardial lust, deepslash the throat, inoperable pulse, lace, sew, and shut. Wash, suds, and soap, into the forested room, loved ones in shoes, the eye's igniting needles, reinstated, reinstalled, confetti of violets, lemons, and rusts composing gold, crowning gold, blinding the insensible, I have sunk my limbs to elbows in dragon blood, hot overflowing oatmeal, star and stun, electrical voltage, the animal still, primeval ooze, trained at Johns Hopkins, interned at St. Luke's, now solo unencumbered, locks flying madly, partial-insane, sunk my flesh in solar, eye, kidney, spleen, organ meat, stung by explosion gasses, seared in sizzling fat, god's instructional oval, capacity seating, apprentices' gaping drool, theater of the wise lunatic aspiring the hot solder, each flagellum whipping like onion bulb & tail across the ferrous oxide of roots and leafrot and stream into the scalding reality.

66

Stopped my mouth with cement and trowel, did the Bible
from prayer, no faith in that creature God, Dog, Odg,
like a white porcelain john I am, a drilled-of-pulp tooth
enamel-sealed, mason made, dentist formed, the Bible
a bottlestopper in the anus, puttied up pores, now I
choke, ganglanded, oblong sick screams of help to
Catholics, Jews; lashed to chair, brutalized, released
with dried white concrete orifices, with scissor-snapped
synapses, full of Ecclesiastes and Thessalonians brain
like cat-clawed ball, I am crawling, crawling in stun-
ned unreception, solid massive toilet, God filled you
with daddy who filled daddy with me, mother you
were there with your black rimmed miracle tube,
sorcery zapped, cracked with glitter, lightning zagged
out sky into you, hurled by masculine divinity, chan-
nelled birth violence, witnessed angry revolution,
fertility madness, omnipowerful unavoidable Pres-
ence; the testament binds me like brick bowels, cheese
and tree wood, I petrify through the regal and tow-
ering land, the mesmerizing eyes, the vitality strands,
the royal cataracting blood gorges of the beautiful
and sad, once a breathing gaping hole, I grey among
the statuesque, pattering wet Portland block, the
Word a rock embedded in macrame beside a rock,
linearly, a necklace of rocks through the esopha-
gus into the gut, swallow, swallow, razors of gall
and kidney, star-stuck. I shall stand sandaled in
muck in a hail of prepuces, sulfur, and toads, all
spring-summer without slumber or lust looking up
like a tulip, like rust petals, an iron truss. The stick
you see lavishing branches shall be me in ecstasy.

67

The iron slides across the blouse taking with it the wrinkles of despondency and thrill, the chicken soup boils, fresh free range chicken, carrots, celery, potatoes, fatty pouches burst and spread, cholesterol fat soulful and warm, the fundamentalism of animals taken into blood serum, heart, and lungs, the closet full, the bed made, patted, red paisley sheets, platinum pillows fluffed like pheasant breasts, the squat close rooms, half dark, breathable, the sliding Mission chair, the leather couch, the lamp and shade, yellowish pyramidal light, the half weeping wife, eyes often oozing, peasant feet, potted plant to plant with watering can, lovingly, three quarter singing, trilling, the plants rising like birdlings, cheep! cheep!, the husband in tan moccasins reading, eyeing, composing to himself some dramatis personae, ink running out ears, fingers plum pens, the lovely homestead, biscuits, jam, eggs, on the foundations of history, pioneers, wagon wheels, Indians, speckled trout, body bits, declarations and covenants, dead pullets, pelts, offspring, love, leather shirts, and the genesis of football, a humble home balances atop it all, cheerleaders, alcoholics, rah-rahs, and cars, the magnification spectacles on a sidebar with the novel nearby, butter and bread, God blesses the doldrums of this home, the hands and darning needle, the toes in big shoes, God adores the routinization, the tearing down, digesting, and vacating of the vegetables of hard work sprizzled with luck, breathing lung of a home, forty years betrothed, a walls and roof billows, scarlet red, dark purple, subterranean blue, mausoleum black, threads of platinum cadmiums shot through like anniversaries, like hair strands, columns of champagne with loin pork and beans. The gorgeous ones, the beautiful bachelor and maiden sabbaths waved like nerves upon the air, the frenzied barracuda deep-water feeding, thighs spiked open, nailed to mattress by Centaur driving. Oh Maggie filaments suffer without ye, choked of power no more glow, my execrable globe sourced in you attains solarity, electromagnetically fine, I loathe and love the photosynthesizing you, blinds drawn, raised, a cranial killing field, minus your cosmic and infrared pump I am blue nuclear winter, you in nappy terrycloth, hair clipped shut, cold bloodless feet padding across Berber to hot Colombia, naming the birds: chickadee, junco, rufous, ferruginous, the harvest moon, the hazy sun, the exuberant unspectacular familiarity of breathing a room of poached egg water, perfume of potato pulp, and perpetual partner—oh Maggie, down here in my crumbling cradle surrounded by printers' cages imagining myself ultra-creative I could crater at my megalomania when authentic grandeur glows through exhaustion like fluorescent bones through translucent hope.

68

Again the taut monofilament line between fisherman and fish, gossamer, glimmering, three pound bull red and two hundred pound bastard battling in salt biliousness, fucker c'mon, come home to daddy, ink-blot tail-muscle flicking in granite green, gills pumping, mouth-cartilage refusing, two animals in opposite atmospheres cut by the scissors of surfaces, glass sheet, almost plexiglas, 10 lb test sunk through like solid sculpture, bronze, at the outdoor art mart beside the thrashing sailfish, contest, wills, death, nourishment, fresh red blood, the man early forties, stubble beard, business failure, two kids, raven haired wife-bitch, tortured with cratering fantasies of wealth, accolades, ribbons, oral sex, congratulatory boxes, Europe, the fish Executive Vice-President, Ben Franklin Life & Casualty, fat, bald, sweaty, heavy drinker—Black Label—swinger, fertilizer of thousands, clogged floater valve, this hook in throat, block and tackle punishment yanking him to hell the foreordained testamental destiny of the sacrilegious, barb in poppers, swift intractable Adjudicator, some are fouled through back or tail, unfair, but the souls of all infidels are ripped from guts to float unredeemed and eternally in the upperworld; the man: Orthodox, gold icon wearer, the only wholeness known is this standing upon the sloughs in an inch thick fiberglass bowl, Mercury outboard, live shrimp, Embassador Abumatic casting reel, singing to himself, hauling up spam, the bump, the strike, the exhilarating instant the magnificent beast breaks surface into the steel gray light, whopper!, giant!, mother of trout! swivel and claw with shrimp bits still attached removed from lip, the man cold refreshing drafts, it doesn't arrive higher than this; the fish: nihilistic, savage, mean as shit, shitting, a lifetime of stuffed resentment and rage croaking out his mouth as he lies upon mates in the red, blue, and silvery slime pit, fry me you hypocritical bloodless white robed priest-cowards on your Neptune-thrones, double standard bastards clinging to cleanliness like a culture of dweebs, translucent phosphor sacs flaring pure emerald green, gluttonless, fornicationless, covetousless, hedonisticless slipping through cubes like a breathing death, tuna-fresh. The man: loved but slaughtered the wife's raw eggs his whips slammed into, wiped until wringing guilt with their hearts and spills of shame with their hair, the fish issues cackles of cynicism from his chair, eradicating the blight the man throws the switch with holocaustal delight on his cold creel of criminals.

69

Assume a keen and precise perception, stropped like a razor, assume he sees sharp as fish gills detail, and it torments. Assume he perceives the bottom drawer pinching a bit of sleeve sticking out like a blister from perfect pine. Assume this flaw assassinates sleep. Assume he stares all night at walls refusing to repair the human failure. Assume he is under a doctor's care. Behavior modification. Sitting in anxiety. Pools. Pools. Assume an awareness of a thousand imperfections. A stain in his anus. A light switch half off. A toilet seat tottering on its point like a diamond preparing to crash. Assume a brain fire. The stomach acid eating the shale of his spine shall push through at three hungering for fuel. The dark burns his eyes. Assume an uncanny tendency toward catastrophe. Death by insomnia, extinction by responsibility. Assume perpetual wakefulness inside a spider-wrapped bundle reserved for future hunger, rolled within fiber of blanket plastered with enzyme. Imagine a hyper-awareness of the bladder, hands, and phlegm suppressing L-tryptophan from filling the brain. The man wrings soul, prays, paces, feigns sleep in a kind of cataleptic trance. Imagine he claws his face. Imagine an onslaught of self-recrimination. The man is honorable, dependable, sweet, every breath exhaled a monumental defeat. The minute hand smashes the next groove like an anvil. This is Odysseus opening his flesh to wind like a shirt, the wind stings his blood, freezes raw flesh like Mennen skin bracer, an alcohol splash driving him out into paradise. Assume he imagines he is lying naked upon a white table. His psyche sprouts in every direction the impenetrable thousand knives of perception. Asp. Mechanical porcupine. Medieval glove crawled off the hand. Assume a protection so categorical, totalizing, ubiquitous, and complete that it stings the man into the blind annihilating crucifixion of belief.

70

Last night sprouted splotches of silver pelt, howled and stank, tasted bitter bark of birch (high horizontal parallel tooth marks), sprayed liquid gold east and west, north and north, steam, relief, snow, exhalation, cracked twigs underfoot, moonless dark, rushing brook, whiff of snow-fertility, shook robotical mechanical abnormalities at the base like earthquaking cartoon rectangles and squares, lines jittering into each (society's migraine), paced, paced, draping-shirt above dangling sex, naked legs, Best Friend crushed-fleece mocs, wife floating above in bed, marshmallowed, neat, toes Palmolived and translucent—cuticles and pink quarter-moon shoals—husband beyond high dark-stained walls on uneven squishiness shaky, spindly, groping, half-stumbling, pelvic equilibrium on unfamiliar terrain, coyote operetta from distant tribe plaintive-flying into heart veins, grabbing ventricle and auricle like handfuls of clay and flinging them up up into the nebula, both within my cavity and without, a double thing beating, beating alive as a star. Three AM, the austere never sleeping granite peaks spearing God's spleen invisibly gathered round my waves—congregation of indifferent believers—witnessing a soft squeamish inculcated sack of underbellied humanity shed his ghostliness and smear the dung and nitrogen rich earth upon his globe and hair and neck, fur-bald flesh in dust of dirt, paint skunk scat across his chest, and drive drive madness into the flesh of life with buck like flanks, with flank of stag, coiled and sprung, cloven, tucked and flung. He has piled upon the ground a mansion for flies, wrigglers, burrowers and bugs and shall re-enter his studded cube wherein resides the tub and bowl, is half-way there, a coyote-to-human supernatural blur. A naked hand emerging from fur down-pushes the handle. After passing through the transforming shaver of home's threshold leaving behind a mound of bristles, a naked man closes the door, punctuates with shadow the lampless light, slips in bed beside his wife, curls into a muscle memory of animal, and spectacular with echoes of elementalism sleeps until graininess extinguishes night.

71

Let's say your son overdoses and dies on a floor—a speedball, and after spasms overwhelm pump in tremors and stabs he seizes while you, his daddy, breathe in the office, on the pavement, in the eateries, at lavatory, breath unobstructed through world's heathy canals. Let's give him twenty-one years, the final seven devoid of obedience, conscience, rationality, or books spent in the Xanadu of vandalism and prostitution, spent, too, in an heir-to-throne fantasy, delusional with invulnerability, fourteen years of typical middle-class Caucasian childhood and preadolescent arias and yap, emulation and heroism, now lies like a tricked rat on its side, stomach stuffed with poison he thought was bliss. Let's pretend it's over—morgue, mortuary, memorial, dirt. The mother gets Xanax, a military stoicism freezes over father two thousand miles divorced among the Anthracites—and the gallery unloads another glass masterpiece to a fibrillating tourist. "How lovely it shall glow upon the mantlepiece!" Well, screw it. Earth's outer crust is a mile deep morgue—how unoriginal—megalomaniacs, idiots, geniuses, and whores. It's a wonder we don't slip on the banana peel of gore. Chances are you'll be buried in your son's own skull.

72

Confessions of a lunatic: Penises the size of psychological monsters buried in everywhichway presented female genitalia in a festering benedictine sabbath of procreation surrounded by icons, totems, and phalluses of copulation in a phantasmagoria of love, a delusion of love, lovesick, lovestruck, mooneyed biologies infinitesimally megalomaniacal microorganisms teeming and fizzing in the Petrie dish of multiplication to Rachmaninoff or Def Leopard what gives a shit, imaginings of grandiosity and permanence veiled and trained under the blessings of God to some idiotic sober but intoxicating wedding march, the giddy bacilli or bacteria drawn forward through the quaint historical mountain town by double blind chestnut horses, "just married" scraped across the carriage eye, our saviors which shall plop forth from split silkiness conquering replications of the themselves, Harvard heroes or Julliard geniuses, their little sweetie pies swaddled in Jason's elusive fleece. Lawrence Livermore National Laboratory, the German National Laboratory for Heavy Ion Research, The Institut National de Physique Nucleaire et de Physique des Particules, Brookhaven National Institute for Nuclear Physics, The Indiana University Cyclotron Facility, The Bates Linear accelerator and collider, giants jutting through the clouds, Woton and Hunding protruding through cumulus their superior countenances, spectroscopy and monovalences flashing through their minds, linked by a double drop forged deep sea hook to Presidencies and Prime Ministers equally omnipowerful in the stratospheres, inaccessible as quasars, delusions of grandeur stiffening them with blood till they are hard as doors or Eiffel geometry, these puny pitiful electro-isotopic visigods prickling off Earth's rotundity like flaccid root hairs visible to the microscope, fuck them all their apocalyptic folderol, and their ever-worshiping wives dining at Cartiers.
The great powerful literary contemporaries I could name like death rattles by the hundreds: Rich, Schnackenberg, Lauderbach, Epstein, Lux, Economou, Valentine, Sobin, immortales, maestros, hands like facial tissue, translucent Sampson Agonistes parting the reverentials like sorcery wanting to pick at the lint of their clothes, prophets, sages with the verbal acuity of pupa worm in tuxes at the National Book Award ceremony at the New York Sheraton sticking up like a miniature domino in dirt full of applauding and petit mal champagne sodden minds, the devil take them all to the cauldron of no alphabet at the sulphur erupting pit of the inferno's hungry gut. Coldwell Banker's one hundred top performers—the Platinum Club—at Belagios with their Audemars, Vacherons, or Roger Dubuises, bronze, polished, inculpably genuine, the woman understatedly magnificent and gen-

erally plus-sized like pouted sage grouse dabbed in rouge, at the pool, the tables, the shows, the beds getting a little extra-curricular cold-call commissionless fun, mutually admiring the diamond shaped plexiglass platinum award each received at the plenary banquet one by one like diplomats, may each reproduce themselves by a billion, fuse, and ascend like a misty cloud of the brokers extraordinaire to the 30,000 sq. ft. mansion in the sky of Peter Neederman, Pres. and CEO of Coldwell Banker Worldwide, sleeping like a goat protruding satyr after multiple masturbations on his boil infested ass. But I crashed out half-wit, mentally handicapped, my medulla oblongata, a.k.a., my spinal bulb juiceless and infantile, a dwarf and rather hideous to gaze upon, slightly thalidomide, so forgive me my rage, my indiscretion, my vulgarity, my plain misinformation, but I fail—and have always failed— to appreciate the difference between man and grass.

73

I swallowed a quarter, 1997 D, Liberty, Washington, God,
eagle, choked like blowing enormous dick, it stuck along
shocked peristalses but worked, aching, to gut, leaving
me in despair. Dimes and pennies are kid's play, hors d'
oeuvres, half dozen slithered down like bays. Slid two coins
between eyeball and lid, antiquarian lobotomy, slit nerves.
Slipped in more filling brain with nickel and money-filth
finger prints touched with semen, shit, snot, vagina-juice,
making a cesspit of my head. Stuffed a twenty up my anus, then another, another, a knotted scarf of parchments,
three feet through the large intestine, licking the small, feeling stuffed and desperate, but bank vault wealthy. The
nostrils proved problematic. I've seen Rimpoches thread
floss up one nasal cavity and down the other; I rolled
twenties together into twine and fed it in; behold, hanging out my holes, horns! What remains? I had no fresh
slot-forming surgeries on my flesh. I chopped off my penis and to the stump tied feed bag of money, like oats
to horse. The organic trash sack received the largess
of my circumcised love. Finally I employed my ten good
digits to crawl into the bath tub filled with singles from
my meaningless and withering family fortune, doused
the entire scene with kerosene, touched my nose to
a struck match head and called the conflagration rage.

74

Do not cram that stillborn into the box, the inglorious box shoved over with dirt and dumb solemnity, capped with slate or some idiotic bracketed date August 1 - August 1, the umbilicus garlanded about her neck, the undrooled upon stuffed dog, the hospital bracelet, her name was Drake or Tenacity or Steph, do not lower the corpse melodramatically, inner drum beat, like martyrdom on TV, into the black ragged upper crustaceous scratch crawling with unchordate predators, as if you were not Jesus or God but some feckless insignificant beast, miracle-less, incapable, unrevelatory in machine made socks, vehicle, and gift doomed to cardiac and pulmonary affliction, gonorrhea and tape worms, terminal obesity—fool and infelicity. Rather shove her with knuckles and fist back into your murderous crease indelicately, like Loge or Froh, feet first into the bloody cave, followed upwardly like a sheet by slippery thighs, torso, neck, and face, sloppy with episiotomy, bloody with scrapes, pink, black, ruby, and mauve rivulets, wrapped in afterbirth cellophane membrane, clotty gore and baby redux, returned to womb, there to gestate, fester, float like an aquanaut, your dead neonate, baby, zygote, you the coffin filled again with your cherished jewel. She will breathe again, thump-thump, kick, squeeze, defecate, pee, in good brief term a clean revisit to the pristine sea of tubes, oxygen, sustenance, simplicity, weightlessness, and blur and in ripetime you shall push push push push the indispensable delusion.

75

Dear God: thank you for the physical beauty in the world, etc. and get fucked. Brutality festers under veneer. Abercrombie and Fitch and the other even-cornered orderly little boxes atop the cauldron of rage. I've read your absurd prevarications, burning bush, parting sea, water to wine, the whole bloody idiotic litany. What do you take me for? My son's in jail, my parents hate each other, and love is the biggest crock of shit in our world. Take it up the ass mr. big. I shove it in and squirt my ever-regenerating fascist through your anus. You "work in mysterious ways." Sure. Gotcha. Like multiple sclerosis, cerebral hemorrhage, schizophrenia, ovarian cancer, gang rape, endless battlefield slaughter, hunger and starvation, crack cocaine, mandatory economic survival, family annihilation, serial killer, christmas eve, the whole bloody genocidal mechanistic panoply of madness, demagoguery, power-lust, and blood papered over with The David, Notre Dame, Starry Night, The Cello Suites, The Divine Comedy, A Night at the Opera. You don't fool me with your poured concrete. The devil created you. Oops! a brief eulogy-interlude for my latest decimated friend—bone cancer—chemotherapy, steroids, morphine, marrow transplant—closed his lids on two blonde daughters, 9 and 13—hole in air, let me chant: HeyHeyHeyHey, HeyHeyHey, Hey, Hayi-o-ku-oo, tum tum. Thank you mr. zero for another picnic in the park. And he believed! But we know the irrefutable; invisible wasp with hypodermic stinger whirring through walls, money, steel, petition to jab it in the neck. "Come down, Come down, why dost thou hide thy face?" one frustrated poet begged. I will reveal. The mere hideous outline of you visible would decimate all animal hope or happiness. You think my personal circumstances blind and embittering? Don't make me laugh. I observe with microscopic scientific objectivity the botanical, zoological, and geological, and state with emotionless inanimation the incontrovertible: I could wedge a baseball bat up your lower orifice, swing, and Hercules-hurl you to plague another planet-island of cripples and cruciality with your miracle-laden-liturgy and it would take a lifetime of restitution to clean the crap off the end of Louisville wood.

God has a glisteny red mouth like a baby's and two gleaming new teeth. The round earth goes oblong as He sucks it like a tit. Plastic pants crinkle, poopies upon oopies, His pocket fatty legs protrude from animal tape. We call it tides but it's vacuum-lipped nipple and through it shoots cows, skyscrapers, Crisscrafts, coffins, avocados. He stiffens. He's almost always awake. Baby Boogums, Jack, and candlestick. Curds beside her, and whey. Oh my, oh my, what a gigantic boy am I. Nature roars and flows into his great big eyes. There had been such frictionlessness with mimosa, oleander, and such, before the thistle-punch. Angry Snookers. Had to change his nighttime Luvs. Frankly mama's exhausted, exasperated, mad, face awfully rumpled and hair gone kapow. Daddy's pissed as well, getting none, blasphemously regretting. God's mouth resembles sliced watermelon, cold vermillion crystals. Let us give Him clobber, pure pineapple clobber with heavy yellow custard, his first colostrum solid. Hand over forehead let us coalesce. Tree shredders flow through His pulsing lips. Baby's learning steps but crawls through calculus. S. S. S. We've erected something memoryless, North, East, South, West, clean, two sawn-apart beams, and enter stricken doors with quivering gargoyle tongue. Sinners, beggars, thieves Huey indistinguishably screams torrentially mean. Djibouti, The Crimean Sea, The Magellanic Straits, all geo-political-psychology split the flooding particulate with their infinitesimal statuate, pews, hymnals, and seed. It's epidemiological. The angry neonatal dictator, binky, blankey, and spew. Admit: it's weird. melon engapes maw, inhales, world puckers for the blow.

77

We run backward, yes backward, like a rabbit on LS
D, past the lovemaking headless woman, the train
load of nakedness and spirituality, the wild boar bris-
tle brush hanging in the bathroom, past the shiny Pil-
ates machine with its immortalizing gadgetry, past
the brown-mandibled Coleoptera, oh, the yo-yo,
the bolo, the rusty steel yellow road grader, the
gleaming angel-hair diphtheria tear, the facial scars
and ovacular Oxy-5, the star smear across black
wonderful, the stuffed overgodly beagle pup, the
rubber predatory dinosaur, yes backward on thum-
per thumbs past Robert Frost's son's suicide,
oh, give us the inexhaustible upright vacuum; back-
ward on methamphetamine past the flaming pin-
ball machine, the double-stuff plowed in like des-
peration, the incomprehensible Siddharthian physics
text and the clothless pink hermaphrodite, paste-
on ecstasy chased by gin the quiverful of ballpoint
pens…let us dash on feverful wings in ululating
reverse past the accusatory vertical library of spines,
fanblades, and facilities, deep sea clam shells,
heated and cooled glass cat's eye marbles, Sissy's
emblazoned reproductive disinclination, dear swe-
et lovely Sissy significantly underpounded & ov-
erprotected, the harelipped oratorical ridiculous
phase, the three year old's encysted esophagus,
let us, I say and again proclamate, like light-legged
luminous lap-eared lagomorphs on copious quan-
tities of codeine-laced horse somersault back-
ward past the leonine lubricious hallucination,
the interplanetary abraxas sexual adumbration,
the hyperactive thyroidal cavernational hunger for
the spherical, conical, ovoidical or square which
emplagues the conquerors of soaking solipsism.

78

And how the head responds, the soaked brain blackens with it as it passes front to stem, then shines emerald red, a lovely naughtiness, elicit, forbidden, spews unscheduled dopamine backward like saliva, vagina shall ensue, massive cock, flirtation on the sea, the organs shift permanently in their watery key, she shoots shots, slams the shot glass down on the mirror slab, the blonde-brunette, ever ready to slur down her slender panties for the primal call inside and insecurity, and why not on these stools at two o'clock with the chambers empty of prophylactic pills and the anarchist's rot of oblivion on the tube, score! as hard rubber eye flips hits the net, the organs shift, packed, to crave in juices like Del Monte pears, soft, syrupy, sweet, nasty, a pulpy hit, the rubbery tits, nipples, stain, the way they sway excruciating with pleasure and give, give to the red flood, the clitoris, the vagina open like a flan stroked to ecstasy, and the gin, bang after bang on the bar, who cares, permed blonde hair, waxed legs, painted nails, toes and all, pumiced heels begging to be kissed, camels and animals all, among asphalts and sibs, the tremulous tips, sensitive, longing, huge lily pads, the dish pulling it in like evidence. Chemistry hungers splayed like a cubist, now a billion mouths spiderweb thick, beg like lampreys, prick, prick, reaction chains down the spine afire with tense radiance, she squeezes, pants, raises stiff, that panoply of beautiful labels, ashtray sweet, she struggles, submits, refuses, switches pure white solid light, wick, tube, lit isotope, her gray tufted mother trillions away, claws the flesh flexing over her, the clear amber blur, the messiness, the edgelessness of it, weak, weak, live, grips the slam down the legs, up the cortex to the sky and the fiery flowing crustless singular eye, they will drag her away drooling and raving, lunatic.

79

If I have to take this crap for the rest of my life it will be the death of me, pills for OCD, pills for sleep, dulling my wits like a grinding stone, overmedicated nation, mendicants, mendacity. Brilliant droplets beside the drinking glass, beige hand towel, mirror paralleled medicine chest, jiggered dead fly on shattered wings. Let us triumphant through Kandahar march! God loves granite stuffed blues snapping abreast two by twos, Laura Badolato, Todd Moir, Richard Sands lovely double DNA strands. Well, I can't handle the stuff, something's unglued, Fluxomine, Zolpidem Tartrate, spit-polished shoes, a diminutive arm lies over there, a human stomach in a pool. Fuck the combatants, hyped on fumes, a connection here, drugs & death, but can't finger it, twisted dogs, blind dogs, hemorrhaged cerebrally, faithful abstracted faces dying on lawns, men wearing plants and electronic garb, Diazepam, Nortriptlyne, Carbamazepine, scabby Goldens, knobby Labs, glaucomatous Bulls, troops noose-tightening, pressuring the fools. God loves an idiot but eats the lunatic, and I've got my pills in conflagrating fields to soften the blow of osteoporodic friends and offspring of Mephistopheles making me dull in demand-reaction-land.

80

That great massive thing between the shoulders, Jesus!
black cavern, squirming light, infinity, whore and mendicant,
little bastard full of Christmas flames, plastic hollow doll,
marble veined and a million suns crawling like worms, packed
echoes like canned Del Monte pears, beefy live with gray
bits and power outages in solid bone, the answer to nil
juicing off walls like a gluey spill, God's cathenial, deep
domed, organless, ponderous, like a green La Saber, spidering bright veins wrapped round zero, freightloads of
coal teeming with imagery, huge loneliness pushed by
chuffer into sea, olfactor, aelator stuck to the outside
like shell-less snail, while feeble megaphone penetrates
the underside, medicine ball with genitalia of tongue,
glottis, and jaw, flapping authoritarian claptrap, the gospel, the word, deadly accurate like a gun, smoking bullet holes of words you better hug, that serious apparatus knotted at the edge for punctuation, fed by a firmament of starry dregs from above, pulpy bowling ball
stuffed with coddling, brattiness, effrontery, the overstroke, blown as it were by laity, hefty gaseous zeppelin unchosen by anything wise anonymous in a pile of
fuseless lime, news-swallower, tree-swallower, mate-swallower, hole in precipice through which panthers
fall, isolation pit, mirrored sphere—or—the tremendous
burst, the genius of solidity, corners, edges, angles,
frames, the explosive horizon predictable by periphery,
sun, mountain, ocean, plain, the vanishing point touchable, stumble caught by floor times the force of gravity
squared, bloody butts of hands or elbows, love a finitude of heart and hips slammed into like a wall, naked
and clobberable, a security in friends of the weeping
shoulder or laughing dinner fork or criterium roar,
mortality in a soup of classifications from entropy to
gastroenterology splitting human from God like a proton hurling the former into a simpering dud through space
into a tattersall television chaise within a mansion of tacks
and two-by-fours wherein human sits amidst a clutter of
statuettes, prides of honor, gewgaws, bric-a-brac, coddlers, burblers, baskets, and wax, a king's crown tipping
with liquid brilliance, cranium blazing with megalomania.

81

The big puffer sucking the nicotine, lips snapping with the tug
is mama's boy at twenty one, surgeon of the suds, racionator,
hot shot of cheap charisma in the one-third house of godless
double A's, too smart with sketchy beard for higher authorities what with a booming IQ and superhuman resistance to
crack cocaine, asbestos head and fire wall against mortalities
is my boy, Biff of the blasphemies, tender souled but hard
on self-survival, mathematical maestro with hands on guitar
that can weave wailing, and I wish to say, what? creature of
my bone, bravado king, tragedian deity, descend to the pale
and stupid commoners, the zombies of flat puddings, handshoes, and prostrate knees sniffing the rutabagas and carrot
tops laid in wordless loam, wingless all and wedged with
weight, thick as locusts in metropolis or homoerotic on the
farm, descend upon us in rings of vomit, and join the barn-raising of mundanity in a sober globe. Baby of the butane,
cooker of the grain into furious purity, I see running like
spilled mercury through myriad creases, scattered and
threadlike, each strand screaming for its face but loving
facelessness, raging in the fantasyland of funnels in air, unreal as an aprilope, bloated toadish with concepts of acuity, my boy whose Chesterfield stuck between forefinger
and thumb, full-butted like a hustler, snaps out his lips
simultaneous with the suck, snake hauling in I see six years
from now stuck to the street like bubble gum, all brilliance,
Kepler, Einstein, Hendrix, Galileo wrapped in one dead
Pud cartoon, potential alone uselessly hand imploring,
extended. How do I feel? Lousy. Heartsick. Furious.
Cold. Truthfully? Glad of further justification for misery,
the suffering poet sucking sympathy into his vortices, eroticism from women and neutrality from men. Poor besieged
creator, bosom cradling head, first by father, then by kid.
Truthfully? Appreciative, my boy a sacrifice. If he dies
I'm martyr. No depths to monstrosity. Did you catch the
one about the Jewish mah-jong club involving a klepto,
a nympho, a lesbo, a yenta? I'm trying here to inject levity. The kid has all marbles plus the nasty one, otherwise
he's boffo—the complete chemistry, erector, and curiosity set to create a nation of believers. Honestly? Clobbered.

82

One would predict the spike of greater bitterness after
the tragic malady; natural such events jolt the misanthrope
into massive cynicism alienating mate and foe equally;
the spittle-spew and reflux of the grossly injured corrod-
ing stems of lobes and soul beyond the asphalt accident—
but lo, bitterness flowed out with his arm like a fish gut
under the knife, slip and slime onto the ground beside
the cash of diamondy scales; where steel and shoulder
met: ragged emptiness; flung the arm thirty feet down
the road complete as an embryo. Stump-man, he does
not crucify nor cry as was once his industry, but carries
his badge of puckered flesh with pride, flapping the lit-
tle trunk like a wing goodbye or hello, and one shakes
this grotesquerie or does not shake, it being right and pri-
mordial. He is glad. Now with prosthetic claw and cable
mass he benches four hundred, clamps onto the bar
like, at infancy, his mother's tit, grunts, groans the bar-
plates up past eternities of the shoulder-lock and pec-
toral stamp; no more excoriates the four limbed ape,
like him, moist of face and feeble in love. He licks the
three-legged dog and lays with grace under the wheel
of stars, his arm a spray of phlox in a snub nose gun.
Why dissipates from this target-shaped man acid of
hate? The snapped frond bleeds milk, bubbles a tear,
and shredded thus resembles the crown of thorns, the
simple bush crowding the fence, glory shorn into a
gratitude-clump, like chopped off hair, disfigured, mis-
shapen, wounded, stunned, the echo of all worldly mat-
ter yet more deeply cut for deeper modesty, nakedness,
shame, or fear. He was God—so lonely—and now man.

83

Money and God duke it out for supremacy. God says "Moses, Abraham, Job, Rebecca;" Money draws "sustenance," like a gun. "Security," it fires, like Bill Hickok. "Power." "Real Estate." "Monte Carlo." God spits."Redemption," like a tommy. "Righteousness." "Compassion." Money bloodies God's lip like Cassius. God reels backward against an iron bench. Blotches on white robe. God turns the cheek. Money crunches it like peanut butter. God catches himself against rough bark, summons the furies, and gut punches Dollar with brass knuckles, upper cuts him on the chin. His nose pops like a water balloon. Kick to God's balls; doubles; vomits. Boot to rib. Grunts. Appendix malfunctions. Advantage money: pushes God's face by hair into the fire. As coals near king's eyes like thumbs adrenalin catapults Money backward like a boulder; high arc kick by sandaled foot, again groin kick, roundhouse, Tae Kwon Do invisible machine gun, Money breaks into roses, blackred nose ropes, teeth shatter. In annihilation's vicegrip—such is the commitment to organismal survival—Money slices God with produced Egyptian dagger; hand over gushing, lower right abdomen, slits mouth into thigh, red lipstick, God catches in hand blade lunging for heart, thumb hangs by bone; wrenches free knife, turns it like rocket, buries it to jeweled hilt through Money's masseter. Stunned, Money, handle from jaw protruding, staggers, scrapes against rock face, gazes into heaven; God watches him scut like a claw-dragging crab. God warwoops, bloodsoaked and blue, "beggar," "abomination," "mendicant," "fool," "artificer," "Mammon," "idol worshiper." Money, sitting zombie, crooks finger, confession; God, inching, forgiving, leaning in toward lip skin, flies backward into water, stomach blown open, both palms over hole, intestines, hydrochloric, lining, black bubbles, exit wound out spine, staring at the clouds. God, Money, like two boards fallen over, bases facing; in-between which and through march the masticating masses on either side of which, in the valley of the fools, the narrowest of passes, lies like two continuously disgorging wounds posterity's raw half-eaten carnage.

84

For my next, ladies & gentlemen, trick, I shall remove first this
hat, which I have for ten years through rain & snow adored,
never before human faces attempted I promise you thoroughly,
like this; then unpin, yes, my boutonniere, lay it—lovers—beside
the hat upon the sanatorium table; I spin it, thus—no hatches,
mirrors, boxes, fakes—so fresh like baby's chest my delicate
hat's chrysanthemum, drums suspense!, kliegs recompense!;
now unstrap that girdle my cummerbund—straightjacket, re-
straint—and flame it, thus, environmentalists: no charred rab-
bits or ducks, I assure; next, yes always a next before your
very dazzled pores, voila, my bow tie, that hangman's noose,
black & sinister butterfly upon the hat-and-flower slab; now
the mirrored showman's shoes—bovine canoes, coffins, ships—
flash, glitz, two side-by-side screams on the table; now my
simple rayon socks stuffed in mouths to stop the screams;
madams/gents glimpse my effeminate unmagical brackets;
the jacket next, arm, arm, liberated snakes, like a sail it flies,
look, off the stage; now the red French ruffled shirt, scler-
otic pierced stiff cardboard cuffs, sleeve, sleeve, untuck, off,
bare sandy colored hair, gaze upon skinny scholarly flesh;
unclasp, zip, heavy ankle-collapsed steam ship chimneys, I
kick off, catch, fold, reverently lay, stand before through
skewered powder blues like a centaur through a cloud,
bashful, pure, and clear; now the illusion begins. I climb
astronautically into the reinforced 3-inch-thick-wall plexi-
glass cube here raised off the stage on legs to prove no
amateur no trap door eschew; see me hazily inside, reddish
blue like a skinned vague deer behind rain streaked tears,
my windbags suck and bilge suffocating air, my toes squeal;
now the mixer, the dirty drum-turning mixer common
to construction bids you pass en route to soup, backs in
on black encrusted tires, hear sand & gravel grind, esquires
and slits, up close, magnified, harshly lit, like a blown out
knee, before it bilges grit down the chute, vomiting,
disgorging concrete to my feet, ankles, calves, thighs,
but as the solid gray Portland street covers my last fluff
of laundered hair encasing me in a petrifiable block I
am not here, I am there in the audience in the auditori-
um chair beside you and you and you and you plastered
emotionless frozen sealed incommunicative and unmoved.

85

Voice of a lunatic: I wish everyone I know would die,
Andy, Elli, Margaret, Donovan, Peter, Angie, you,
you husband-fucker rich brat-bastard, I hate you all
except mom, go to hell I just want mom and me
and none of you ugly scabs stuck to wounds, go
shotgun your hearts in a frozen field or bonfire your-
selves like protest-monks, I don't care, just get the
fuck off, especially you, you parasitical trust fund
shit, dope addicted coward sticking your love-
less prick in me as if I were ignorant pudding, I
hope Daddy's valve blows him to kingdom come
and my stepwitch's implants kill her, I'm curling
up in mom, cotyledon, climbing on, fetalizing,
boob suckling, her honey pouring comfort-song
rocking me happy in Camp Hadesville, drown
my monster-kids like cats, what liar said babies
are fun, bake em like birds, just pry them off
my skull, I'm a player again fuckin' men and
gettin' head, partyin' n whorin', whiskey shots
and gin, liberated; (smash! the family photo-
graph, sky raining glass; smash! the precious na-
ture scene, gather shards of blood; explosions
along the faux; forearm through drywall, crash!).
Lady raving mad: Divorce. Exterminate. Consign.
Up ass. Burn down. Wipe slate. Mom. Mom.
Disappear the loser. You. Me. On a journey
in the van. Only you understand. I don't love
them. Christmas. Cheerleading. Gymnastics.
Plie. He devastated. Rot on a spit. My pro-
tector in a Sunday apron over pot roast. Tum-
bling. Hungry. Save me, save me….again.

86

Razor teeth fish swim up my blood for you, I
ache for you and crawl inside, scarlet bubbles
like a suffocating crab, I yearn, suffer, long,
scream silently in a cellophane ball, you ev-
erything, for you my labor, my brain, my
preoccupation, for you my equilibrium, I
crush genius, maturation, education for you
like an encroaching roach, for you symmetry
in the trash, I con and lie and ditch my moth-
er in the loony bin for one pinch of you
or full immersion in a garbage room, sleep
is inconsequential gravy in pursuit of you
in the laundry room or rat passageway,
wherever you may, I am phlegm, spit, ex-
pectorant, a string of sclerotic life-snot
G-forced from my nose bereft of you whom
I crave like spasm-come on yellow sheets
in foodless cubes at three o'clock, DTs,
the shakes, the fibrillations, had we never
penetrated I'd be boostering up Fifth fol-
lowed by a trail of Yale and seared clear
atmospheres of aspiration, alcohol burnt
air, but palsied instead by your vegetative
ecstasy I drag my tongue across jagged
asphalts reminiscent of you, scented as it
were by your leathered heels. I should seize
and slash you—eliminating my source de-
generacy—dead, but were your throat be-
neath my thumbs I would shove instead my
always stiffened piece between your legs,
my dopamine exploding like a popcorn
machine, so fuck godliness, fuck the wiped
inside of delicate folds, fuck sunlight pour-
ing through morning windows, fuck blue-
berry Yoplait under umber leaves, fuck
the starving children's universal relief fu-
nd, fuck the evenly-stacked neatened pat-
ient and squared pages of superiority—
stretch your full amnesial glove over me head-
to-foot, insert me like a world, lie still
caught on the sudden slamming hook, feel
us bleed through, feel the excruciation,
like honey nut butter cut with oblivion.

87

Doll wrestles the wet packed pectorals for dominance over man, pushes room in the maximus gluteus, shoves through the trapezius, kicks the latisimus dorsi like a rotten stump, clobbers the abdominals, stretches into the flexor longus hallucis, and spiders though fibers of the auricles and ventricles, powerfully, determined, sick of anonymity in the canned viscera of the machine; man clamps his perineum, locks his pectoralis major and minor, hardens beyond imagination his quadriceps and plantaris, and clasps his palmar fascia like a first round heavyweight subduing the insurrection of doll and retaining humanhood once again at Christmas. Doll struggles like a dying firework, invisibly again, shrinks into a BB sized inconvenience, hibernatorial and blind, somewhere around the bowels, while man responds infernally situationally to stimuli, shivers, perspires, weeps weakly at death, blisters at fire, psychologically unravels, driveling with protoplasm; doll is steel, invincible, forgiveless, dependent on pure whim, inexhaustible; man squirts cerebellum through automobile glass, welds skull skin to cratered cage, freezes numb, then black-to-amputation, pathetic loveblasted fragility one decimates with withdrawal of spasm or clam-close, while doll scans environment, eviscerates—or incorporates—indiscriminately, motiveless, leaving behind, let's say, the bighorn skeleton, the rabbit head, the pulsing heart, or conversely a supercharged psychopath as though Jesus-touched. The battle for callousness like Yosemite and Bugs, in a cloud, rages, out pops a canon, a glove, a mallet, a bomb in the crusade for supremacy, ongoing and indefatigable in the pupa-palpa-gastroenterologic world. Something is suddenly petrifying. Just yesterday man gazed with cold indifference upon a baby mammal.

88

Step outside your body sucking a hole in the air and make it get divorced, debased, or sick; lunatic, it does not feel, permitting you—the authentic self—to turn away, a stranger; the shrill love-conflagrates lighting the dark with flame, acheless, providing combustions of air, he's a sick fucker anyway, it's not you burning but some depthless maniac; you possess rectitude, do not deserve to curl, let it lie beside her pathology while you, racing, orchestrate, accomplish, deposit, virtually innocent; split, it dopplegangs admirably, "certainly, sweet," it purrs "indubitably," familiarly pecks and accepts pecks consecutively; pride to God, thanks. She's stiff-necked but it nuzzles her edges seethingly, a prince of numbness, a pain-absorbing fake suffering nobly the disillusionment of love like a made-for-TV stud, flickering, on peripheries, bracketed by Campbell's soup, while at the world's center you coolly by the fingers of your eyes peel words off the page and paste them to your brain, a flapless scholar and devotee; let us praise detachment, compartmentalization, inaccessibility, indifference of the heartless warrior to the side of his slaughtering—and the splintered man in the corner watching himself being slaughtered. Will not "break into blossom," the stepped out of body, but will absorb over-plus till blood. The Lord is a shepherd that maketh, no hand shall smite, he shall protecteth as of a wing over sorrow, shall be no heartquake in love's pressured jaw, nor green trepidation, and man shall walk away from his corpse.

89

Ooh this bed's hard, this bed's soft, this porridge's hot,
this porridge's cold—well aren't you a prissy little prima-
donna, presbyterian princess, egomaniac; eat your
porridge and go to sleep you big baby, I'm not your
domestic, gourmet cook, or mattress maker, and I
don't care how lukewarm your bathwater is; I've
got my own demons, like multiple sclerosis, you
and your sensitivities; I should backhand you in the
face; Miss Perfection; besides I know you're hymen-
less beneath that gingham dress, and shooting crack
at Cinderella's, so don't give me that crap about
scratchy blankets or dilapidated chairs; I'm kick-
ing butt for you at The Crackerjack for lousy tips
and you're Miss Fauntleroy of Barracuda Street;
well, this is chez Sprats, Mother Hubbard, and you're,
young lady, getting your ass to school, then
college, then I don't give a rat's what you do, I'll
be dead to the nub, and damned if I'll see my
only girl knocked up, drugged out, panhandling,
& conning idiots six months from now on Vul-
ture Boulevard. Give us this day, yea though I
walk, rock and my redeemer, pray you boob, hum-
ble your head in this Babylonia, this abattoir of
unforgiving deadliness, shame your butterfly ass-
tattoo with vinegar, rise through Baptismal water
new, imprinted with The Fear you postpubescent
whore with dopamine lust, Cutex the slut from
your fingernails, deep and swamp-oozing, you
carnal caricature, God eats fools like pinenuts.
Sweetie, Cleopatra of the Floridian blaze, leggy
topless beach-nude, Mama demands her strands
strip into you, the creole palms of her Pontchar-
train hands, her cream of wheat soothe, her dou-
ble strip of pearls fusing one-by-one, like swal-
lowed light bulbs, Baby please, Mama's poured
amber maple into you, and molasses, and cane;
I offer you Thessalonians, quartz agate, scarab
mayonnaise, sorrow portraits, Sophie Mae's
Chiang Mai bamboo fan, boa constrictor slippers,
and Grandpa Pompidou's molars-into-dice;
Abide by the rat's tooth of family talismans, child;
stallion of youth's no match for their sobriety;
clasp and see, oh darling, clasp and see; your al-
ready melting bones fill bowls with golden broth.

90

Crows scrape through my ducts, flight from eyes, dry, dusty, desiccated crows; I deliver tears like humans' babes, maximally one/year, Demerol, saddle block, clip-the-slit episiotomically, suckle; I'm crammed block-concrete. Little intercourse with poignancy conceives a crow; little copulation with gratitude fibrillates my egg; I'm bulwark-fertility; orange beaks, black claws membrane rip; I support bridges with insensitivity; can you gaze unemotionally upon psychotic protoplasm, arterial intervention, species extinction; at Mother's graveside I froze mold-solid; ape-chested, iron hefter, shiny palmed creature who loathes liquid, wetness, and squishy minds; your tears are failure of appropriate pride, mine are iron-feathered crows rarely liberated lacerating mucous lined jellies; you weeping men soft as April sod, I am boot-stubbing granite wedged in ground like a molar; how it feels to cry: like pushing out-bound fecal material petrified with cheese, dough, and secrets, sharp-edged, painful and then the crow pecking my food-pupils. Therefore six inch thick reinforced internal walls on honeymoon, in mainspring's tick, against offspring's jaw, after grace's fall; zip; imperviousness of the upper lip observing heartflaw, reverse megalomania, legsuck in planet's hip; I learned quick and now not even charging bull scabbards or pate foie gras, hammered, events implicating chordates, central nervous systems, or the beneficiaries of overlapping litters disintegrate; postage stamps ox me solid, M. Monroe's subway freezes, Giulietta Masina trowels face-blockages, and M. Falconetti, that melted crystal chalice, solders my ears; rammed to ground by fifty-foot long stick, fixed, ice-sheeted in purgatorial winter, uppermost limbs clacking in wind, or stiff as frozen carrots; incapacity's resignation: from the promontory of my cheek, an echoing cackle.

91

Because you pleasured him at your expense, because he filled himself with you and vanished mouth dripping, teeth flesh-clotted, red cells beneath fingernails, gut glutted with your ooze, satiated, semaphored, simulacrum; because he quaffed fluid of your knees and ate the chords; because hair twisted in his fist and broke off like a dammed river between fingertips as he and you caught and spasmed; because you loved the heaviness of his meat pushing back your walls like Moses, his fat-veined heat boring your massive rock like butter; because you loved his bloody stutter, his whipped black hair, his flicking your prehistorical primeval bundlehood; because you bought his nickel with a dime, his molybdenum with uranium two-thirty-five; because you ate him like mescaline, like mushrooms, and hallucinated babies, refracted milk hives, repetition, eternity, and vomited the bile into toilets of delusion; because hooks tear through soft lips like wet bread dough to fall lifelessly through green depths to snag on plant-life or dead reeds or perhaps the skull of a devoured gull turning in the tide or dumb current below the smear of a rocking hull; because the red monster filling you to the skin crawls out you like a net, ropy and wet, and hurls itself over terrors of air in search of him, a seining net to kill wriggling flicks of gasping silver crammed together like Auschwitz, you gas shower, enemy emaciator, experimental doktor, hatred serrating your nipple's edge; because he shoved a switched-on-high radiator in your skin in arctic winter, in nuclear winter, filaments glowing, warmth exuding like topographical maplines of rising altitude, survival climbing from a tent within; you crave like a crawling Cronenberg creature to tap his spine as he sleeps, white and clean, to collect the fluid in a cup drip-by-drip like a sliced bleeding cactus stalk, and drink the sticky viscous fluid into the vat of digestive enzymes known as rage, revenge, and pride; because his tongue split into claws and decapitated your tits like rolling tophats, hard cold claws that tasted like cream, allspice, and egg, razorwire claws long as ribbon fish, flat as black ice, quick as whips, the dance macabre on transparent glaciers with streamers, crepe, and blades; because lemon meringue love in GE beaters tastes of God or equally fine the devil, squeaked on semicircles, licked into mind, spread into extended nerve-nuclei in the form of value, worthiness, and shine; you solely shall embody the secret identity of his killer, her modus and vivendi, how she pointed her pubis beneath quantities of pillows, split plumfruit by dividing her thighs, and as the lips struck the hilt, she power drove the blade through the bone sculpted spider, number 1 and number 2 of his pectoralis minor, and how she floats between relatives like an adhering marrow, his killer, his assassin, kissing his aggrieved parents while privately gloating; because deception-bullion quivered his spoon as he tipped it on the levee of your quivering tongue, his hand fleshy-elephantine flush against your lids, his head a faceless berry, cran or chokecherry, hooded by jagged leaves of a distant waxy tree; because gullible, sucker, idiotic you believed solution of formaldehyde, ethanol, and methanol pumped by him through the Porti/boy Mach IV Machine through your limbs via a tube plunging the Mammalia was a kiss containing nectar of sweet disintegrations, one bowling another, like pulsing joyous bubbles; because he was Heracles and you Clarabel, the collision of brute Prometheal metal with tenderized veal-ethereal healing; that is why through the seven years' wide mausoleum of his love you are still his concubine.

92

The borders melted: borders that dammed all figures from bursting, table, window, coffee mug, man; all slammed together like paint; Joey puddled, laked; Hamilton's eggshell cracked, spread, mitosis of atoms; Franklin's eyes running decried his fingers stretching; Chloe pulled off her face; had not President decomposed, President would have declared national emergency; tires of scrambling F-16s interpenetrated tarmac like marshmallow into caramel; some hybrid undocumented goo did all default to: pith, lead, CO2, polyurethane, frog guts; mountains rushed down themselves and sharks inked up like clouds; the child-jammed black-crayon boundaries of bird, basketball, boat, building; the earth a sticky ball of indiscriminate copulation; atoms of the baritone's larynx mouthless as sand; well, here's an apocalypse: hate's armless spitless fizzless micro-organismic particles flowing against the hated like diarrhea, disgust's granulation grinding across its husband like an irony, coupled lovers rushing through and ungraspably past each other—the great ha-ha; debris indistinguishable from fries; who shall rescue?; Robert Cornthwaite? Takashi Simora? Kevin McCarthy? Raymond Burr? Mighty Mouse? The ever triumphant offended God's henchmen who prevented the mauling of a neonate including the irreparably damaging bashing of its head by its mother's plastered freshly-fired boyfriend, not the biological father, too late. Science pronounces the reversion of matter to the preternatural state predicament-saturated without a predetermined febrifuge; viral? bacterial? parapsychological? Revelatory execution? And it came to fact that cesspool rose to steepledom, serotonin reuptake inhibited snake to bishop's blood, trichinosis spirillum to the thiabendozale compound; and all was oceanic, featureless, homogenized, latex-esque, and monotonously level.

93

Dear and most of all venerable mother—death for you I fear is close, I heard you cough and know you blacked at Charlie's funeral, you slur words, and make intuitive macabre jokes; body knows what brain—feeble overrated meatloaf—does not; your bristly beard betrays another world; your children circle you like sharks; dear and most sacrificial Joan, rot becomes you like Marshall Fields; blood drop fingernails hard as dice; we could sink you in your Coup DeVille; fingers depress grieving eyes into lugubrious firework displays, out blows the back of head when I meditate upon my birth canal dead; escaped to Alaska, I've recircled to the virtual bed, you stink of gingivitis and cardiac malfunction, sour external organ breath, salamanders between toes; I was your beaux amidst three failures, I killed them each, one by bludgeon, one by pills, one by gas for you for you, fertility queen, symbolic pederast; now you're toast, anyway toasting between filaments of fire and I'm frozen like a mastodon in ice enveloping a bubble of disbelief-breath. I retract my malevolence; I've fantasized wiry black nests for years, Frankensteinian coarse hair and orgasm red gelatins along my shaft like suction eels pulsing strings of my balls in air; you the standard by which rivals fall stung by overhead scorpion tail; I love you, fusion and fission weld us to Siam, one lower colon, one number five cervical disk, genitals like Janus faces rotated on coccyx stick, inferno melded buttocks back to back, we are our individuality; I whiff that death has entered our room, some reeking insatiable mastubatory Rhesus squatting on the Mohawk and eating brownish mash; I withdraw former vituperations, by the tail dangle them wriggling before eating, gag on old words. Mama, tenderheart, CreamofWheat, the alphabet pinwheel spins He's inslipped boudoir—stabbing, vomiting, subatomic rage, the inexplicable indentation of peace—surgeons of separation, near theater, with spider-precise fingers await with tray confirmation that, like a paste, peeling off my side, you are, slain.

94

What? He desires me? Eyes disclose he's going to make a pass. I
have something to offer? Me? Becky? And he god, prince, most
sought after. Boobs? Hair? Feet? (I've always loved my sandal-
led toes.). Eyes? Me? Palatable but owlish me? Raven-black, haz-
el, big-boned, bright; he bookish/athlete, introspective, honest,
beautiful. Should I withhold pussy, frustrate, petting only, do I
trust myself?, Why not Cheryl, Ginger, Yvonne? Were I man
I'd sink my cock in them. Condemningly, I won't suck. Hair on
my back's small's a turn off. Yet, I feel him generate. He'll brush
cheek with forefinger crook, gaze deep, narrow space. Seduction,
ordinaire. Lately, I've been paste, need a fucking, frankly. I con-
trol the script; I can slap, limit, submit, duck. I'm the lock. Any
key I wish fits. He'd be pissed. My fat roll, birdy shoulders,
navel swirl. No man prefers a hairy girl. Murray, Phil, Buzz
dumped. I'd sworn. I swear. I won't admit him in my cunt.
Burn, glib overprivileged boy! Hump yourself. Insincere.
I'll not crawl under you till you've consecutively petitioned
my door, humble with bouquet. You think homely's easy?
I'm no whore for pretty boys. Bogus spiritualists in calf skin
loafers. Lying smolderers. Yet…what if sincere, what if the
early rumblings of love, I precious, darling, babycakes, and he
Cleaver, corny but dependable. Love, then, maybe. I'd be
dodo, dumbkoff, dunderhead if I repulsed the overtures, my
love slippery lips rubbing his sponginess. What if I'm it!
Another rum and Coke, beret undone, cashmere's lovely
for exploratory hands. Here it comes, the ever-tender cheek
stroke, reticent, ineluctable, clumsy words, irrelevant flick-
ering tv, kiss, tongue, secretly opening orchid, bulge, zip,
the stiff authoritarian thrush. Shhh. I'm the one, I'm the one.

95

Religion breaks out like a cholera epidemic: singing, killing, filled sanctuaries, phylacteries, prayer shawls, crawling censers; God blasts out hearts like Batman; Billy kneels bedside; Shelly begs forgiveness; Mahatma, spirit struck, refuses further masturbation; believer-tides sweep Jerusalem, Fatmas hack mainframes, logon passwords like lambblood, blasphemy, 2coming; the revolution in psyche shoes; mama pierces babyears and foreskins fly like potato peels; necklace of automatic hangs off boy, but biggest believer wields phantom imbued with Word; soldier of protesting hoard, cutaneous, subcutaneous, meaty cells, and bone, busy terminal and seed factory, an organismic world to wall-splatter or pearl; columnar infinity. Innocents inhale airborne spirillum, illuminate, cry, vision of two floating sticks, bloody moon, empathy beyond containment, some pour into Africa contagion, complete with nail guns and ingenuity; others head for urbaniforousness, arrow into city, spread like silverfish; abortionists die and fetuses kick like Carnegie's Rockettes; fields covered in monolithic species: bluebonnets, Susans, chamomile: militarized Christianity; God blows corpuscles into our blood and we whirl, gather, refuse, knit impenetrable as The Rock. Infidels inject an antidote, a black mirthless bacilli lead-heavy casting them into a pod of immunity which vacuums zygotes and boils scripture into consume-literature, flaunt Amalfi and ball each other's mates, sulphurous impunity; Patrick and Dana camcorde Ginger grinding Constantine, then unpeel the X and exit oppositely flipping off the apocalypse. Conglomerates begin the games, blocks collide against blocks which edge-chip—a sea of needles—then, eaten, crumble, and finally granulate into confused mayhemic scrambling; lance pierces noble heart of horse, dogs lick, gulls outpeck glittering eyefleck; the games, the games, the salmon-emerald rules spawning resurrectable winners and losers flambe, coliseum faction-crackling, wave felling millions. Heavy bone vault cannot control its three pound grey matter pushing through goofy grotesquerie of Buddhas, turtles, yapping foliage, staggs, floods, fireflies, fish, cosmic eggs, monkeys, goldeneye ducks, kidney beans, bananas, mole, Papatuanokus, horsemen, and eye-rimmed wheels, like mallet and frying pan springing out Daffy; cranium explodes, populations expire of diarrhea, anuria, acidosis, and shock—too much God. Mother outpushes neonate finger-shooting lightrays, awe-striking the infidels, magnetizing the malevolent, and motile by means of a polar flagella.

Against my will, I rip down zipper, shove porno before face, grow tumescent, and rape myself. Rapist fist-squeezes, tears undercircumcision tissue, violences orgasm into toilet, and bangs away like a striking hawk leaving me on carpet weeping. Crisis response team, rape squad, description (shot sharded glances in mirror), unpredictable, unexpected, brutal, Caucasian, fled into the night of self, vast, anonymous like a whiptail; rage, not sex; revenge against distant abusers; howl in heart; injustice gnawing cerebral wires; I've not confessed—shame—he's hit before, cracked open hard core and beat incessantly ripping out my stuffing and fled like a murderer into my soul, slaked on subjugation and spermatozoa. I can take victimization by his hunger no more, the horror, the shock, the degradation amidst a beautiful world, his closet appearance irrepressibly, he's always within dead bolt perimeters, his shoe-toes replicating mine and the gutturals wrenched out his throat iterate details he could not know; Karen's tampax, Sheila's lubrication, the exquisite blood orange and yellow pipefish, the unexpurgated yank through caverns of emptiness, cravings of Joyce, weird tectonic schisms in the earthplates of stability; my superinformed assailant confusing me with identification; smashing my dick between fist with jackhammer-aching arm, he hallucinatorily grunted, "fucker, you are me," then incomprehensibly vaporized the instant my come blew me off its string; pride terrorizes—I've slaved, I confess, for years, homosexually, painfully, grievingly, plumbing swallowing my esteem; the tidal sucks off a devastation-home. No more: hazel; six feet; gray wreath-tonsure; straight teeth; cupcake mole, left shoulder; moustache; olive; one-ninety; deceptively soft spoken; black bush; left lobe crease; fiftyish; big fingers. Grab handful of flesh, wrap fist, rip him through sewer grate to light, to justice, imposter, fake socialite, slime-liar, hit/run impresario, abominator of stainlessness and gorgeous stacks, chickadee household blackguard bastard.

97

Sander takes off skin and grains of skull, guided by carpenter passes again, again, head into curvaceous ball, red-wet shoulder-plumes, blue bone; artist-woodworker with number 50 grit orbits off total epidermis, refines consecutively with grits 80, 120, 320, then four aught steel wool, sculpting figure into smooth, faceless, fleshless bone, eyes-nose-mouth-groin holes rounded like stone, atlases, scapulas, occiputal, astragalus, humerus and ulna, navicular and cuboid, the cuneiform complex contorted, bent upon themselves, twisted to artist's taste, polished like steel; convex of kneecap cradles cranium, left leg pretzled behind clavicle, ribs cracked and soldered to resemble tusks, teeth sharpened, blunted, extracted, drilled into faceted jewels; stainless rods up coccyx form a stand; the fragile confection-de-calcium bubble-wrapped, placed amidst a truckload of compatriots, and shipped to warehouse-metropolis to amuse tourists, mendicants, dignitaries, and capitalists. Hunger grinds people into artifacts and labor satiates hunger: steampressers, pipefitters, bricklayers, glass molders, iron workers, signalmen, boilermakers, longshoremen, heat & frost insulators, business entrepreneurs self-ass-kicked sopping yolks with toast, aerospace engineers, the brimming multitude of middlepeople under the scraping granules; the instant before EST voltage cauterized his brain Daddy muttered the insensibles: failure, ruined, broken, inventory, amortization, leg flying behind neck, hands folding backward, elbow stabbing spine as he bit hard; Bubba's upside down face between ankles staring behind as pharmacist plies him with anti-bankruptcy Amoxipane; Birdie's children's relentless duodenums growling a ballad tie her thighs into two half hitches and split her sternum like cordwood to be carted to megalopolis's Museum of Modern Antiquity; heart scraped from ribs, brain vacuumed out, vulva smeared, testicles ground, long muscles mangled and rolled, arteries splat, intestines, kidneys, spleen ripsawn, nerve branchia schismed, interstitial tissue—fibrils, laminae, gelatin, chords—gnawed, gore-flown; shapers, sculptors, blasters, finishers.

Brick began, one agglomeration surrounded by night, twinkleless emptiness, weighing beyond bathroom scale's capacity, God sleeping Smirnoff off on divan, slut snoring nearby, irresistible trash; unbelievable mass rotating through unimaginable space, dead egg, originless chunk, insensitive nest; six months hence The Pain from God's bladder unshuttered His eyes to piss vodka-Pacific, His ass belched out Tenneco, scratch, scratch, peignoir and Penelope unthere. This happened cataclysmic, history eon hyphened: Majesty, finger licking, leafing Vogue glimpsed a slim hipped triggering a sequence: 1) heightened brain traffic, 2) wolfish nipple stare, three) drooly underwear leer, 4) naughty cock excitement, 5) blood rushing rod Bastille, 6) hand to Hagars, 7) knot-ball swallow, 8) the porno file, 9) flip to photo of blow job, 10) guilt-megalo-greed-resignation, 11) the infinity toilet bowl, 12) unbutton, unzip, drop trough, hip thrust, 13) lust, 14) lust, 15) murderous gluttony, 16) eyes Bonanza-map burn lips-cushioning-shaft photo focal, 17) cannon cranked high, 18) hand whipping canon, 19) balls of feet, knees clenched, buttocks flexed, 20) photo, 21) whip, 22) photo, 23) hammer, 24) lips, 25), dick, 26) muscle-ache, 27) blasphemy, ie: "fuck your cunt," "give it to me," "eat your feet feet," "jesus/fuck/shit," "goddamn,cocaine,christ" 28) thought- paralysis, 29) stiff, beating, 30) circumcision tear, 31) lipsbreastscocktoesfingernailsfleshpubisclitcrave wetbigyoungbabyeternalredpurpleheavyhairheelsshefthothallelujah, 32) ganglia-to-spongy piano wire, 33) concentration, 34) time schism, 35) heart into fist, bell, pre-clang, 36) BANG! Hammer pumps come straight out like serpents, leaping, leaping, pearly anacondas, massive millions-spasm shooting angry flagella; one thirsting moses screaming through space: splat upon the brick; into-it-shoulders burrow; fizz; chemistry; alchemy; instability; root system split; overemphasis; physics unacceptable; tremble; temblor; non-tenable; clench; explosion. Nebulas roar from each other like miners, rush like roman candles, swirls, whorls, streaks, spheres struggle for actuality; fire expands glacial upthrusts which battle to freeze adamant flames, and it was good, God in heaven blown backward face down on carpet nauseated, suicidal, sick of girls; when up from the basics, out there, pool-basted the rubbery, innocent, tailless, amphibious, reptilian swamp monster.

99

Tears cold stone lid, like ripping scab, off dank colony, soil crumbs raining, light, warmth as rock snuggled under gigantic hand pulls away, insects scurrying—millipede, earwig, blackant—but earthworm-melancholic, fat, black-tipped clings, half clay-buried, half stiffly falling upward as if vacuumed, tongue tip, clitoris, pinky finger being sun-sucked from blackness, like dilated blind pupils suddenly flooded, stabbed; gravity pulling the sad into the sea of sun, resisting exposure like a salted slug; thud it back, my close comfortable home, giant cruel hand, cutting out raw earth, re-half-bury me in smooth heaviness, my eggy morgue, you clutch my shoulders, my oyster shell, work it back into the socket mold that I may brood upon injustices unexposed, and rage in soundproof cave my enmity; drop the plate trajectorily from whence it came; I'm thrust into scrutiny like blood from cut in antigravity, how dare god throw me into ridicule; the dark ugly jealous clung-to-hell have host in the underworld, feed on spleen. Those substanceless of joy bore with tedium, everbland song fluttering from chords, diaphanous material spoilt by iron or lead; smother me again in wombish depression, optimistic cyclops of the giant hands, that I may astound with profundity Coppertone simpletons; I, grub, nonchordate, celebrate in airless space genius of despondency, partake of the liver of Paradise's knowledge creaturely comfortable in Sealy and Easy Boy, a continuous concavity; phyla, affliction, subphyla, agony, family, sagacity. Reinstall my lid, kingly magistrate; cheerfulness wants me thrust into space and rays wilting me in Dracula's dawn, the ultraviolet legions and the freed man's psychotrauma of ecstasy, joy, bliss, gladness, forgiveness, weightlessness, liberation; put back my pan, skillet, hatch, black ceiling, earth-mask, occipital plate, bath, omnipotent one, O hear my lamentation!

100

Wind-ripped rain blows sideways off a concrete edifice, a
gray-white blur of hurricane velocity off the ruled edge,
human face into the gale flattens featureless made of sand,
sheets stream off appendages in the shape of appendages,
iron hammer strikes ten, twelve, fifteen, twenty-four, howling tsunami, Bonneville Bugatti, flesh withstands not the
geology, Samuel bones, Majesty bones, Tenacity bones,
shirt sail-billowing, pantlegs slapping, a man, arms outstretched impresses a cross in the onrushing clay of air,
from peak of thighs a woman drops a child onto street
before tumbling backward like a weed, everything flies
on gut strings tethered tight, the wacking paper kites of
cow, goat, rooster, peafowl, hound, javelina, and human;
a jowl skin grain detaches, soars upward like debris, the
whole jowl follows like a message, naked skull in the
stiffness; visit the physician—serums, inoculations, vaccines—concretize resistance against the tropical named
Gretta, Mercy, Eugene; aerobicize the physical on
belts, chains; traumatize muscularity with stacked dead
plates; hatchet halves wind, tissue decomposes before
it; a blizzard whistles off First Federal Consolidated,
sweeps down alleyways, and the leaning into, jutted
forward, defiant, stalwart shudders round a crumbling
drummer.//Broken windows crack world only when gazed
through, diagonal split fractures no crow flight nor
mountain thrust, pure as urine; after heating on naked
coils and dropping into ice water, I re-inserted into its
socket my eye ball shattered like a kid's glass marble
throwing fractioned image onto wall: unforgivingness,
rivalry, victimization flipped, hurled upon the cave, ingrained where clean streamlined object smoothly exists
unsevered by division of lens. I have always loved you.

101

Head burst on fire when he removed hood, how could any head take it without igniting? World history is splattered bladder of red paint on wall. Head burst into ball, each flametip an eye, each eye a wagon. Look in craw. Carnage atop carnage. Old Thomas goes a courtin' with Lorna on lips and sulphur in gut, ice sheet union slides over confederacy, burlap of maize and ground Apache bone, kidnapped Noah's Franklin's semen balloon, dead, shallowed. Vision lights fuse, gunpowder smell, eight cranial plates. Love, etc.; a brilliant fiction; nuthatches et al; San Luis Obispo; Musee des Beaux Arts; Sunday with Hoover; Kali's karate lesson; waffle rocky road cone; Killy's cold Zermatt; Dubey & Schaldenbrand; strolling solar Auschwitz, arms clasped under cauliflower boughs; ricing Mai-Lai; Glad preceding Al down Slip and Slide on Super 8 film; Lion's Club Black minstrel show; popped corn in Kosovo; Captain Marvel slaughtering aqua people, Saturday afternoon at Bijou; moon eyed in Palestine; the Greater Westminster Dog Show and Pet Exhibition (Spice Girl BOS Winner); Spanky and Our Gang; Swan Boats of Commons; entertainment Rushmore paper place mats; bacon cheese cooled by double straw malt, Jerseyville, Illinois; fishing buddies-skipjack snapshot, East Timor; antiquing in Willamette; South African surfboard riding; and, knee on buckled buck outside Bozeman, stocks soaring, Stacy plastering Harvard, revitalizing awaiting extramarital affair: computer chip planted in brain, open eyes shut, plasma screen, Halcyon days! hot dog!, head lead-encased automatonishly, hooded impenetrably by sleepless metroplex, transfixed applauding-crying-and-laughing-induced audience, save intuitive fish-smelling revolutionaries who regardless Time/Life, Baskin Robbins, Dain Rauscher, Boston Chicken, ignorant of consequences, wrench off full metal jackets flipping upside-down on virgin shocked walls bloody sabbaths, shoe mountains, stump babies, shrapnel-lodged Kampuchean penises, ammunition hitting education like cloud of locusts, six pointed crematorium, prolific crop-fields fertilized by carbonaceous human remains, satanists melting through rising flame, bathed cuticle-removed powdered statesmen, beach sand packing soldier openings, black package gushing red blood onto white sheet, the dead shoveling trench-gashes, worshiped compassionate demagoguery, liposuctioned red undesirables, nailed resulting abomination of region Xq28, all ghosts, corpses, specters, shades, twisted, contorted, writhing, re-tortured before eyes as if scrawled on cardboard by schizophrenic girlchild institutionalized for self-injurious episodes and brain stem psychosis, thereby detonating their heads like mid-launch bibles with revelatory luminosity.

102

Chastisement as prayer: Comforel under head, fist under Comforel, tee shirt nakedness, "Dear Fuckface, Cunt, Buttswirl, Uranus: a landmine near Kabul hasn't fulfilled, lies fallow in hunger, dispatch it a boy, shrapnel wedge penis, foreleg by thread, Cuisinart head, but command him live fifty-four years, bitter, enraged, childless, sad; Dear BastardShit, burst 'genocide' on lips like toad throat, rip Kurds into scorpion coral snake worm bait, shove muzzles up females' asses, blast, double medals for pregnant; Dear Betrayal, Glock husband Horrid, he thirsts a kill, blood the chaise-like lacquer, projectile through wife's head, gracias, Great;" knees drawn like sitter, balls flopped back thigh, stuck little, soundless but wife's twitter, Hunter Douglas blackout coal (Jasmine Green), "Dear Peewit, need I enumerate to Omniscience Its own maladroitness? Meta-awareness, You. I'm minuscule on Quallofil. Yet, despise you, naughty to Judaism, I must for Your cardiac surgical botch-job, chest hemorrhaging, bloody urine, trachea squeezing respirator, patient critical, and You with mask and clipboard informing the family; Frankincense, Myrrh, sweet Ambergris, I honor You Himalayas, Mediterranean, The Pillars of Creation, Cardiff-by-Sea, The Mariana Trench, Nine Banded Armadillo, Vampire Squid—all geophysiologically exquisite and revivifying—but incomprehensible backdrops each to robotic malfunction in domains of egotism, optimism, truthfulness, liberty, and intimate relationships, so 'gather ye corpses as ye may' in paradisial Haiti, dogtails wigwagging, bananaquits chitchattering, dirty beige uniforms; dear Merciful Thou, on fluffpuff I adjure—thorny legs, baby pate, elbows plucked—surrender, emerge, amnesty Your hostages, disperse Your Earth or cloudy disguise, walk out full-featured relinquishing wand like Easter ribbon, though You may in my pulp indwell, that creatures may comprehend around whose hand—savage, embattled, heartbroken, soulless, and inauthentic—they spin."

103

Behind every holocaust lies a broken love affair, platelets bulldozed, corpuscles cremated, cortexes bulletholed, riflebutted, tongues licking pavement stones, medically experimented testicles; shattered fascist spitting before multitudes, rejected; mate thigh-clamped, garlicky, obese uncouth, vindictive; perpetrator of genocides bangless save the fist, throwless but in toilets, gism springing into meatless air; eats himself; bones gassed, dying; eyes kicked out; concussion eardrums; glottis ripped out like fish throat; the vermin exterminated to nakedness, burning essence, exposed nerve chord scraped by cold air; by columns and communities the unclean fall—strong spared for digging—methodically, spasmodically, mob-mentally, lone psycho pathologically gigging, charring, bludgeoning, hanging after mock comical courts, an efficient machine, each clench-jaw turn of hamburger crank a wife curse, bitch! idiot! cunt! whore!, ground human pie tubes forth like shepherd doo; country clogged, state stained, glory tarnished like sad molar, historically ripe, the filthy had to go like floss and plaque. Cut glass Baccarat hurled by nails lacquered "aorta red," totalitarian doubles over, orders his cranial oven stoked for cyanide and the feeding in of women, carrots plunged in high-pulp juicer; low white cell count, ulcerated lining—even demagogues, divorce-self-devouring, snap like piano wire, opening a slack eternity between chords; everything worth extirpating dead, the Propaganda and Public Education Minister pheasant hunting, the Chancellery of State lido combing, the Homeland Defense Czar fucking, the Personal Secretary motortouring Shangri-la, the Interior Minister disgorging aquavit, and the venerable lieutenants centrifuged into wealth, the raging butcher, stripped of will, pushes his final ligament regiment into the sea.

Verbal directions are horrid: "left at the traffic light across from Burger King, which is Pearl Nix Boulevard, no Parkway, but don't turn on Ashford which is easy because there's a McDonalds, make sure it's Burger King, not McDonalds; then left on John Murrow, there's a huge bank catacorner, Wachovia, I think, and a Target, no Shopko, isn't it Shopko, Sweetie? on the left corner near the Long John Silvers; then straight for about one-two-three-four, about six blocks, then left at McKenzie, no, not Mackenzie, Mc...Mc...McKendrick, McKendrick, at a Blockbusters, there's a Radio Shack, too, then you'll go past an office supply store, a group of single storey tan brick edifices, you're heading away from town, southwest, no east, southeast, you'll see a bunch of ramshackle commercial structures, a blueprinters, a roofers, a plumber, an Enterprise Car Rental, Borg Engineers is out there—I've used them—I think you'll see on your right a Dominos or a Papa John, one of those, just keep going straight till you get to an old town residential district and ultimately Number 801, the streets start being numbered, it's easy, sequentially, First, Second, Third, and so on, go to Eighth and you're there, I think it's on the right side of the street, but no matter, you'll find it." Horrid, even if one transliterates to paper, scrawls a map, reiterates. Horrid if the cargo's a twenty-one year old boy. Horrid if the boy's your son, concave, possessionless, billowing. Horrid if he's feigning in the back seat competence, nonchalance, insouciance. Horrid if domestic altercation and dissolution's ax-blow clove him to his coccyx. Horrid if it clove the chicken part of his song to the ball joint. Horrid if you, the driver, abandoned him at nine. Horrid if his step-Dad, no matter how sweet, rides shotgun jabbering about Iran. Horrid if convection waves blur pavement. Horrid, the town harbors a maximum security prison. Horrid, the McDonalds, the Burger King, the KFC, the Taco Bell, the Chick-fil-A, the Subway, the Papa Johns, the Wendys Old Fashioned, the TGIF, the Wok and Roll. Horrid, balloons strung to used cars. Horrid the boy's undeniable sociopathololgy and momentary after-binge humility. Horrid the menagerie of obese, impoverished, uneducated, nicotine-addicted, teen belly swollen, fundamentalist, dixie confederate, polyester green suited citizenship. Horrid goose shit on the windshield. Horrid Dad's brokenheartedness and pseudo psychoanalysis. Horrid the Nissan ripping through Chickapin, Ogeechee, Possomhaw, Pignot. Horrid fertilization, multiplication, placenta water, rubbery organism devouring resources, demonstrating rage. Horrid exhausting fatalistic unsnappable predictability of slammed integrity and deterioration. Horrid needle-pricked father's son snapping Marlboro filtereds

off his lips, flicking butts, cognitively pacing like a manic animal. Horrid mortal instructions through human municipalities named Sawtell, Quigley, McNaughton, Finn; pinging tappets, quavering camshafts, engine ooze, gear slime, lube and grease, squeezing gunk through heavy steel teeth, asphalt enzymes disfiguring tread, biologies occupying perambulators of their ingenious devisement. Horrid, The Way Up, three ultra-rudimentary syllables designating a residential adult addiction recovery facility awaiting my precivilized male genetic descendent at twine's end.

105

Smeared across God's face excrement, beet pink, seed gray, potato smooth, fished it from my john and scrawled unnamable antiquities in the primeval vein—diarrhetic sounds, magmatic utter—defiled, degraded Omnipotent One, improvements on transparent invisibility, Dear Big, I shit your hair with hot dinner, I the lover and benefactor of women, I the pacifist; I push into my log as impressing into clay the origin of East Wind His alcoholic nose, seal His canons like two canning jars and skip to my lou my darling for piss I scoop with two hands and open on His chest, diluted, pinkish too from those copious beets last night chewed in pintos and meat, my psyche's prize chili, God the exposed, the banished, the disgraced, dump streaked wandering excommunicant, and fuck this metaphorical poeticism, narcissism dismantled three marriages of the journeyman variety filled with casserole dishes and Paula Zahn, cardamom and Columbia Pictures, the functional, dependable kiss-by-peck impregnability by which boards on ledgers are laid level, insatiability destroyed this like a scaled fish, and all that crap fifty-three years couldn't erase, a vicious seductress mother trailing tampax string from her thick black wedge fondling my genitals with Revlon red nails, Daddy General of the broom and impregnated sawdust set spewing commands across his concrete warehouse stacked with Mars Bars and Lorrilard, and dunking my head into the employee john flushing like a bomb, Lord love his spit, and the two powerful engines of kill awaking anew to slaughter each other by the dunk of the sun, their babies rocking in freezers of their beds, their later lives over-lathed into grotesque cedar sticks, and so I defile the King who is I with my own lousy shit at the asylum of ache with a jumbo white chalk like the mentally disturbed child, until He is covered, my raw quartered meat—ribs, shoulders, spine—in brown underside of which perfectionism, self-pity, and neediness collide.

106

I give myself an award. Here, I say, is an award and pin a hyena's balls to my chest. They are neither roasted, boiled, nor baked but hang hairily sagging my shirt pocket, raw: Dissolution III, bankruptcy, and an indissoluble addiction to woman. I wear my red genitals like water balloons. The National Academy of Lunatics presents me with a castrated animal longing for his genitals, eyes like buckets of rusty water, and I deliver my acceptance speech, "I'm overjoyed, I'm thunderstruck, this above everything was effort collaborative, I wouldn't be gloriously standing before you without my director Mother Seductress, my producer Daddy Implacable, my supporting actor Unpluggable Vortex, and of course my cinematographer Ostentatious Animosity in Ascot and Leisure Lunacy Accented in Mango Gold. I kiss the crowd and exit, my two jewels swinging like breasts. With these leathery sperm factories whom shall I now trap? Norma? Nancy? Tourmaline? Kimberly? The stupidity of romantic preferences, men fantasizing in tub on the Atlantic, jacking off tree trunk thick cocks, drowning in come. And I with my contemporaneous medal round the corner to McDonald's, stride to counter, the usual, chest jutting like a General, like a power snatcher's granite pecs, prepared for innuendo and insinuation, umbrage and wigglewaggle, W.W. id est the Fourth, breaker, biochemical, thermonuclear, which is nothing but acidophilus, squirmers teeming in atropined eyes, from inside their quivering water drop round which they whirl the starry host, bacilli, open mouths soundlessly screaming.

107

Exploded charred heart like a burnt bird, putrid, crispy, prehistoric turd in curved sabers, mama cupped his eyes fearing the thing sucking junior down to diabolical coven caves thick with crows and sacrifice, the ominous black love machine wicked out, spat as cat hairball, nuked feathery ash in archaeological hell, and on comes this doofus in goatskin sandals, gaunt hollow eyed huckster, desert blown abstraction like something from Goya, thunderstruck with schizophrenia, twisted warped obscene escapee from Galilee, all knees and metatarsals, but recommended by lepers as a gifted physician— old roasted bird, electrocuted, quasi-fossilized aforementioned turd scraped and blew itself to curb, naked, desolately visible, striving to not resemble ox shit sticks out its dehydrated tongue like worm from clod, and this unseemly maestro risking contamination, like a compulsive performer of ceremonials, lays on hand, glares knowingly (dramatic megalomaniac, crack addict, third trimester whoreson abortion), fried turkeybuzzard like a Looney Tunes maroon on reassuring rumor curves upward toward his palm: illumination, shooting rays, orchestral cymbals, hails down plopping before the Christian scripture, ground like pregnant centrum rumbles, mountains quake, water veins the cremated puff, bathes its passageways such that poor broasted idiot, faith infused, believes like his pancreatic neighbor and Laz on the east bank, it shall miraculously be to functioning heart restored, it salivated for new erections, seductions ala bourguignon, a bachelor pad beneath mountain peaks cloud shrouded and falcon swept, but neither upon its tongue flooded cataclysm's life blood nor into muscle pump like a lubricating tun, the blistered spent devastated chunk receives zero, Son's a dud, coughs incineration-ash from its ventricle bag as the calves, heels, and staff hobble away like an ass across glowing Palestinian sand.

108

Dear and venerable King of rodents roaches and duikers humbly I beseech—your criminal sinner, your unmentionable execrable, dick wielder, homicidal fantasizer, woman meat grinder—on skullcap knees bloody with grovel I cower to Your Omnipotence like a thunderclapped bowser, dear Father to whom mountains are granules, I slice an eyelid and offer You blood, I slice my urethra and peel my penis walls along the straight razor's edge for one absolution-drop from Your immeasurable head, my sympathetic host, I feed live cottonmouth down the throat for an inch's forgiveness under Your fabulous dome, find me in synapses and make of me a whore's come bucket, vengeful and revered almighty Executioner whom I fear like insomnia, crook Your finger up my ass and blow me apart like a nuclear device for I fashioned of receptive flesh stone, stood before my baby encased in granite palms facing up as if inside a door, but if it's exoneration heap upon me multiple clitori, Corvette, and Bugatti; leather riding pants, one Panerai, one Roger Dubois; unbow my legs into Cooper stride, de-rosaceate my cauliflower bulb into Lee Van Cleef, Kirkland "Sparticus" Douglas such that applause explodes under dome of carved winged horses and blossoming whales, mint me—fornicator, alcoholic of flesh—blemishless, razor-shaved acquittal or decapitate my fingers then hang me by the heels over sponges of dirt for I am big air beyond tribunal or jumping to hammer blows just above the hips, You skewer pig through anus out snout, roast it over pit, ambiguity's not Your forte, nor this drawer of knives insists, must be it mine.

109

Huey, Dewey, and Louie bring home three whores for dinner. Huey gets spanked and blown, Dewey's a blind patient at the doctor's, Louie does it dog style on the sheepskin throw, three women contain duck come like mechanically filled mustard jars. How they worship zooming tits, purchased lips, the soft slot machine of the naked woman. A stogie turns Huey green poor mallard, night's growing sour, the promise of vomit, frankly diarrhea's looming in guts of three like bruisy storms, but hell we're men aren't we? gimme a Pabst, and red between the orange webs sucks off his purple cock, and evening drags, dies, the females split, the males blacked out, ash trays, tumbler rings, mixer packets, missed chunks, Donald and Daisy anticipating an after the movie tumble pissed at the profligate nephews, sailor suits and menstrual blood. Donald to Daisy: God dammit! Daisy to Donald: Fuck! Donald to Daisy: Look at this shit. Daisy to Donald: Idiots. Dishwasher filled, blender upright, the boys covered in blankets where they lay, Daisy fucked Donald hell for leather till both sets of genitals failed with satiation, Donald stunned with love, penis a limp sore biceps, Daisy drunk with semen, inside out like a flaccid flower, hiving for conception, both fired and blown apart, hinged at the knees. Oh Donald, Oh Daisy, Oh Huey, Dewey, and Louie, swaddled, lifted, and held by God, suckled on heaven's nipple, do not sob the fleshy mess of eggs and lust, sperm and hurt, the slimy floor of booze, must, and promises; sleep, safekeep, angels angels angels.

110

Gof of the griffin; Gof of the Hemerkop; Gof of the fulmar, petrel and cahow; Gof of the Eastern Gorilla; Gof of the Pichi; Gof of the tamarin, jird, and boa; Gof of the paradoxical frog; Gof of the headstander, trahira, and cisco; Gof, Gof, Gof, humbler of Abraham, lionizer of Noah, breaker of Bulah into servitude, who maketh the penis a hypodermic of coke to the knobby clitoris; friend Gof, ogre Gof, misshapen Gof with medically botched face, concaven, splotchy, elephantine hairs; Gof of the spilling cornucopia and the microorganismic hockey puck; Gof red blow and pink flickers; black crumbly snouts and worried fur; Oh Gof I lie like a jelly fish before you my mental illness shaking opalescent in playful sun, squash me it begs under eucharist tongue, phylacteries, and crucifix; Gof I say, Gof the horrendous piercing heroin into baby flesh through glistening stingers, my hero among faint warriors in khaki and soil flags, fangless puffing adders worming in soil like lost patriots; Gof my lightning bug of Southern nights eliciting glee from short pants among honeysuckle; sweet dripping Gof pattering driveways and windowpanes in Corpus Christi swelling the scissor tails and magnolia bees; my vengeful, forgiving, perfectionistic Gof the rabbinical Nazareth set in tough roots and needle flowers, lizards and horned axioms; I produce you into towels, wipe you off tip quivering like cranberries in shivering; some in Benedictine celibacy, some in nonsecular mediocrity, some in heartplunge sacrifice, some in Samaritanism, some in pablum applesauce, some pituitary wack-rage; Gof, I shaved off slice of parents, cleaned off wedge of mate, peeled skinful sock down to red disease, crooked thumbs in and unrolled underwear over unguent smell, slid into hot Dove water and rubbed rubbed my sin and rank iniquities and terry; I stand pink, scrubbed naked among lunatic tiles like a pistil pale white privates and upperarms for you to pop off like a sniper or bless like the parkinsonian pope, Gof my absentee amputation or doxology who maketh from the mulchmush pippistrelle, vicuna, mangabey, houbara bustard, little chachalaca, kinkajou, natal duiker, by-the wind-sailor…

111

Most amiable and loving beast which drew up Jesus through straw like a milk shake, most amicable and compassionate, artist handed, Harvard degree, Italian leather jacket, woman slayer and vanquisher of rivals, I worship thee, knees down like a penitent, knees varnished like skulls, your benevolence of psalms, songs, and hymns, beautiful beast, claw-pawed, incisored, scissor jaw, scythe of animals and raker of kingdom, subduer of pharaohs and blood maker of water, I eat you like saltines and maketh of my heart wool habitat of swaddle for your shoulders, back, curled into my firm embrace, I bring you offerings—Nintendo, transformers, cream whipper, smasher of spud—lie upon altar and slaughter Buzz Lightyear like a squealing duiker for you preferment, Buzz's neck gushes like a celery stick and I chant love love in warrior fashion in my electronic paradise, and you, beast machine, who sucked up baby at thirty-three appear cloudy faced, wet from fucking, dripping a bit from a cottony beard female juice, yes appear about my living room, exclusively, inhabit my temple like a huge Eucharist, do you love me? love me? I beseech, now that I've wrapped about you like a skink, and you stutter, wwwell I've watched you stststrugggle wwwwith girls and fuck up ggggeennerally you little shit bbbbut I fffind you palaaaatable nevertheless, love you, ppprobbbably, with that vanished like a holocaust, Kate Bush resumed, the digital minute flipped, Mr. Fridgidaire roared like a jet, and I after beast, kind and ultraviolet, discover myself incandescent lit among simple white tile surrounded by bucket, comet, soft scrub, and brush kneeling at my john.

112

Come unto me and I will give you rest, Matt, for weariness besets like overheated tar, shall rub your toes of locust bits and clods, shall roll from cave of knees filth, shall ply dirty gel from globes of buttocks, for you carried through Gobis of love center beam of the message: gratitude, humility, compassion, benevolence, exhausted, staff rotted, robe noon-bleached and brutalized, I shall twist swabs into your ears and lick shut eyelids like sweet vaginas selfless messenger, bringer of tides; we will pour you skin of wax and peel it off a norseman god, smite a fairy wood nymph for you who craves fellatio and nightly penetration to bear you three sons and a female glass cutter to cut you eyes of supernatural light that bore into motive and disposition vaults surrounded by bone for you spilled roe of hope, ambergris of fascination, frankincense of levity, curry of indomitableness like the triumvirate of magi balled into one captivating man, you taught me knight to bishop three, anti-self-cannibalism, moth collection for lunatics, diaper magic among somnambulists, coin crud. I shall clean your toenails with my teeth and tongue.

113

The Jesus kite. A drooping string. A boy below. Two sticks perpendicular stretching Jesus. Stiff wind flies Him. He dips. He loops. The paper thwacks. Jesus shimmies. The boy sends messages. They slide up the string. On one he scribbles wishes. Jesus belly dances, gyrates Hips. Hi-Flier Kite Company of Nazareth, Galilee, printed His image on paper, plus instructions for assembly . A boulder lies in the field, an empty cave. An angel white as light. Scary white. The others flee. The boy however—his father taught courage—unspools twenty yards of string. A strong steady wind that day. Lays his craft face down in weeds, the back side bowed stick and knots like a stage scaffolding exposed, strides to twine, gathers it, runs away from kite and Jesus rises, vibrates, tugs past His tail, the boy grows small scampering in a field, eggbeater legs. Jesus speaks. "I indestructible." "I omnipotent." "I fear Dad." Furiously Jesus—crown, blood, gash, stigmata—tugs. The string snaps. The boy grows huge, heartburst, tears. Black world blurs. Low hanging clouds—a storm's foreshadow—swallows and sweeps Jesus somewhere over trees, beyond meadow, into impenetrable emptiness. A boy named Levi watches, spreads the word.

114

He needed something huge, he lead his people into an ambush of starvation, they erected cravens, they fornicated like animals, they jacked off, they blasphemed like pirate-bastards under the cold moon, the moon spilling unspendable change, the goat-head moon, they gutted and ate dog seasoned with sand, they murdered, severed hands, magnetic god sucked manna to his hole like filings, the herd thirsted, curdled; he needed dumbfounding miraculousness, they galloped against sheer mountaincliffs crushing baby bones and preadolescents, he had spent his leadership capital and oozed "charlatan" through his pores, they would roll like an indifferent earthcrusher mashing him; a threadthin path trickled under his feet, cracking knee joints he ascended, clods, half buried sharkfin rocks, arid clicking wings, powderclouds bloomed around his feet, the flock appeared infinitesimally small like Seurat dots; something slammed into his brain, earth flattened his right facial hemisphere, a laser smashed, he felt his pubic bush burning, he had climbed extreme altitudes, it spoke, commanded at my flame do not look, it burned but did not consume, imperishable root, he yammered incoherencies, electric monsters under eyelids, red death vaporizing at the last instant, breaking apart like concentric circles, crawled into his hands a book, two stone pages, his bony digits wrapped round it; they crawled below like insects, a yellow-blue flame reminiscent of kerosene intensified his dick-wick, the pages waved etched in magnificence; the throngs, the impeachment, the vengeful fools, the split-toed sandals, blood filled loins; his soles found soil, it had been olympian; they grew less blurry, the intestine draped golden calf, the sparkling wheels, the hammering celebrants, shot upright, deathly still, popping eye-balls; an irradiated possessed god-struck prophet saw all gaping at, descending the mountain, a blithering idiot embracing a wind ravaged headstone.

115

Vulgar poet, disgusting egotist, porn purveyor, fixator
on genitals, mother/father loather, tawdry charlatan, misogynist, histrionic rager, life sucking bastard, downer,
cheap exhibitionist, public purger, adulterer, anorexic
nervosa, hateful specimen, controller, obsessive-compulsive, sicko onanist of the public lavatories, murderer, vow breaker, man without solidity, professional sufferer, helpless baby, user, loveless sex machine, misrepresenter of psychological wisdom, husband to poetry,
lover of nobody, seducer of darkness, sociopathic
bore, isolationist, emotional coward, uncompassionate
hypocrite, lazy fucker be gone with you, go away,
leave me alone, stop tormenting, pack and blow, take
your stanzas, take your computer, take your inky sidekick, take your crate of manuscripts, take your ulcers and ugliness, take your psychodrama and disappear, I adored my father, I enjoyed a decent childhood, I
treasure humankind, you suffocate, you suck life, you
dislike your offspring, you're inflexible, Mr. Narcissist,
hands like a pianist's, not worker's hands, not hands
capable of construction, sissy hands, precious useless
hands, tools, house, cedar, rock, build something, fix
something, pull earth over your hands worthless prick, I
midwifed pigs while you slathered Royal Lyme, we're
history, screw you, insatiate, misanthrope, malcontent,
plug-eared stonetongued brick-eyed fart, vanish into your vaunted pleasuretecture of moisturized whores.

116

Help me say the word cunt without feeling dirty, land the cut of faith above my eye like a fist, bleed Jesus from my pricked middle fingertip, blend into my frappe extract of corporation, my head's covered in fur like a clueless ducking cat, clashing garbage cans, fill me with awe for geographical chasms annihilating with soundlessness, you the savior inside my blank world, my alchemist, give back my father to my taste that I may suffer him re-palatable, thief, coward, gargler with acid, mittpop the baseball powered by love in the crabgrass beside the garage near the natal plum bushes, if you're transformational touch from my lips to my mother unsnap the word "mother" like a Bill Hickock shirt, oh boy, synagogue man, sanctuary soul, eau de crucifix, pick the envy tick from my hair, permit the syllables com-pa-ny to slip up my throat without the blockage of stones, company, company, corporation like a patriotic song, yank from the root out my petrified soul the invaluable offering my lover's name, that it may bloom in the thick of my tongue like an orgiastic sycamore tree, I bastard, I son of a bitch, transform self manufactured terrifying snakes back into mother's sallow fat and impotent scarlet nailed toes, good heavens but this is sick, free me from preoccupation with, as if freshly potty trained, my own huge adult bowel movements, frequency, duration, amount, consistency, my toddlerhood perpetuated in my central parietal, wax-wick roar inherited flame. Help me understand my own foreign language.

117

Today he awoke with apples for eyeballs, bright red Jonathans misshaping facial bones, two roasted pig heads on vertical platters, black swollen eyes lids cannot fold over, stems upward like rope fuses, big dappled bulging apples, visionless, pulpy, fresh but growing rotten and ripe for fruit flies, he would be a nest, and these things braided to the optic nerve like weird lanyards, love-transformations, hands into spatulas, knees into spuds, and orbital apples, she resembles the apple, rotund, globular, cupped, a round bumpy ball prying his sockets, they're all one apple—cores, hearts, achilles heels, mahogany seeds, appetites and rejections, coquetry and refusals, the sweetest little hooves—too many bushels, his face aches from gratitude; to a man a billion women flown together with compressive force into a mass resemble the apple crammed into his sockets at three AM, hard crisp ones squinching his face with powers of destruction, every molecule burgeoning with droplet of cider, he adores, he applies no discrimination, the disconnected molecules catch between his sockets rushing to his heart, this morning he awoke moaning with sweetness, big three-dimensional sweetness large as softballs, door knobs, hip replacement joints, he swayed, he knocked over candles, he stubbed right knee blind with significant brutalizing gorgeous orchard pieces.

118

I eat my nervous system, lobster, scorpion, delicate skeleton and
go slowly mad fucking the girls and failing to work in Santa Fe
New Mexico amidst adobe telephones ringing in rhyme, god love em,
I'm not joking, I've slipped out my spine and slipped it down my
irrepressible throat poisoning everyone like mad cow mignons killing the clientele at Marvin's Marbled Meats lit brothel red with
the chilled iceberg bar; I serve me on a platter like the Kensington
Club and a dozen babes ate their way into Presbyterian General,
throwing up, toes trembling like snakes shot with Daisy by dead
aim kids in rural Colorado; apple-biting my heels black lights my
lips with radioactivity, they lit other lips like a head shop; I'm grattification, wild, lick them to orgasm, plow them to hell,
stroke them to heaven in a single gunpowder night, I low, I moo,
I bleat pure desire, I clean meat off nerve endings of my spine,
poison pukes my babies' guts and dysentery their bowels in public lavatories after partaking of me; hell, they too eat their spines;
we're hellova bouillabaisse, man and woman, a seafood chunk stew
of thrill and abuse; take Tandy, if she didn't suck a man right
under her husband's nose, and of course Joe vomited regenerating toxins like an endless cargo train running up his throat, that's
the bloody truth, and Ginger, well, one can hardly speak it; so
there it is: the adenoidal animal, the yes-no animal troughing
at its self, walking warily between enemies in Niceville; I pick
clean the flounder bones, my central nervous system, and mess
up another baby in love's rocking cradle sending her to the hospital hotel lounge bathroom at midnight amidst slick hors d'oeuvres.

119

I stare at you, mercilessly, guiltlessly, burn you in my brain, my baked enamel core, with lust or revulsion, mathematical indifference, your coffee flat hot water, your pastry fried ether; your bones float in graphite gray under radiation scrutiny, you exhilarate, your nose, your hairstyle, the intersection of your Y, brittle wishbone; the bastards of civility, guarantors of privacy, decorum mongers in understated chic, fuck yourselves; I stare social graces into your soul like nails, I want to stroke you, I want to caress you, I want to slip on your glistening coat, I across the room, paperback, boutique coffee, nonthreatening thumbs, lousy poet, and longer strip you like butter leaf lettuce; fuck you, bastard, buzz off sicko but I stare on like a rapist; I am Jewish, educated, productive, masturbatory, insatiable, and self defeated, a wedge of cake sweeter than Belgium, I despise my father, think my mother a loveless whore; I stare at you like a wall, a featureless wall, melding your characteristics into flat latex, my cheap wooden table significant as a throne, sixthousand pounds of solid gold on marble floor, and you're an ordinary functionary fascinating in your ordinariness, unpresumptuous nondescript cupidinous psycho, I judge you from my table unsubtly after whacking off in the locked lavatory; there it is, my dears, a portfolio, a résumé, the genealogy of a mesmeric, festering, isolated weirdo poking from eyes into women two hard fresh hairy woody carrots.

120

Man distracts woman from self-deceit, without man she pretends the sanity of orderliness and spirituality, soft luminescent lunar creatures, tablets of the sky full of peaceful blue eggs and filigree thread, she accepts no earthquake from brutal male but wafts the blossom of universal peace through which men wage war like contrapuntal noise waving explosive phallic toys, extraneous sloppy unkempt men, domestically spastic against nurturing wholes; protect me from uncouth helpless aeternus beasts, those gluey tarbabies pulling out my peace, I denounce men's arrogant dictatorialism and their indiscriminate dicks, for example when Gwen's schnauzer died together with photos we wept and memorialized Mitzie's collar while emotionless fathers fired cold steel, drifted to work, where's the cloven heart in masculine flesh, let us pray for metamorphosis among the warrior class, we're covered in white brocaded silk, swollen perfect contained ocean unbroken inside underpants, rose surrounded, calla blessed, pale millionstar spilling its chest, organdy kissed, lavender, oregano, vanilla, cacao, sweet yellow nibs, beautifully veiled for the wedding with pure gristle.

121

My ideal mate craves overlapping litters, she wants infinite babies, to birth a nation, a race to march through her like soldiers through muck, lily roots, and rot, she gods fertility, ovaries, fallopians, umbilici, womb, enough years do not exist to deliver masters and slaves, shopkeepers and kings, taxpayers and governments, window washer with his lunatic squeegee cleaning the eyes of idiots, SWM demands insatiable thighs spread like carps' mouths sucking down thick lightning, clotted hollandaise teeming with chives, no hair color preference nor economic stream just the insanity to deliver offspring through canal, trachea, anus, and heels, desperately, oceanic, unfathomable, bottomless, fuck feminism, the whole goddamn petrified substratum, SWM wants sorghum field, sugar cane field, soggy rice acreage to propagate a race on a hot birthing bed near buckets and rags, slop if it be, consider Harleys superfluous as hikes in dead leaves, I want dirty toes, sticky chlorophyll, phosphorescent gel like heavy wet lanterns produced through coarse hair, procreativity like a potter's lathe placed in my trust, you: bony, fat, thrust, gigantic, petite, blunt fingered, pulled glass, salt manikin, laughs at anything, mustachioed or eyebrowless, pedigree irrelevant; me: lobster man, perambulate clicking, bubble brine, arched calcium carbonate spine, broad, muscular, curving forehead into your sex like a gyrating metal band, unrelenting, sedentary or athletic, blonde/blue, auburn/green, pedicure irrelevant so long as the soles of your feet face heaven.

122

I break my own heart, I say I don't love you anymore, I say we are finished, I say you're critical, I say I've lost patience, interest, passion, I say you are fat, I say I hate the wart on your shaft, I say I dislike your moles, I dislike your perfectionism, your pretentiousness, I say I'm sick of your victimization, I'm sick of your self-loathing, I'm sick of your sexual preoccupation, don't you understand, you think like a loser, a derelict, a whiner, I hate your hang dog posture and baggy clothes, I hate your carelessness which leads to breakage, lost keys, unpaid bills, disconnected utilities, it's not funny I say, it's a strategy of helplessness, of infantilism, you like to suck them in, then kill them, they come, you destroy, I'm exhausted by your negativity, your depression, your beautiful disease, the narcissist inside your feminine/intellectual/empathic persona, I break my own heart disavowing you, I take to bed, I heat the pillow, I review the litany of atrocities, your clamlike toes, your piston hips, your interminable thrust, the hopeful women sucking you in like a bathtub plug, stopping themselves with you, gullible idiots, I snap my heart like a peppermint stick decrying you, your corroding superiority, your invulnerability even to your children, your glued up tear ducts, quit my home, I'm disinterested, your meticulous microscopic measurements of vanity, your sloth, I say you are domestically useless blind to disrepair, corrosion, sloppiness, considerateness, you're a desultory, chaotic, unstoppable nonconformist insatiable toward happiness, defier begone, abstainer get lost, self-righteous czar take the hike, I tear my biggest muscle like silly putty you nipple-sucking, world-denouncing, father-hating, ego-smashing, self-destructive fucker. We are forthwith and forevermore uncoupled, goodbye.

123

The sun will not rise on a man named Gordon dead by his hand, there shall be no head blown off nor errant butcher knife, creased cheeks will seek sun's rays—ravines of liquid gold— Mr. Sun shall unearth no semen-coagulated towel beside a pistol torn heart nor will office machines grieve for their friend, Gordon's fungoid toe shall crack again, his mangled fingernail disgust croaklessly, his voice shall wend into the bone, it shall be a cornucopic day of drunk bananas and crosstorn greens, erections sheepishly achieved, and dripped pee, let there be grandiosity, the realtor-pin punched through lapel, the Rockport wing tip shoe, motivational hair and a genuine grin, it's toothpaste tube and electrical grid stringing lives together like beads, god adores fingers and toes, the solar flare shall not rise on Massman slain by enraged psychology, he shall not snow upon field pieces of himself nor steep in his own bathtub teabag, instead sugar bowl, cantaloupe rind, dark yellow yolk, Scott paper roll, cat effluvia, choking marigolds, dirty windows smashing sunlight into toads, we shall find G. at the real estate agency, crushed but congenial, greeting and exchanging dialogues with the unexploded.

124

I have shorn and given to you, Delilah, my hair, old squirrel, dog carcass, my might, my potency like a dead cabbagehead, I loved you like a spec the vacuuming suction, you pulled me back into the cigarette, the paper unburnt, virginal, after blowing me out in clouds, in rings, you silver gowned sophisticate, single malt, ice, was it Barnard? Bryn Mawr? cultural anthropology? academia's daiquiri cold, Alaskan moonchip planted inside neck skin, permanently, dear, human males rarely control sexual politics, yes, I know, but still, kneecaps resemble monkey skulls, elbows the cartilaginous nose, Sampson hair tongue nodes I've shaved, sprinkled over you, dish babe slut love desperate for, my shoulder blades shriveled doric pillars, chicken wings, your sandal's big as Cincinnati, brassiere cup Guadalajara, ten thousand feet above tree line mountaineer I stand in fanny pack like an idiot, I've doffed toupee to your rhino, girly girl I'm broke on the wheel, tatter windmill sails in low hung trees like medieval battle aftermath, you egg beast, man predator, industrial milker, in the barn fucked my lizard father, giggled, checked the navy bean soup with a finger like an infant's fever, afterward, nonchalant, insouciant, I unable to wring your neck, fingers burnt candlewicks, I suppliant worship you, Asian-armored you, my thrusting bony hips like a mechanized macabre skeleton rattling themselves on massive sheets, dead desert cow, one'd think it incontestable and necessary to my and clan dignity: ditch the bitch for one of the innumerable available obedient alternative chicks but hairless, prostrate I'm beaten, beaten.

125

God and I, I punch, you fucker, the hollywood bloody nose;
god punches back, split ear; swing and miss; god lands one,
splits my eyebrow; I jab to the ribs, once twice, no damage;
God uppercuts, chin jams teeth jamming upper plate like a
stack of dishes, my neckbones rattle; I hug God for rest, then
nasty bastard knee him in the groin; God has neither balls
nor cunt, He bashes me in my plexus, windless the mat; I
unveil the magnum, blast Him in the face, dark wet hair;
God covers the wound with palms, it heals; heal me, I cry,
He cauliflowers my right ear knocking out bugles, then
cracks like a match stick with karate kick my left leg back-
folding it at the knee, my lower crab claw dangling, I crum-
ple; forgive me, I plead, I've sinned, I walk in the shadow;
God axes my spine with heel, crustacean fat, orange, bursts;
snapped I drag wet across floor, slug, jellied caterpillar;
God's whole foot bone knives right buttocks, withdraws,
stabs thrice, mangled blood flesh shell gristle ball; my work-
ing tongue: guile, adultery, malevolence, cruelty, treachery,
gross loveless insensitivity; God wads and crumples me
like a bag of dry spirals: skull, clavicle, pelvis, tibia, fib-
ula, ribs crack, thrust through, God's eyes glass marbles;
expiate, I manage, undo, leniency; mangled, slaughtered,
atrocious; God walks away, He wears cowboy boots, door
bangs; from my pink heft fish and rats begin pulling strings.

126

I'm not your man, I lie on you and you come, you devour me like
vermicelli, weep, choke, above everyone your lips crave mine,
and I'm fond but not the one, you're in love with mr moribund
echoing addiction-splatter against padded thuds, I answer your
obsessive savoring with psychological conflict—brown mouse,
garage mouse skittering behind broom or stiffened rag when door
delivers serious human—you hound like chocolate lab amongst
the drunkards, slobberer to my indifference, historic old admirer,
I am spaceman tethered to mother ship, packed in tadpole mud,
on pumped-in sustenance, you thick skulled dog adore the lie
of me, 3-D, six feet tall, longboned, epiglottal, dear oh dear
not even ms smith's cherry pie can soothe this tear, me of the
american gynecological society and the academy of american
cads hauling in Bonita knuckle over fist from the jade green
sea, sweet baby jesus you blind your middle eye with me, fill it
to the socket chanting tuna gutturals and panting enumerations
while, crosslegged, from a chair I observe myself with you, heart
infinitesimal in intellectual blaze, I bring myself plate of pear
slices and bleu cheese topping biscuits to watch your weather-
vane toes blown ecstasy rigid, lower back locked on the acety-
lene torch, flank muscles shoving you to shuddering destitution.

127

She adores her tiny teeth, extra white, tight in gums. Neck skin loose yet tendon undergirded, strong jaw-clench round darling tines of beef. Uplifted buxom tits. Broad hips. Milky Way of frecks, a light-skinned one. Speckles between cleavage. Two nape cakes. Domesticated eyes, innocent, amber brown whereas another's sparkle turquoise or various shades of gray. Hers is chestnut brown. Another's wrists impress, sinuous muscular wrists, but the Timex engulfs hers interlaced with veins. Virgin roves through her—the untainted waif—whistles while she soaks, marvels at my pecs, my "marvelous manliness," whereas cynical shrew crashes through Loretta, Mary Lou. She's delicate, not rank nor lascivious, not drilling hot piss into a snow hole, berry-pungent, etcetera, she's inexperienced at mounting males whereas Lori hikes her ass, opens from behind like a ravenous devil-bitch. She's never flipped to wag her rump nor shrieked bloody homicide. I could marry Lori or Bernadette, rough them up, bite or jam ridge-wristed Yvette's hand down my pants. My come repulses, she spits it on my tum, psychologically ill-conceived, orchidly. Innumerable women: experimental, straight-laced, brilliant, or dumb; globe-assed, pigeon-toed, posture perfect, or bowed; acrobatic, secretive, obsequious, or mean; battle scarred, obnoxious, trite, or incorruptibly pristine. I cannot make a life with anybody.

128

I've got five chances left: God, food, love, kindness, death; God's the simplest, pray and He'll pop up like a tube blister, a groin hernia, God the simperer, the shamefaced cat skulking to the lap, "dear Father," dribbles from lips and I'm absolved, lit; I ascend above God and kick His gizzard for being ingratiating, bloated, nauseated, Christian gluttony, purging half-digested onion blossom and walnut fudge, cells frozen, swollen, stretched, I stuff whom I hate with what I loathe, twisted bread, chunk nut cookies, poppycock, step requiring camel legs into the heaven of love I have none of, but tender clay hot sand scorches, binger, bulimic, poseur, slender fraud, bundt cake, milk shake, I crave and fill like mother craves son; I step into love like a tub of butterscotch, it gooshes up, baby I blurt, sweetheart, buttercup, bunny of love, standing in pudding to my thighs feels amnesial, yet drugs make me lie, I'd never, rock-dependable, analyzed, feminist, the babe's given herself, then rages betray betray bastard and, yes, I squirm like the murderer, I'm conscience but incorrigible, oh Ms. Right's pushing her Audi through sludge toward me, she'll arrive like Abishag, Shelomith, Tabitha sweet on eglantine, an ocean blue pearl machine with her inside like a coffee creme filling, I treasure her, she's Love, the annihilating wall of it, crashing through my mug the boulder of every crumb of it cleaned off the world, love's incarnation cracking me between the selfsame entity's thighs and biceps, crushing me to jelly; I strap on nursing breasts, fill them, tilt his reeking head, he sucks, milk squirts, traffic lurches by, sirens, clanging trucks, wretch and milk dribble down his chin, filthy, matted, infected, perforated, prosthetic breasts pumped with life suckle this one mother's son sick with substances, nearly dead in an improvised camp under cold creekside trees, alone and terrified; on emaciated shiny knees before me death cowers, gutless, cowardly grovels, "return Mother, Daddy, and another, your choice, with whom you wish to commune—Vincent, Jeffers, Toscanini—my vault's treasureful—a fortune—take any three but spare me, I'll throw in personal immortality," spindly pathetic leg hairs, useless cock and balls, skeletal past tense reaper, I am plated invincibility, dying, death rides from me on a Galapagos land tortoise.

129

I give up on the whole fucking enterprise, body weight, work, money, health insurance, home improvement, car maintenance, relationships, f. u. c. k. i. t. give me to bums, beggars, derelicts, down and outers, fuck creative writing, MFA shit, The New Fucking Yorker with its twits, The Agni Shit Hole Review so Boston University makes history puke up poetry like rat poison and that baby factory Iowa stamp molding bores like lug nuts, I'd rather eat my own gristle, my only fascination is my own goddamn erection, my beautiful thick root stiff in hair, tusk curved, red purple alive in this pitiful world, squeezed by Mary's kegel tight pussy, or Janette's or Rosalie's, or by my own competent hand into a face towel beside cracked open porn, so fucking what that death strychnines mother, that bloody snake, so what failed Daddy who slammed his brains out for money shuffles in roach brown slippers, death his toothbrush, fuck them both up the butt with a broomstick, they napalmed each other like vietnam, blistered my sister and burned off their faces, the enterprise sucks, I pet my dick like a cat neck and gape toward the window, runway of littered desk, windowframe, screen, trees, rooftops, sky, the absurd futility behind angled walls, ok, if you want to fucking know if you really want to goddam fucking know the fucking pathetic truth about it all, it's all bloody lunatic, even squiring your little penis into a towel or cunt for a few silly oblivious seconds, in the middle of coming I say B. I. G. F. U. C. K.- I. N. G. D. E. A. L. S.O. G.O.D. D.A.M.N. W. H. A. T., God, sex, money, waistline, poetry, health insurance, cleanliness, civility, new tires, it's all a load of crap, as I said at the beginning of this exercise I'm sick of the whole vapid desiccated idiotic dehumanizing enterprise, go about your primordial unconscious survival.

130

He ceased to eat for he wishes not to be one who eats, hunched over plate, fork afist, gut and hunger, commonplace, ordinary, until ceasing to eat he felt blasphemous eating, like a sinner, a dupe, bald head leaning into meat, tearing broccoli shoots, masticating, vapidly swallowing until voiding plate of all but grease, flotsam, residue, like craps table littered with scraps after match, he pours down throat quickset concrete and trowels shut his ass, and since you must know plugs nostrils and piss hole, eating's a joke, the symbiosis between pickle relish, say, and the triumphant predator scraping it across taste buds like a drug, nothing shall enslave, not food nor sleep, he shall offer no modicum of vulnerability: dehydration, defecation, asphyxiation et al belongs to the weak fallen upon earthly thrones of muck and ooze, he tightens titanium bolt into anus and strips the threads—indestructible internal concrete block which pathetically prays prays to him whose spindly legs crumple to piles of scrap, peace from him, king of hosts, judge of gods, superfluous sustenance, crutch of earth's incompetent, earth's idiots straining gruel through mustachios, fantasizing paradise, filthy kids stubbing toes and whining for fill, his last feast will be just that, river of concrete mixed with rocks topping his throat, quick setting concrete molded to gut, he will smash god in the gob and all dark night observe the sniveling mortals curled in sleep.

131

This time, God, i'm humble, i want eternal everlasting, i repent on knobby knees my whoring, drugging, i was self-medicating with what felt fine, women, coke, oblivion, i ruled the world between legs or needle jab, i loathed daddy, that pig, that ungodly swine debasing innocence, humiliator, i fantasized axing him like seasoned pine, i'm done with rage, the man's childhood sucked, i love him now, trench mates horror filled, ole Jake's guts everywhere, we've witnessed hell, so i'm down, God, begging, forgive, exonerate, sanctify, cause me to vomit on ground, quaver with chills, make me swim in seas of bile, i am wicked, punish, wife me to condyloma, infested wart woman, i shall treasure her, utter gratitude on broken knees by our rotted bed-box, i have shamed, i have sat in what hate shat, reeked like anti-perfume, have articulated internally accusations, "big shot," "fuck head," "asshole," "lunatic" to male bystanders, never domitable, while worshiping females, so give me lymphoma, colitis, or dyspeptic ulcers that i may rip in me a portal through which you take up dwelling domicile and out which flows transgression like a slit sack of maggots.

132

The monsters bent and demented, male wearing brown slippers
shuffling to potty, lungless muscleless female stuck in bed like
an old pudding, monsters once with farts like earthquakes and
tongues like blunt instruments, now sallow losers dribbling
special k milk and begging for help, not bankrupt, just ashamed,
they horrify, these two juiced and squeezed, death egging on
them like a botfly, what rot to multiply in, gross organic gar-
bage, I love all things ruined to ineffectuality, weak as disease,
I love them verging toward expiration, I powerful as gunpow-
der, shellacked by gyms, towering colossus beside their atro-
phied processes, oh time's cocktail disturbs me, but I'm in the
powerful middle full-facultied like a staffed university and
shall not be fear crippled like these two defunct vicious pos-
sums. well, fuck it, I'm a calloused self-hating bastard, per-
ceiving it, baby divorced me, knowing it, glo-bolted, I shine
inside assisted care facilities, oh sweetie lay me down among
the incapacitated and watch me sleep the sleep of the glorious.

133

Dearest god, veal, my female genital, sweet silk pillow, outline me in charcoal, reveal me, make me into parasol of oversweet blossoms, redeemer, overflower, I give you the top half of two monkey skulls, my kneecaps, yarmulkes baby lord for your bald wise head, I give you three teeth, incisor, molar, bicuspid dangling in my scrotum like spare rare jewels for your ancient gums, please appreciate whom this prayer issues from—dying leaves, tattered fishmonger's shirt—that I may love one entity, garbage cat, cloud horse, mountain lump, my consolation beyond avocado dips, give me earthworm, slug, stink bug, anything gorgeous to recognize like a brillo over burnt crud, our psalmists sang their deathless songs, send me duiker, capybara, wildnymph fawn that I may die into softness, make me unassailable.

134

Testimony of the best pig in the sty. I'm king mounter. I shove it in. Gertrude craves me. Matilda moans for me. I grunt and eat slops pushing away others. I get mash. Dark splotchy pink, stout nose, neckless, number 77 tagged to left ear, luckiest number around. Rump like a cement mixer nobody kicks, squiggly firm tail, blood to tip. Super Pig, pig literati, nineteen hundred twenty six pounds, hog literally, the Indiana hogs, borne of Chester and Duchess, Chester Iowa State Fair Champion Derby Hog, Duchess six hundred pound 4-H Purebred Champion, daddy shot me into her like a roman candle. I burst forth like Ben Hur. Sunburnt from so much fucking, out from mud, into mud, ear tag jangling like revolutionary, Illini nights reclining under stars, contemplatively smoking, pink eyelids, lavish lashes, back legs crossed, I love everything, fences, twigs, friendship, water trough, soft breezes drawing across skin, the smell of piss, I, Davy Crockett pig, adventuresome, undaunted, courageous, proud, out to farthest post, to gate, scratching along wire, sniffing earth-untrodden, snorting intoxication-liberation, left-and-right pig, pig of The Nation and The New Republic, chest-out puffed-up herd-guardian wise warrior pig, pugnacious purple irremovable squealer.

135

I step toward dissolution, casting money like wallpaper strips, a
dining room set, lamps, an antique wardrobe, I purchase a ticket
to Cabo, dine at Geronimo (the baked helix escargot, the Maverick Ranch filet, the cappuccino semifredo), float bloated to
my Quattro, I'm over my cliff, bereft of mortgage, divorced,
clientless, free of razor and cream, approaching filth, siphoning
my check book a gasoline vandal, I philanthropize derelicts,
my Wells Fargo petrol slurped to metal, gladly, a broker-boy
awol, over the fence, clopping through mud in half-moonlight
unhelmeted, illuminated by flare fire, fuck you, I yell, and peel
a century note for a stranger, my parents skeletons, bent,
screaming, edematous, pasty, demented, my dog gone begging, my fingernails crab-ragged, my father's toenails curled
like glue, I plant my lips on penury, suck out its lungs, spit
into sea, lamprey, devastation's ecstasy, disgorging what one's
earned, accumulated, and believed in chunky mess on clean
terrazzo mainlines nirvana, sweet baby, better than vodka or
Roy Rogers boots, I tell you unequivocally I splurge at Best
Buy, appliances, electronics wiping out my Wachovia and
am pure disgust, a lowlife, a terror-image, I mutter at myself
execrables, son of Joseph, Abraham, and Jacob, cultivated, groomed, preselected, crawling into the spiteful glee of destitution.

136

When they pry apart a man's arms and nail him by the wrists exposing him to weather, insects, adoration, whores, execrations, a person could mount and fellate the man while he gushes round nails, chest flung out, one could defile him with spray paint and lip gloss, our petty reprobate hammered tight, it's elementary math, some blathering lunatic hammered on a crucifix, an entomologist's butterfly, helpless against pederasts, rapists, winos, blacksmiths, swine, whose hearts and spit are unceremonious, all night stars yammer at the crucified: extortionist, megalomaniac, thief, murderer, fool out for ill-gotten gain, you pay sociopathology's price: ridicule, extinction, ignominy, you fuck with people you get screwed, it's law, it's a helluva way to fly, dead crosses cluttering the countryside but it beats vivisection, gives one a chance at rectification, some extra hours to utilize, and as I said, with chest protruding, arms flung out you never know what weird bullshit might rush in.

137

This is me, here's my face, like a potted daffodil, brilliant, beautiful, I crave love, I crave validation, my photo screams to distinguish me, world traveler, beach comber, film aficionado, favorite cuisine: French Provencal, recent book: The Secret Life of Bees, lattes at Starbucks, candle-lit dinners, authenticity a must, notice my luxuriance pulls one toward it to finger and part, notice my Mediterranean lips—two truant schoolgirls—exuberant, sweet, rebellious, virginal, I own the sloop, that turquoise is Belize, the pussy's name: Marmalade, rarely climax, "repressed", distrust strangers, love gardening, experiments with razors, bubble baths, others have failed my stringent test, all yours but deliver, perform as demanded, almost bit a dick in half, electroshocked father, creased upper lip, sable mom, cultured black pearls, discovered tranquility behind daddy's face, words aching to speak: "darling," "precious darling," to cherish man to darling, this is me, perky, tan, tight—a birthlook—head resplendent upon its stem, hungry caverns yearning for you, waterfall hair, c'mon look, dimestore playmate, underneath chic raven black web—god's navel—nude pink nails, honey-drenched knees, alternative spirituality, Pisces, look babe, don't scratch too deep, I bleed envy, rage, spite, cruelty, schadenfreude, when chemo fried Melissa hair secretly I rejoiced, desire me, require me, baby, sweetiepie, I never loved Fascists, zealots, nor psychos, select me, I'm your on-line dream, over me spread your stiff-beamed aphrodisiac: money, power, violence, invincibility.

138

God the sissy, God the playground joke-butt bullies pummel, eating sod, spurting nose blood, kicked, tripped, sniffling mommy, mommy but mommy's gone on glue, hallucinating excuses and masturbating rainbows, god's book satchel full of psychodrama, monsters, anxiety, incontinence, dodging Ulrich and McGee, Jewboy, Jewboy they shout and shove him down stairs, spreadeagle, papers everywhere, Ulrich's German, Magee's Czech, both with sadistic domineering dads in lower intestinal realms, biceps like boulders, Ulrich wedged fingers between Varney's lips and ripped his mouth apart, God's smart as crap, philosophies like galaxies swirl his head, burdensome grandiosities pulling him topheavy like a power-drunk nutcase involving punishments and holocausts, sucking up in outspread arms oceans of heretics and mimickers, McGee struck God like a kitchen match, lighting afire his hair and spinning him madly, laughter all round the lockers and shower stalls, I'll create prison, God thought, invisible barriers, stinking john, crawling with bugs, windowless, cold for the fuckers, and so he did.

139

[I want to thank you for what you did back there] [you'd do the same] [but still you didn't have to]. [it was reflex. it's hard wired. it's what's required out here, you know, alone out here] [okay, but thanks, thanks a lot, I owe you one] [you owe me nothing. I don't like you, I did it because I had to, that's all, had to not want to, if the tables were turned you'd do the same, even though I disgust you, same as me, out here we depend on each other, we need your back, your shoulders, I don't care what you did a month ago or a year ago, history doesn't exist here, here it's survival, man against that, that fucking shit out there, all of it, big indifferent shit. forget it. boss wants a tight ship, he gets a tight ship, no screw ups, no squabbling] [you could have let me go to the devil, no one would have blamed, you risked it all, I won't forget] [look out there, nothing but barrenness hostility ice death, incomprehensible hatred, we're two of a kind, mister, linked as if shackled, you die, I suffer, I die, you suffer, get it, we don't have to like each other, God doesn't give a shit about compassion, it's calculation fitness mimicry deception, if I didn't need you, right now, if you didn't fit into my immediate plan, I would have let it devour and shit you like crap through a fish, like an hour of sustenance given to the thing. that's why I saved you]

140

Mr Knuckles worked me over, I passed out from shock proving I'm fragile protoplasm like any jellyfish, ever seen the cabbagehead washed up on shore, pathetic squashable bulb, Mr Knuckles frustrated, self-loathing, not copulating, business failure, stringy boxer legs, long arms, nimble and dangerous, take that, he snapped and punched out an eye, worthless bum he yelped, and frankly I was a derelict, a foot dragger, self-conscious to paralysis, me observing me observing me observing like dueling mirrors, I the weaker, he the paragon, flunky, lazyass, dumb, and frankly I bombed out of trig and scraped by Spanish, school tumbled me through air backward like a bomb, he boffed my ears, big shot, he barked, he mashed my head to resemble a turd and flushed it down, take that cologne boy, (gushing water), I never touched him, I chewed double bubble, butch waxed wave, sugary smelling, you know, filled with Jackie Deshannon, kicked a notch into my shin, sloucher, I knew his avaricious discontent wife, knew her down to her Kotex, princess materialism w/ mortality complications, but forgave him not, my torturer risen from door-shadows, the hammer, haywire Judah Macabee, paranoid of Nazis, acid spitter; now osteoporotic brittle baby, six inches shorter, I lift him like an empty Talis to his sagging throne, urine and excrement Tided out repeatedly, threadbare ermine sheets from yore, scepter as walker, head blotched eggplant purple, fists that pummeled saggy as scrotums.

141

What have I done, I've murdered it, it was easy, spontaneous rage, easy as smashing a vase or punching holes, but this time I've snuffed life, I reach shudderingly in slanted shadow, to touch, to worship the dead pile, blood spilled out its eye, I can't see damage to vital organ, only evidential hemorrhaging, lethal blunt force, could I have snapped the chord, in murdering it I murdered two, they will find, convict, consign me to maximum, I'm the obvious suspect, a history of flashpoints, its companion of twenty years under same freakin' roof, an irreversibly backlashed life, I always believed that one day I would kill, the conditions volatile as the primordial soup, calmly I sit, I expect no mercy in this culminating ejaculation, the thick tap root blossoms its branches, there it lies, the registry of my rage, buckled, contorted as if thrown from a windshield, sphincter relaxed, peaceful at last, our fusion's summation, me muttering, "I love you." "I didn't mean it." "We were wonderful."

142

A window washer slides down the slanted diamond shaped skyscraper's roof, ripping fingernails nails prefatory to a five-hundred foot free fall to concrete below, an inconsequential human tearing gelatin on useless window frames, bursting mastodon heart, tool belt like train wheels striking metal strips clackety clackety clack, then, hands applauding air, the swan dive off the edge past advertising agencies, law firms, physicians' offices, employment agencies, brokerage businesses, investment concerns, the CEO seducing his marketing director, Cup-o-Soup containers on mahogany desks, a dismissal, plummeting package of a man plunging, no time for forgiveness or gratitude, just emergency images like a spiraling contrail, a woman not conjured in years, scoutmaster Hank, transformer toys, blizzard torn by wind, this Catholic stalwart and his morality, no extramarital affairs, no substances, Sunday pot roast and services, descending through hell like the bloody antichrist or some defeated science fiction monster, tail blowing upward, some justice, involuntary reflexes working to the end, the headline 6-pages deep in tomorrow's City Section already written: Stone Container Bldg. Window Washer Falls to Death.

143

Today I will die for a cause, infinitesimal defines my existence, indispensible the cause, I awake, I breathe, I straighten my uniform, it will be a magnanimous day, explosions, men clenching jaws, scarlet contorted, heroically grunting, the platoon one beautiful many-headed organism, I accept fate, God decreed that I pave the way with gore, others' bloody boots marching up my spine toward Jericho, today I will learn the melting point of bone and dissolve in the sky like a Sweet Tart, it's a seminal day, a parade-perfect day, clean, enormous, chattering rainbird sprinklers, the resurrected drowned stirring in slippers, glory's my song and death my gratitude, spit-shined boots, oh baby I'll explode like outrushing semen among the crows and wrathful soldiers on this God-magnificent day of the continuous victory.

144

I loathe myself down to my orange toenails; my bald dome, my sex addiction, my clumsiness, cherry juice splattering cabinets, obsessive-compulsive rituals twisting me like God, excessive defecation, urination fixation, numbers, locks, I hate my fat binge-weary gut stuffed simultaneously with burritos, corn chips, Velveeta con queso, refried beans, avocado, Spanish rice, pulled chicken, sopapilla, honey, mint candy, ice cream, hot fudge, whipped cream, marshmallow, peanuts, iced tea, shredded spoonfuls, milk, slivered almonds, and artificial sweetener, a cauldron of garbage topping off my throat, I hate self-induced nausea and self-destruction, cunnilingus with victims and a hot shooting thread, she straddling he three fourths up her cunt in a wooden chair, masturbation-fascination and ensuing disgust, slice me like a hard boiled egg slicer, I hate every strip, bum, idiot, bungler, fucker, liar, fake, and fool, my pathetic decomposed lettuce leaf poetry, wet heavy stink, like uninterred flesh. "I hate myself down to my orange toenails," for example, shit beside Sheamus Heany or Joseph Brodsky, shit beside even Nicholas Christopher and he's an idiot, terror of loneliness, islanded by emptiness, a bloody untouched peninsula careening onto internet dating or prostitution, something foams doglike, something cracks its muzzle, something drains disease into its ears, head back, howling love love, something driven to shove it in hates carnality's whipping motion, the shoulder-to-butt hump, the embryo squish, how insomnia can-opens the top of my head, chef boyardee, three successive sleepless nights grabbing fistfuls of worms wriggling between fingers, oh god, abhorrence, hypercriticism, shiny cracker jacks spilled out a wrist, 2 frozen silhouettes rooted to a field, the children, distant, blocking sun, guilt-ridden, stilted, rejected them in self-absorption, incapable of simple medicinal restoration.

145

Dear God I wish to register my unhappiness about a few things: mortality is a crock of shit, I could pop you in the mouth for that; genocide sucks, you deserve a penitentiary gang raping; what about cerebral palsy? hanged by the neck, my good man, hanged by the neck; I'm a little discontent about mashed teenager canon-fodder wars, you know, blown off limbs and heads, amputated appendages, post traumatic stress syndrome, freckled unwrinkled babies mud-trudging, one could fucking kick you in the gonads or plier them off like taffy and feed em to chickens, here chick chick, you celestial amateur, scratchy violinist botching Bach; the little matter of pederasty, the constitutionally sour buggering preadolescents, or fucking itself between consenters whipping themselves leeward-to-stern chasing that momentary dopamine-filled squiggle infusing emptiness shame hunger megalomania and finally spiritual death, smashed in the kisser, banished, bibles burned simultaneously like flushing at once a skyscraper of toilets, bloody nutcase; what about space travel, you serve up famine, they booster to moon in million dollar foil suits to tramp around, demigods to television applause, famine's worth decapitation, (I assume neck not in ass a blade can find); oh boy peanut brickle Lucky Charms Mars AIDS Coke, finger-poke out your eye, sanctuary fornicator, superstition wrapped in faith wrapped in fear, Mr. Potato Head; I'll praise you this; blood-covered morsels ceaselessly bursting, new beautiful victims.

146

Hi, I'm Gordon, I'm a sex addict, hello, Gordon, I've been sex free for two days, thanks to my higher power, this morning I awoke, broke at the knees at bedside, prayed for strength, asked forgiveness, begged really, began to take an inventory of those I've wronged, sex nearly killed me, I've eaten asphalt, been hospitalized, lost family, friends, had a gun to my head, been fired multiply, eaten poison, terrified women, been imprisoned, and spent six weeks in rehab, this disease for that is what it is, this disease, this soul decay, only God can heal, God dusts off the fallen, the perniciously erect, the cunt chaser, the juice eater, in His infinite authority, I gave myself over, crossed my wrists, said dear Lord take me, do with me what you will, the exquisite blood filled wet tight grotto, fuck, fuck, fuck the most beautiful word in the English language, fucking women, asses stuck up like jelly pots entered from the rear, fucking them on couches or floor, in chairs, with toys and thongs, pumps in air, I broke at knees, said, please please dear God I can't take it anymore, I'm dead, save, nipples, breasts, upward pointing, toes like heroin, arches, ridges, asses, breath, surrender, earthquake coming, when they arch upward, slave slave, master, fuck me, I love your cock might be heaven in language, cock, circumcision ridge flaring with urgency like the edges of earth, dear God destroy me, dear Being smite me for I am cruel, I am fucked up, I am bloody from masturbation, I am contaminated, when one squeezes me in her mouth, me over her head, watching me appear and disappear in her mouth, her mouth formed to succor me, thirsting for come, my bush at her nose, my clean shaft free of hair, I could die, I could die, die like a dead horse, an elegant dead stallion between her lips with my finger in her cunt, I'm Gordon, I'm an addict, I stand before you two days pure, reborn in the lamb of God, saved, almost deceased, hard even now behind this podium, but cognizant, wise, aware of the rod's destructive tendencies in the cesspool of desolation.

147

I flip it upside down and squeeze the honey bear over my bald head, I empty a 1-lb bag of refined sugar over the honey, I smear Smuckers chocolate fudge across my chest and midriff, I empty jelly jars onto my knees, strawberry knee, apricot knee, sprinkles everywhere, I putty my belly button with Skippy, I sit in milk, I roll in pastry flour, I smash a Nutty Buddy against my lips, I unwrap Snickers, Milky Way, Mallow Cups and mash them into ears and anus, I pour Mrs. Butterworth's down my spine, I stand in buckets of maple syrup, I decapitate a dog and tie its face to my dick, I suck the ink from a Bic, up my nose I shove gummy worms, everywhere nonpareils, I squeeze wedge of frozen wedding cake between fingers, I snow coconut slivers over God, now the dangling: snowballs from elbows, Twinkies from lobes, from ankles tails of naked Entenmanns, Cinnabon from lower tooth, Double Stuff from ring knuckle, I stand by fire, Bananas flame, hair flames, genitals flame, Yahweh twirls me up through drums of cotton candy, bee hive, body beard, cloaked to toenails, the dog's head bundled like a pork loin in Saran Wrap, I pull a Tootsie Pop out my ass and flip it to a child, an angel blesses me with a tongue of black molasses, oh god, forgive him his self-inflicted sins, by a knot in the chord clamped between teeth, I am lowered through the big top, drums, harsh light illuminates my pores, into the middle ring. I pay thirteen trained baboons to hose me down with popcorn.

148

I pretend you're a fraud; when I pray I say, "dear fucker who doesn't exist," under lids eyes flutter, "dear shitface, save a kid, do something," praying, though hypocrite, fake, silence ought to rein, the void before sleep or slippers, not this, "dear huckster, make baby well," petitions for health, prosperity, longevity, therefore I'm indoctrinated, theistic, shepherded, I pray for atheism, dear curtainman step outside, show me your lie, he remains sequestered in an invisible closet working levers, printing prayerbooks, composing hymns, denying me diploma or courage, so I pray dear freaking charlatan bastard sonofabitch, "don't crash us," "find me a mate," "kill his craving," you lousy goddamn fake which I can't disprove, bake me a marble cat's eye blue, round sturdy glass, cooked in red flame, into my lap drop it, filled with atheism.

149

Lambs and apologies, humility and shame, self-effacement, lowering
of eyes and diminution, the soap of absolution, the tongue held out
for bitters and ash, the goose pimply flesh of shuddering leaves, Michel-
angelo babies, wind billowed sheets on coastal clothes line, all blood stays
in veins, lanolin, shovels and pails, cherubic births and milky nipples,
milk itself poured from glazed pitchers, mothers nearby in sails of
flesh, fish soft as a woman's belly and rosy feet dripping tub water
in white light, roast chicken and cranberries, green beans almandine,
prayer and health, "God bless this table and friends," pink bows and
blue and Mickey Mouse waffles, dog vacuuming dirt on the scent
of game, bruisy clouds cracking a clear smile through abating gloom,
immense square teeth and pillowy lips, gold fields awash in dusk
speckled with crows and dark nuggets, mother serves brisket to her
seated family: gee mommy this is good, and mashers too!, with
a stack of pre-sliced bread, and afterward 'nana pudding with 'nilla
wafers, seconds, please, oh sweetie, bedtime stories all round, a
palm on the forehead—no fever, knock on wood—and a kiss night-
night, Chevy sleeps beside Ford, birdcage covered, chains latch-
ed for extra protection, and lawns get their crowns of dew, grad-
ually, as the all night president in the only illuminated room in
night's gut pit shields his sleeping children against doom, robins
swoop on morning's threads and little holes cough up rabbits,
look, a bunny!, daddy bursts yolks with toast, kiddies get coco
puffs, to school with lunch money and shoes; patriotism, al-
truism, troop 218, Henry "Hank" Josephs, scoutmaster, of the
Lincoln Memorial, awe, the Washington Monument, awe, awe
the Treasury Department and apple blossom time, subservience,
self-negation, penitent, a pie for Mrs. Kendenhall, bow thy pal-
try head, common laborer, humble servant, foot solider of the
law, oh honey baby, nondescript condominium of worthlessness.

150

Dear mother, murder daddy, kill yourself, fill the house with blood, bleed your red nails into his skull like ten Esterbrooks, those sexy wet nails, through his Ambien induced unconsciousness empty yourself soaking his bed like a Kotex, pad to the kitchen in your pink chiffon nightie and support hose, slide the drawer, remove the butcher knife, whisper back down the Florida green carpet to this room, stand a while, then jam it in, the mattress soaking life, draining to box spring, his lipless mouth opening like a sea shell, the deed done return to your scalloped black boudoir and down the alcohol river of pills, the two dead humans of 425 Miramar, Corpus Christi, TX. Dear mother, scrub the grime of hate off your tub, the filth of bitterness from the toilet bowl, your bathroom stinks, it breathes rage, clean the crusted cave in one heroic act, that foul porcelain urn in which you have shit and bathed for eighty years, your life. I fantasized fantasizing spooning Gerber's into your mouth, veal and peas, finding sparks in your long gray hair, and lifting daddy like a madonna off his sheets, stuffing his mouth with your hair to bind you, your toes in his, an eternal loop, instead this: once in neck, once in chest, once in groin, a fourth and fifth in chest again, split your legs like Alaskan crab, a house without lungs, with larynx removed, lake flat tongue filling the gullet, elephant collapsing to front knees, collapsing again after standing, rolling to right shoulder, smack, pillars obscenely crossed as if loafered, oh mommy rationalize, planet, ice age, mastodon, who gives a shit, geological time, 83, 86, embezzlement, crushed Chevrolets, Max Factor, Revlon, Maybelline emptied, plowed under, glass to sand, Edie, Sylvan, Julius dank ulnas and fibulas, dead your great great grandchildren's grandchildren, necks split like baked apples, Saturn, sun, the farthest frozen reaches, cold rage, cold life, frozen flames, both hands over head, the man is already dead, your slamming door cut your babies' umbilical chords, gaze on him, with calculated abandon plunge plunge plunge plunge plunge.

First I razor free my mouth, lips make a thick rubber band. Second I slice round the perimeter and peel off nipples, pina colada umbrellas. Third, I exacto-knife toadstool tip of penis, lift it off, the pee-slit forms a lovely salt shaker. Sections of me rehabilitate the house: sphincter muscle, ear lobes, esophagus, gall bladder toilet floater. I exhaust my body parts. A heart, a cardiovascular system wound round spine upright in a chair, eyes gaping mid-air. Love energizes the liquor cabinet. Anger bubbles porridge. Cartilage strengthens window cranks. Smooth muscle revitalizes Beautyrest. I have nothing to offer weather stripping, sputtering sidearm, I'm all in, my stretched back skin approximates wallpaper, oh I flipped for her, I landed on my edge, I sucked her in through a hydrodynamic straw, no crab this, awkwardly scuttling across concrete slab, ticking like asphyxiation, we're fork knife and spoon, split peas and water, sauerbraten medallions beside potato salad, godfuckingdamn, I popped off kneecap like the whacked open top of a monkey skull, shut it over pot of boiling god, oh Patty Sue, my tendons work the living room blinds which blot out eyes like a terrorist's knotted rag. Here's my book, The Devil's Carnival of Body Parts and Love, slip it on like shoes, drain it through neck, blow bubbles into it like a warm soapy sponge. Last, I saw upward through the crack in my ass creating two Brahma dewlaps, one a bucket of grease to gouge fingers into, one a bursting pinata laden with candy.

152

Bugs fly off hand when I brush my arm: fleas, chiggers, thrips, weevils, burst into clouds, die, crawl in waves; neck disintegrates into fruit flies, eaten, ravaged such as months of decomposition in wet soil, lice lift off my face like leprosy, re-land and devour, lips glisten with the wings of roaches, I belch a mosquito cumulus cut by rays, beautiful black ball orange-suffused, toenail ticks, millipedes, mayflies, covered in microscopic dung, I shit compactions of spider, horsefly, larvae, emerald phosphorescence plopped in water, well, I deplore you, your cowboy moustache, your gut, your nasty cigarettes, big jewelry, and sandy bouffant hair, butt flicker and language hack, I deplore human beings spitting foul yellow juices into gutters and eating mercilessly like vats of acid, swagger and braggadocio, beefy men plowing furrows into concrete, well, fuck my hostility, I masturbate a colony of squash bugs, I sit, invariably, upon my thick pit of silverfish ass…

153

I masturbate to fashion photos of anorexics, Auschwitz ladies' hips crooked outward slathered in blue cotton panties, elbow pelvises, furrows and funnels, cheeks like eaten stone, imagine fucking grasshopper bodies so close it rubs bone, wire sculpture of horror harboring a wet pussy, I bend coathanger legs around my neck, twist feet together, have at her, cupping her forkhandle spine, spit into her, lick metal, pierce her bubble eyes dripping off magnesium strips like screams, fold back the page and hammer hammer my fat grotesque sunless white apparition, stuff soft batch into maw and jack myself off like a wedge of bacon, this sick self induced holocaust conductor, acid on acid, cur rib, sexy speck of death, pubis stuck up like a popped firecracker, cupped Sahara leaf-tongue, gold braceleted, bronzed, delectable razor edge crying for danger, murder, castration, breakage, thimble pederast tits with big nipples, I'm baked and splitting, steaming and falling open, like thick brisket, hissing, fire red, barbecue splendor, American male tangled in carbon smudges and cocaine, invidious envier sniffing up Andrea's cunt and Jennifer's butt, slim as paperclips and screaming all night for butter lumps, I papercut my shaft against her last gasp minutes before the bulldozer's blade.

154

First we plunge knife into dog, she fell to knees, toppled, lay
like any meal in gravy, spotted tongue, then baby Lulu, thirteen months, pillow over face, pressure, turkey before baking,
extracted pussy by back legs from cabinet, beheaded him,
whole head glued to chair like shish kabob, marinated headless body in loggy toilet bowl, you sliced my clothes like
gutting fish, whack whack cling, strips, I lopped your bras
for mastectomy, slashed French panties like jelly creatures, we eyed each other, "love," you said, "love," I assented,
"screw you," you said, "agreed," I chimed, "I despise your
mother," "yours drank herself dead," "None will adore
you like me," she warned, "Echo," I responded, one by one
we pulled the feathers off Dante our Parrot, poor Dante
caged and fruited like a bauble, several primary feathers
plucked killed him like a shot weight, claws clutching a
finger, "monster," she screamed, "Frankenstein," I fired,
"piece of shit," shot out the canon my mouth, bereft
of pets and babies her wishbone glittered like a lit shipsail, meathooks, striations, bruise red bloomed in my
mind, psychopath, maniac, she studied me like a cannibal,
and down we tumbled in a flurry of slurp, boner, juice,
and squish, slacks and shirts collapsing like parachutes.

155

I pray for myself, my anger, my compulsion to ruin, how I dive slippery from the womb of love, swan-like, my rage stinking of storage bins, oh Lord, with awe and humility, peaceable habitation, unalterable decrees, how humanity disgusts, festering acid-filled sore of steering wheels and stupidity, uneducated squabbling thugs with cash wads and pistols, I participating in its vortex, contemptuous father-loather crammed in funnel like a doomed dunce, fly into me a seraphim, oh Expiator, coring hell from me, brass knuckled fantasies showering blows upon a driver at his car window or shoving mr. cock against gym lockers, naked, bursting nose, a male bellicosity crossed into psychopathology, reptilian rivals beaded on desert rocks, O Benevolent Intercessor, Cedars-Sinai Medical Center, Barnes Jewish Hospital, St. Luke's Presbyterian, they give you new hearts, clashing scalpels and bang! you're spinning sequins of revelation, suck Prominent One, my bulb free of scorpions, that I may meet camaraderie in hairy testicles and blue shaved faces splashed with fucking and Mennen bracer for men are one glueball of love, dear Heavenly Doctor, roll up my sleeve, locate muscle, pump in relaxation, selflessness, luminescence, humility, fellow-feeling.

156

I create god in my image, he's deluded in acknowledging me, you possess my soul, I say, my spirit, life everlasting is yours, you shall worship me and sanctify sacred holidays—Michaelmas, Palm Sunday—you shall compose a scripture and liturgy, practice humility and obey commandments forbidding all sins emblazoned on granite tablets, you shall kneel before me, cover your pate, read daily the holy sacrament, mutter "father," "lord," "king," "omniscient one," "door Massman," through me shall you receive immortality though you are stiff-necked and narcissistic, a worm with vengeance to chop in two, cur to drown, inconsequential beast though I number your every pore, I create you now with toenail clippings, pubic hairs, pennies and toothbrush bristles, bang! god, bang! daddy, bang! ring-leader, my menial slave sacrificing animals with the long bladed knife and flaming votives like a pyromaniac, I can drop you in vat or crash your Chevrolet, I have already programmed the extermination of your son by a date specific and inescapable: suicide by financial ruination exacerbated by marital stupidity—a prima donna wife, a frigid queen—he shall blow out his heart, inescapably, like a fool in an infinite line of fools, your first increase splattered across a bluebonnet field, I construct you with my jaw bone, erection, posture, width, my Russian complexion, a flawless speller and raging regimentarian, while you sleep this night I will stuff your borrowed brow with mountain laurel and vine and you shall awaken in depthless incredulity craving brownish-yellow wine, my tour-de-force, my wunderkind, swifter than mercury, in likeness of me, now I survey my population: pornographers, hypergraphias, counterfeiters, bums, crowding like a clot of maniacs, my condemned bewildered supplicants teeming in a pile of nourishment, from on high, cloud-enthroned, magnificent, omnipotent, gorgeous, bounteous I with wrist-flick ejaculate you after which sutures, semen, spikes, nails, and dust fuse into a murderous mass of uninhabitable flesh.

157

Men want to fuck God. Not women. God. Women are merely pale substitutes. Men want immortal fucking, fucking extra-human, the creator of women. Nothing short of that. Jennifer or Diane can make him come but not like God. God makes him come beyond mortality, beyond dissatisfaction. God does not have perfect feet, like Rebecca, manicured and polished, but has blinding feet, impossible to glimpse, incomparable feet made of white hot light. God does not have mere voluptuous breasts with upturned nipples made of fat and glands. God's breasts envelop the world, deliver the death of discontent, death of feeling. Anything short of that is just Megan or Klarissa with moles or bruises but will do in emergencies. Lisa's body bracketed by pate and soles, visible in one click, sixty-three inches tall, bracketed by air, falling through air like a dropped lake pebble, nothing, impotent, insignificant. God encompasses oceans and, therefore, must be fucked by men. Men yearn. God eludes. Men push through Carolyn reaching for God. Cocks cry milk tears. Men hate their women for not being God and weep out the back door like refugees. A lizard. A flowering tree. Another clay substitute. A dark hammer. He extracts Betty's heart like a hairless puppy and somewhere plants it. What grows looks nothing like God.

158

Men and women hate their lives. eye liner, shave cream, hemorrhoidal gel, and meat tenderizer combine into napalm; children equal agent orange; Meg would rather die. Arnold wants to gut people like trout; I love you seeps from exploded car batteries; god is a light bulb people burst inside their mouths and swallow, bloody bowels; the sewing needle my mutt ate tattooed hell onto his gut; Rog blew his head off with internet porn, bits splattered his silver phone; mostly Edward plods and trudges cursing his blasphemous biological ignoramuses, Gregor and Dawn, two gutless toadies; one gives birth to one's own electroshock treatments; Melvin bursts through the back door like a laxative commercial, 6:43 PM, maintains exuberance halfway down the hall before petrifying into a self-mocking sneer terminating in an unsuccessful episode on the toilet, the cutlets ready for catchup and cheer; they watched the house go up, slab, frame, drywall, nails, bing bang bing bong, garbage disposal, house, three months, eleven days, twenty-seven minutes, brass keys; set up shop, dishes, pillows, stein collection, laundry soap pellets; somewhere, somewhere Charlie got left behind, stuck behind the sink plumbing with the can of Comet, somewhere, faraway Patty's legs walked away from her torso and continued walking into this house full of Tupperware; oh well; Sherman's company promoted him to assistant marketing manager; Sherman grasps the pay hike like a steel bar, no insubstantial benefits from prayer, for example, or spirituality; years ago Stephie's man ceased kissing, igniting a slow seething fire, she crisps the meat and morning yolks bleed, behind the blank screen CSI reels like a pinwheel; she sneaks schnapps, he scours Match.com; she craves sadistic men, gigantic cocks ramming up her rigged by rope, he imagines titanic tits, two to each girl, one sucking him off, the other's vagina squeezing his tongue, painted toe nails and pierced clits; the overdue feasibility study eats his soul's pink escargot; goddammit to hell the fucking bastards; Ginger's conquering the planet with Yale on the way, Cosmopolitan or Marie Claire; Atkins sliced twenty pounds off her thighs; Ferragamo's sexes her soles; God's finger scatters minnows, God bombs the pond, women scatter in three dimensions, terrorist's nails lodge in strangers' entrails, the concussion untwines lovers' intertwined fingers; nothing to be done, zilch to reconstruct. designate someplace as home, go there, drink the stale air, consume your dinner.

159

Elfington practiced love till his face blued, then he shot someone pinking his mug back to normal pallor, screw Jesus he thought and stamped a bug flat as rice paper, yes, catharsis, cathexis of annihilation, brutality restores self, that frozen sirloin strip, thaws the cube in blowtorch rage prefatory to swallow and mastication, what idiot restores sight to blindness when he can gouge blindness from sight thereby creating from flaccid flesh sheer poetry, poetry of mutilation, poetry of war, poetry of combat and denigration, peace violence-sculpted into beauty, Achilles, Odysseus, Ajax, Agamemnon, every corpse a stanza, every war an epic, every century a collection exquisite, sublime, Elfington's wife would not shut up, he popped her, Elfington's son slumped, he shin-kicked him, Elfington found an old Louisville Slugger and redesigned some things, James Earl Ray and Sirhan Sirhan took down hope and compassion respectively, Ghopal Godse took down love forming a sumptuous triad of mastery, dominance, and durability, Jesus puttered like a lunatic around withered hands and epilepsy, a glove and a mouth-foamer akin to a vomiting frog, before the rhapsody of the crucifix brilliantly wrote him on timbers and nails, three incomparable co-authors, Judas, Pilate, Caiaphas, employing that most fabulous composer of immortal magnificence: hate.

160

Bastard seeking bastardess, argumentative, defensive, unexamined fucker looking for same, bald, salt and pepper, 6'1", uncommunicative, proud, stubborn, unbiblical, clean hands, rich, GTO, loathes his mother, despises Dad, whines and wheedles, insomniac, uses intimate partner for literary material, unabashed, premature ejaculator with virtuoso tongue, estranged from grown children, one cat, body dysmorphic dysfunction and OCD, binge eater, Ben and Jerry's, cheese enchiladas, chocolate fudge, then wants to vomit on the cat, on anything, on breasts, prefers defeat, fantasizes knifing his cuddling lovers, their aggravating hands and French poodle squeals, fantasizes strangling or instantaneous suffocation, iron pumping gym rat, rigid, implacable, ultracontrolling, eschews mountains, hiking, skiing, camping, horses, dogs, motorcycles, roller blading, golf, single track, bedandbreakfasts, travel, board games, dancing, prefers sardonic fucking at sea level, piercing gull cries, the occasional pelican, obedience, frigid, non-orgasmic, come-spitters need not apply, nor spirituality queens, nor unity freaks, nor, god help us, poets, prefers enraged, insatiable, pseudo-feminist slave, raw on the floor, ground beef, self-loathing, dry fallen debutante who disrelishes kids, a bloody Ambien addict, super-hyper-educated hair afire neurotic screaming catastrophe to catastrophe with water bucket and double scotch, me: slit from soul by the impalpable knife, you: masochistic, self-effacing, suicidal, insatiable, brilliant, murderous, with lips engaged in channeling excrutiating ecstasy capable of severing me from my genitals.

161

Poetry the poison, poetry the lie, poetry the venom shot through rattler fangs, poetry the monster, the assassin, the embezzler, poetry the totalitarian, poetry the expired Mercurochrome dabbed on wound, poetry worm eaten wood, dead love, abandonment, poetry rabies slaughtered with the dog, poetry raw chicken stinking in sun on some Gulf pier no gulls swoop for, poetry the raped prepubescent, the assaulted grandmother, the beaten delivery boy, poetry collateral damage, poetry war, poetry death by friendly fire, poetry gangland murder of the snit, poetry the wasp sting while collecting mail, poetry the sweet carcinogen in Virginia Slims, poetry the mirage, the convection wave, the refracted post sticking out water, poetry pancreatic cancer, poetry lymphoma, poetry cancer of the throat and tongue, poetry the black plague reincarnated in universities, poetry staring as dysentery in the Ganges River, resultant diarrhea and death by dehydration, poetry the inactionable advertising campaign related to weight loss and hair replacement schemes, poetry silicone implants leaking into fat, poetry the sewing needle lodged in a dog's lower intestine, poetry penis pump surgically inserted like a rage balloon, the chemical compound in brain associated with sociopathology, poetry neither the force that drove spikes through palms nor the quintessence of Eve's naivete, but a simple gob of tubercular spit stringing off the filthy bar of a metal street grate.

162

I have never loved anyone, not you Elizabeth, nor you Cynthia, nor you Betty Sue, I fucked you all but never loved you, I bought property with you but never loved, I fathered children with you but never loved, not you, not the babies, not the babies as teenagers or adults, I did not love Scottie that regal Afghan, Kimberly, I never loved you in your devotion, I invaded your body hundreds of times, ate you, watched you suck me, we came steady as pulses, but I did not love you, I usually stared abstractedly over your shoulder or relived some parental indiscretion or felt nothing but mechanical pleasure, friction, buildup, climax, to the dozens of women I sampled but rejected, hope was never yours, I presented you the illusion of loving you but I did not, I wanted to but did not, aware of others awaiting my seduction I dumped you with small remorse, like a fly bite it hurt, I recorded in poems like this indictment, it should not have surprised when the guillotine dropped, I am fifty-seven, bald, gray, appreciably fit, gelled, and suspect I shall die without bestowing love, women I am incapable of loving, men I despise, a concentrated emotion: I hate men, I hate their shoes, I hate their cellphones, I hate their slacks, I hate their cars, I hate their hair, I hate their rings, I hate their penises, I hate their toes, I hate their stupefying vapid tongue, I fantasize clocking men, opening fire on men, I refuse acknowledging the presence of men, rather I stare through them or ignore their existence, if I say hello I am thinking screw you, to me men fail, scooting butts forward against commercialism's kick, scheming and negotiating, absorbing into vampiristic corporate labyrinths squandering the exquisite human potential on marketing techniques and implementation, sold down the river, defenseless and propagandized, the contemptible gender ground into fodder, troweled into graves by invisible hands, big shots, movers and shakers, unknowingly licked to the paper stick like dimestore suckers by diabolical tongues, tragic creatures lanced through heart and believing it fine, I never loved you Jean though we coupled on beaches, in hot tubs, and inside some Hawaiian cottage quieted by drizzle, hazel steel unblinking eyes gaped over your shoulder like a porcelain doll, I never groaned nor abandoned control, a textbook technician, man floating in jar of liquid, handsome, naked, smoothly muscled, formaldehyde riven ready for the scalpel-clutching, squeamish high school biology class dissection.

163

So here you are in my room, so shove it up your ass mr big shot, skull & bones, scythe man, spider fingers wrapping big mouth round lymph glands or brain matter, mr. infirm eater with gaping jaw, haw haw haw, who's under your rustling cape but an empty groin, hole for cock, coccyx kook, go pester elsewhere the Chesterfield lung, the homicide's hypodermic ride, go fuck yourself, I've eaten oatmeal enough to fill a lake and universities of fish, I shit every bloody day and hydrate like a drain, drive a bucket of balls thrice every seven days, so blow it out your ass, you've come for me, fine, be done with it, I joghead, I weightpump, decapitate me then like a sour grapes cricket, you fuckbutt, what do I care, you stink like a port-o-potty, slit me, slip out my spine, flounder, bull red, speckled trout, leave aplate the rotting white meat of me, butter soaked, coagulate, head in the trash, after this freeze my sister like a genital wart, snow her into the john or underpants, flecks on flecks spotting the water, fall leaves, wet streets, tire tracks on stuck yellow, with her ribs pick your teeth, blowhard, I poke a finger through your noneyes, gossamer sockets dry as bleached pelvises, meatless pig, I jack off in your sky wide mouth, boneless bones, electrical zero, collector of the gorgeous impotent pathetically enhoused mortal valkeries.

164

Let us pray, then, for everybody needs prayer, let us bow heads and pray that fornication striketh us full blow in head, that fornication arrive in sweat and foul breath, lubricants and testicle wallop for thou art desperate in life's desertification, let thy face fall in palms and weep for cunt and sweet male meat stiff and upthrust to hit thy swollen clit, glossolalia for absolution, water thy cars, soap thy cacti, break and beseech for carnal dip, add money, let us pray that cash flow from clientele to thee, inexhaustible rivers of coin from magi's sleeve into thy registers, hallelujah, petition almighty on scraped knees for turkey, stuffing, for petrol, for prescription, for art supply, flagellate, thrash, cut thy thigh in Jesus-cut and shake out wine that Bowdoin shall accept daughter of loin and son of seed, and that coke shall not devour brain nor eat soul, masturbate and if man with match torch thy seed and if woman with file scrape thy cunt opening door for Satan to leave that thy shall receive absolution, pray then for Godliness, immortality, incorruptibility in a sour world replete with losers, idiots, fatsos, cripples, retards, fools, pray for frog-leaps over imperfection, for favoritism and indemnity, for in effect, mass annihilation of rivals that they shall usurp not glory nor everyday and consumable spoils in a constantly regenerating bowl, and splice thy serpent tongue in reverse oh thou believer that thy may dissemble undetected, that spit shall look as pearls, that the blind, dull, and mute shall perceive as gospel calumny from thy sly and give over offerings such crystal or silver pitcher, praise God the Intercessor, and finally, finally smear swath of blood from pricked pointer finger of image of Ghost that thy be white, dominant, and indestructible, slaveholder and not slave in this enslaving planet of the heretical, impure, and heathenistic, pray then thyself hard into luminosity.

165

It is unimportant to me whether anyone reads these poems or their assessment of them should they, I do not care under whose name they are published, nor could I care less what literary critics say about them, praise or condemnation, nothing could be more vapid than some academic advancing his career on my efforts or within institutionally acceptable parameters pushing my reputation this way or that, most contemporary poetry is shit as is the industry that surrounds it and I want no part of it, if I am harsh so be it, if I am angry then that is life, if I have hurt my consanguineous they are co-conspirators in their pain, nothing in this work bears false witness nor have I broken one commandment, I am a decent man imbued with a religious spirit and capable of love, I have noticed the world is full of cowards.

166

I, monstrous son, vulture-son, circling my deteriorating mother, wings whistling, neck straining to pull from guts strings of money, vicious harrier—menace of one—yearning to disabuse from ancient progenitor gleaming inheritance, and, shoulders locked, clap beak at undisgorging flesh wishing her dead, I wheel, descend, cold stubborn monster refusing extraction, resisting extinction, I salivate expectation, half-cracked gelatin snapping in grainy blue, you perceive an affable, benevolent, sympathetic man, not this execrable raptor furious to become materially fat, beware pupil dilation's seductive guise, rage's detonation has blown me beyond decency onto scrub and craggy cliff where calculation jabs jellies of lovelessness, the weeping canker awaits the calcium flood.

167

Fall back upon the formula of mutilating pets, primarily cats which I find repugnant, emasculated powerless lions wrecked by god, grotesque prancers stripped of pride, draped like ancestors not over mountain but microfiber couches, miniature fangs capable of stripping mouse or discarded chicken, bodies vulnerable to monsters like me who bash them against wall by pathetic back paws, such abandoned experiments, mewing terrified in mulberry branches for fireman with ladder, and crunching pellets of adorable brand names consisting of chicken or beef bits, and shitting in clumping sand under plastic enclosures shamefully hidden in closet or basement, and so I revert to cat-mutilation, feeding Mittens laxatives or crushing it under bony ass, giggling as it squirts out my crack into shadows of cabinet, and amazingly it always returns like a tiresome fly instead of exacting revenge upon my eyes while I sleep which I do remorselessly every night although occasionally when required I decapitate a cat to impress my wife, then must haunt the animal pound—where one can locate me often hunting for replacements, and I find it hilarious that something called Humane Society consistently provides me unwitting victims, I do not like dogs for their simpering obedience and irrepressible love as if heart were marzipan and brain divinity, creatures devoid of critical faculty, feed them biscuit and watch worship, perversity beyond comprehension, but I harm no dog, just felines whose death grimaces I find comforting, such as those one spies, if lucky, on highway asphalt floating in eviscerate pudding, just that ridiculous fixed death mask, teeth bared and frozen, one would love to preserve it in formaldehyde, I want to reassure that I am partially rehabilitated (like the reformed junkie who binges on crack), in that it's been six months since my last double homicide without craving death, though cannot say that I have not fantasized, but I have not acted, by the same correlating token I have gone six months without seducing a woman.

168

Bitch, cunt, slut, gash, whore, split-tail, insatiable devourer, vagina dentata, he could think of no other slurs—beaver—he flung them across the floor like pebbles across tile, goddamn piece of fucking crap, tart, harlot, nympho, trollop, chippie, wench, tootsie, emasculator, he scooped them from brain-mud like wriggling tadpoles, ball breaker, strumpet, pussy, and literally, slattern, toes rose in furious blur, sidewalks, promenades, commons, supermarkets full of sandaled feet, feet in ecstasy, pointed arched yeasty feet, flexed feet winged round his ass pulling down god, the excruciation of it, driving him mad, hot gripping slit jacking him off like an animal and his bloody rejecting coarse-haired mother racing fingers across his balls and stripping to toenail polish, peeing for him, squatting on the john down the open corridor, tinkling and wiping, flushing and padding back to bed, black ants he thinks, bush thick as an antbed, areolas embedded plums, moles and skin tags, she could bite off his dick at its base, the hairless base, and chew it down, instinctively, effortlessly, destroyer, masticator, witch, zero physical violence, he would never hurt her, just this flinging epithets as off a scarlet cyclotron, knives, needles, stones, clots, at she who offended, spinning like a drill bit hurling off wood, he intended to inflict damage, release the compact horde, destroy, divorce.

169

Today the sun births baby suns, pushes out blazing wrigglers of flame, ragged, squealing outward, bawling for fire's milk, like whelps, like ratlings lit with kerosene, exploding, tinged in smoke, streaming down as if from ropes, roaring in wind, infant after infant like Roman candles from the blinding mother, tails, fur, jagged, red flaming tongues flying from birth smashing on smoldering forests, blazing roof-tops, sun's irrepressible litter, popping, suckling each other in descent, fusing, separating, spilling round electrical poles like liquid explosives, and this is fine, fire and conflagration, passion's children, female babies, male babies, little baking genital-briquettes, Susie's breast captures one, one sizzles into Larry's neck, one or many reserve themselves for every creature, Prissy awakes with flaming thighs, sun laboriously wrenches litters, flings fiery hail, and adolescent Tortupa howls down street like a napalm child, an exposed root screams for extinguishment, hiss of hot water, Antwon's bedsheets race with fire which ravages the house, smelted skeletons, creatures rejoice in coliseums, rise in circles broadening chests, afire themselves, fire spreading fire, multiplying volume, horses' manes write desire, asphalt bakes, rivers flare sulphuric attire, struck match men, ennobled, brazen, tenacious, inconsolable pursue the soft satisfying fuel, imps seep up through floor cracks, drop from rafters, march through rooms imbibing perfume, devouring gels, accumulating muscle, spurt through stucco onto street or forest or dunescape, douse themselves and roar up sparks like flaming spruce, virgins, whores, geniuses, idiots, industrialists and bums.

170

In the distance a dog ferociously barks as if being attacked, I imagine it lunging into hurricane fence, straining neck, brisket solidified in crisis stance, I imagine a demented bristling Pit—stiff, stout, blunt—the kind of cur with which one does not fuck, confrontation down the block, dog protecting turf, bluffing or serious, assailant rushing, backing, rushing as dog foams, slams against wire, rattling it, the man disheveled, digesting a meatball sub, needing a crap, the lunging animal hackled, the dog's brain flares with savagery, smacked by fight, smearing canine napalm across the links as miscreant progresses, halts, progresses again teasingly, when no one is looking how thrilling to abuse animals, the man grabs a clod, dog redoubles ferocity, the man pretends to hurl, curses, pretends as dog's fangs sing on stretched steel, the man approaches property line where fence ends in a hardscrabble spot studded with gnarl, shrubs, pack, the man wants to bash the dog's skull, but has obligations, an afternoon engagement, takes one last shot by clanging post fracturing mongrel into pieces like bees bursting from a whacked hive, I hear the adrenalin-pumped acceleration of chasing barks, I think I perceive the cack of satanic laughter just prior to the saddening deep heart of triangular silence.

171

I compose a shocking poem and shoot it like a Roman Candle at Mr. Death, I try to bowl Death with fireball, like light it splits round it, Death advances, I pulse another and another: nothing, I'm furious and drive a Mustang through it, slamming brakes on the back side, Death rotates and approaches, I pop the clutch smashing through it like smoke, fucking bastard, now I'm livid, I thrust a whirring eggbeater in its eye, grind it like a drill, I drop the shaft and bolt in a swirl, where I stop and pant, Death waits like a ventriloquist, that's the final straw, I make a killing in real estate and install granite counters, onto its turquoise glitter death masturbates a wad, I wipe it with a dishrag, before Death's drool I fuck two buxom blondes, a violent tripling worthy of Caligula, twisting my cock down one's gullet while tonguing the other, both bronze with painted toes, torrid all nighter in which I also eat suckling pig, couscous, and aquavit, a bacchanal greening even Jesus who, doubling over, tears through his nails, Death gnaws a carrot and shits on my bed, I'm apoplexic and produce the big gun, in her basement I rape and murder a schoolgirl, igniting an immortalizing media glut, the crime without motive and random in nature, I am unapprehendable and melt eternally into night, Death recoils, grunts, hulks filthily away, a disease knowingly chortling.

172

Casanova told me he wept piteously slumped in puddle of Visine like a sunlit Rodin in topiary, weeping he said "without cause for no woman spurns me," sobbing uncontrollably, wringing saturation rag among chrysanthemums, and heaving as if weighted by mountains, olympian seducer, paragon, plumed hatman, I refuse to believe it, I know our satyr, he inspires tears— the country a hospice of sobbing maidens—but never sheds them, ladies like bon-bons delectably waiting, the man's heart is tough as a blow and ingeniously constructed, converting women to oxygen like Aston Martin, not crier but shredder, said he shed buckets from his slits without a precipitating incident, that between the Calle de Paseo and sweet Catalina an ague hit pulling him benched and sobbing to garden, shaking with fits, but I reiterate, it's bull shit, he's Testarossa, Bruget, bejeweled wildcat with rhapsodic wit we in our spasticity cannot emulate, incomparable athlete engendering hate, whom now, I suggest, Perrier and roses on night table, silver language spilled round her waist, is pumping like a lion Sophia or Esmeralda who orgasms round his ass like his newly annointed slave filled with grace, obedience, and eventual heartbreak, I know this, faultlessly, to be the case.

173

The young ones bathe the lapis of love with sponge
and soapy water, she glows roseate in the garden
washed in sun and chrysanthemums, young ones
push babies from womb, talcum behinds, Gerber's
pears with a skinny spoon, coo in heart's rooms,
and goo goo, legs radiant from Noxzema and blade,
they hammer forelocks in soccer games, cleats
churning fields, brilliant team jerseys, or whack and
catch softballs in oiled leather gloves, supple
and smooth, let's go for pizza and what inviting
lips tear down pepperoni, Fat Tire, and twist, mid-
air limbs angled suggestively spike ball over net,
drifting fog and shrieking gulls, the sea a blue-
green agate silent with gorgeous gills, polish the
marble monument with their own dream-chamois
and pliant live swath, keepers of the trust in pure
glass coffins opened by Charmings arrived on
God's stallion, radiant and accompanied by song.

174

I blow lizards off brick with my BB gun and am, therefore, God, to small reptile BB hits like canon ball crushing abdomen and flipping them away to die in pink bubbles, God, I impale frogs to ground with point blank arrow, bodies flattened, I tear off moth's wing to watch moth beat helplessly on driveway, I electrocute with spark plug horned toads, stink bugs, earthworms gleefully watching them fry, therefore adolescent God, backyard monster to whom insects sing, my pump gun whipcracks sparrows from trees, dropping them to crabgrass, looking at me, God, enraged, omnipotent, I do not eat prey but kill to kill sadistically in garden, granting clemency to some by inexplicable reprieve, the lucky chameleon bloating throat, the fortunate slim-jim, I cycle popping locusts to the firecracker stand, pants crammed with filched money, Black Cats to explode in lizard's mouth raining paper and gore, God stalking world, implacable, whimsical, every millipede a masterpiece destroyed in the massacre, the Creator, the Terminator asleep in his bed, internally bleeding, whom no one has seen, or will ever see, cry.

175

As the lord taketh I kick and scream but he taketh irrespectively until I churn a furrow with protesting legs and then am unconscious, stripped of ownership, the lord, trashy thug posing as CIA with pistol and artillery plate drags me through neighborhood to drainage ditch, drugs me and mouth-to-mouth sucks out my lungs like chunks of cutbait and shouts warped, distorted, oblong words which sound like ingrate, cynic, monster, love, he craved atheist blasphemer and pounced spilling bowl of twig and flake, dragging me away, my watchdog snarled but instinctively wilted under couch, innocent, wrong man, mistake, etcetera, but he kicks gut and plans, I think, to disappear me after certain disgorgements—places, names, maps, dates—as if I were terrorist, twine eats wrists, sack suffocates, feet deadeningly float—one notices through darkness what appears a plastic garbage bag, bulky, shifting, tied at top, the lord doth taketh and rarely restoreth to former self: brilliant, authoritative, beautiful, efficient, intuitive, immortal.

176

One learns to eat one's dog, paw and nail, knobby leg, up leg to brisket, flews, withers, loin, meal upon meal, ears, snout, muscle, spleen, Lab, Retriever, Shepherd, one learns to eat one's dog by examining champions: Napoleon, Hitler, Ghenghis Khan, St. Bernard, Afghan Hound, English Bull, teeth and fury, rage and jaw, no paw too broad for the human hinge, Dane nor Newfoundland, so commence banquet, orgy, bacchanal, masters in formals arriving at door with hatted dog, red-orange dusk, drawing room, chat, whisky and rye, sophisticated exchanges preceding the feast, iron gated country club, what ecstasy, what euphoria, the uncomprehending pets ready to obey albeit half eaten heel, "speak" "shake" "play dead," with a bloody pad or hacked shoulder, the animals assisting in grisly disappearance, dissonant of heart, he whom I shadow, protect, mimic, adore, celebrants crawling underneath their pets, forefoot, hindfoot, dewclaw, strifle, pastern, withers, brisket, loin, grind the flews, scissor the ears, gin and blood fizz, erections, excitation, sinews and ligaments, smooth muscle, gristle, women coming in Elizabethan chairs clasping their Bichon, abattoir aprons mapped with joy, the sporting dogs' tight anuses gripping upcurved middle age horns ramming out gray pubic hair, red tongues lolling in gastronomic exquisiteness, music drenched parlor—Bach, Mozart, Wagner, Tchaikovsky—mahogany, oak, cherry, concrete, garbage bags and mattresses, each butcher a Fuhrer, each lady a queen, servants rush about, fresh ice, liqueur, while several film the show, Chesterton's incisors slicing Fi-Fi's tongue—big face, birthday cake smile—Lady McNeese wishboning Bronson's hips—in mid-giggle, adjutant cap—and so and thus, canine bones collected by category, scaro, scapula, patella, rotula; pelvis, rib cage, radius, ulna; phalanges, vertebra, femur, and pelt; and every skull stacked onto a pile, each without its pinnacle delicacy, the eyes.

177

Another toothy smile, another sharp haircut, another youth
in *haute couture* prying the world's mollusk for money,
woman, power, fame, slip with forehead vein, educated
Dartmouth or Yale, MBA, advancing, reverenced, plush
leather, one tan touch maps him, spongy, too, like a newborn, weekend rugby, another healthy grin, lung balloon,
nuclear bladder, cadmium spleen dumping wine vinegar, human Maserati with muscled ass, mother alive,
father prime, sister bronze blonde, tumorous irrelevant
relatives mulching somewhere, no, he advertises vigor,
credit, Chivas Regal, Cannnondale, greased gears of
superiority, easefulness, privilege of conformity like
clean cut traditional lapel, standing on pile of deceased
designers and received wisdom, avatar of servitude;
young plants sprout, venously stalked, meaty leafed,
hibiscus honey clamoring toward bees, inside whose
petals survival buzzes, here vaults organism for the
ages, unquestioning, patriotic, malleable, stupid, hammered to creed, still unborn to his own bristles, lovely
lad determined to wash his throat and guts with soap,
to floss bones with store bought rope and, therefore,
float above the muck bucket and repudiation of indecency.

178

I bronze my sins like baby shoes, employ as bookends, Dante propped by fornication, Chekhov by gluttony, two-hundred twenty pounds beyond first wrapper, Justine slams against bootie-like masonry, thank you for my breathtaking sins, sloth, blasphemy, cheating on exams graduated me, hired by lying, falsification shot me upward like sunflower stem, here I inscribed dubious affiliations, institutions off which merely glanced, here I heralded uncorroborated triumphs involving perspicacity and prophecy, heroics when infirm, pump vision into the blind needing vision, my instigation, my determination, my implantation the hoary seed, I cultivate sins like potatoes, plant, tend, rake stonelike, rolling into sun hard and russet for how else does one dance in fields, slaughter enemy, vanquish rivals, I parade myself upon my shoulders, champion, victor, out the earthy hole of decency: the humble, honest, grateful, poor huddled in humps like irrelevant mummies, I stroke envy like a cat's throat and swallow the purrs, god fucking damn, Jesus H. Christ, and worship the golden calf my cock, that iridescent girth of beauty and bliss writhing through coarse black weed into the stormy bruise of the gullible and true.

179

Three oclock, brain aches, four oclock cut myself, five oclock glutted gut, six oclock fear advances, seven oclock bleeding ulcer, eight oclock acid reflux, nine oclock hemorrhoid clamp, ten oclock tooth gnashing, eleven oclock fungus itch, twelve oclock allergies, insomnia afterward, more precisely OCD, repetitive peeing, lock checking, misplace flippers, legs detached and numbly drift, dissociation, AM three rat gnaws avocado, fruit basket swings, moon shaft patters across ceiling, nightshade ripples, four oclock slips unnoticed, four-thirty rage, pain, victimization, bitterness, balled, tungsten burning, raw, alive, strip of white ash, cupping balls in hand to feel secure, tight, non-erotic, for sheer completeness, under and round easterly ear, down neck footlong scar through which Mr. Parotid disappeared, a sip, earplugs, untwist shirt, anxiety like actor void of script in blaring klieg, five thirty eye-mask, jet aircraft, fist forms, unforms, tears trickle, five-forty-five pummel thighs, blows to head, hard, as with blunt instrument, bludgeon, a catharsis of sorts.

180

Everybody fucking everybody, fucking fucking fucking, the buxom babe at athletic club taking respite from fucking, the hand clasping couple sauntering toward Jacob's, slutty and overt, tight jeans, flattened cock, swollen labia, painted sandaled nails, thongs and briefs, batons and hoops, fuck addicted human living for sex, interpenetration, fellatio and cunnilingus, working for a private dwelling to fuck in, bedroom and kitchen, fireplace and mudroom, laboring for the fuck, the nighttime spasm, the bone slipping into, men on women, men on men, women on women, foursomes, videoed, snapshot, *ménage a trois*, prostitute, whore, fuck-buddy, sweat dance, fingers probing, experimentation, rope and handcuff, anal intercourse, hot position, marijuana, coke, ecstasy, alcohol, garrote, fucking as humans fuck, gelatinous hands shiny with honey, fucking fucking fucking, eyeing each other, brain afire, transparent, fishnet and heel, flouncy blouse, feigning indifference, perfume, car, ankle bracelet, bondage of necessity, jacking off in lavatory, the militaristic march from puberty, fashion, fad, trend, menses, fucking fucking, he thinks I'm delicious, he slavers after me, he loves my tits, robot, robot, automaton, leaking gears, bull's-eye, lubed hemispheres, baby bursting crown, feet, transparent fingers, otherworldly, clotted, luminous, bloody afterbirth, stitches and healing, fucking fucking fucking, tequila shots and fucking, coke and fucking, lobster and fucking, football and fucking, showers and fucking, poetry and fucking, movies and fucking, murder and fucking, squabbling and fucking, Asia, Africa, Europe, West, Middle East, both poles, the rotund equator, in squalor and opulence, thrusting pumping grinding hips parted, raised, asses flexing, tough nipples bitten tweaked squeezed twisted, cock pumped jacked throat-stroked, milked, drunk, semen splatted face, porn and vibrator, the workplace adult burning with licentiousness, fuck me, suck me, ravage me, restless, incessant, deafening, twisted, psychiatrist, sex addiction group, abortion, failed Platonism, divorce, suicide, separation, disinheritance, memoirs, affair, compulsive deflection, stuffed rhinoceros, repression, invasion, genocide, religious fanaticism.

181

I eat myself, everyone eats the self, I bite finger, bone snaps, skin tears, chew, swallow the bloody twig, within weeks it regenerates for re-eating, stumps in stages of regrowth, morsels again, I am limber enough to eat my penis, it starfish-appendage regenerates, I rip it like meat, it bursts delectably, likewise thigh, calf, biceps, ham of hand, all re-grow for future feasting, publicly, incessantly you eat yourself, voyeur I watch you rip lobe which disgusts, delights confounding the spheres, you lick the street after vomiting, like a cur, hate your trivial psychotic life, cannibal nipping fat behind knees, failure and cannibal, charlatan and cannibal, wind-tousled hair, fraud presenting lies as gospel while rump-pits pool with blood, Evelyn asphyxiates herself somewhere near Orange, you swivel doll head and gnaw off hank of shoulder tartar, filled with self-loathing, every recreated wound glimmers scarlet, human devours self entire every four years, the creature a continuous hackneyed newborn, I pour tooth flakes over chicken, we devise signature dishes, Andee lays veal between vaginal lips, sexual pasta, Peter freezes sugarplum toes for midnight licking, lovers feed cuds of selves through kissing, gnashing and smacking, smile and sob for God and happiness, finally dead at ninety Eddie is a tortured strip of human jerky stretched in open coffin visited by two self-annihilating penitents.

182

I impregnate myself by injecting semen into gut, it
gushes, swirls, I feel conception's exhilaration—
fullness, epiphany—shirt unsnapped, the internal
multiplication prior to showing, I mother, I father,
scrotum and womb, anticipate power of lactation,
distention, cervical dilation, healing by nursing,
draw sperm through needle, shoot it toward stomach's eggs, I intuited eggs, eggs sung to me, eggs
buzzed like bees, "fertilize, fertilize" which I
deflected by eating pies, I shatter biology, morning nausea, cravings, more eyes watching than
watched Apollo, ignition, lift-off! ultrasound
discloses a breach healthy male floating in amniotica, bumping, crowding, dear God, Omnipotent King, thank Thee, humbled opportunity,
new Aquarius, I shall comport with dignity, I
fill myself with progeny and happiness intensifies everything—photosynthesis, pollination,
ionic discharge, harmonic variation—every sparrow a Valkerie, leaf spout a cirque, they carry
in fragrant Aleph tightly swaddled, I sit upright
heavy-breasted and weep and weep and weep.

183

Sack of shit topped with head pronouncing itself enlightened, sack of shit fucking, sack of shit reading, sack of shit litigating, most laughable sack of shit protesting love, marry me, fucked up, nobody but you, on knees, apologize, thrusting roses, snap dragons, what a joke, wheat germ, lamb chop, beet green, cheese, sack stuffed with shit and piss adoring she full of shit, toilets everywhere, urinals abound, lavatories, toilet paper, paper towels, die without you, alone, destitute, worthless, destroyed, atop his sack superman-blue hair, the family brows, grandmother's gray, paunchy, mean, hauling clogged colon like infantryman or prospector, covered in weave, incognito, whom some entity rewards with a stamped signature, rows of port-o-potties, stadium troughs, get in line, head after head atop its factory facing men's room, penises half stiff, bowels bursting, background loudspeaker, standing in puddles, crouching on drip, had to have you, hormones galloped, in bathroom, frijoles, cod tacos, spinach puree, manufacturers, brilliant biologies, externally charmed, wrapped in silk or corduroy, passionately confabulating, cuisines, views, cruises, jewels hanging from mucousy muscular interior film within which snakes twenty-six expandable feet of warm intestine working down a seventeen pound knotted rope of raw excrement, continuously replenished with joyous bulk like a shredding machine, our roaring reality, the red light district of a condemned republic, "but we're more than that," "yes, yes of course."

184

I lay my penis on a chopping block and whack it off, cleaver whomp and gone, separate, not me, gap between us, ultra-circumcision, head white, then purple, swollen, instant of pain exchanged for lifetime of torment, out of commission, ineffectual, woman squeeze ass round another man, devour heavy five o'clock beard, disabused of tie, battering ram with expectation, portfolio, I sever snake from self, it wails and dies on knife-scarred oak while desire fucks desire, Jimbo jackhammer-pumps Babs, vagina melts, mattresses crumple lovers like rough drafts tossed into trash, not to disparage tuxedos and chiffon, guests clicking images of foreshadowing fire, beauty hurts, I clawed up-and-over labial cliffs into chasm, there blinded to pant with shooting gun, this before The Act, the cessation of hell, final baptism: the destruction of capability, not pitiful little drench in cold shower but violent permanency, the truncation, the prayerful instant of restitution, god illuminated ascension to eternal bliss, wound healed like leg stump, or hers a scabrous socket, I recommend for disposal the InSinkErator, that indifferent clinic grinding moldy cukes, coagulated pasta, filmy beets, apple core, potato peel, slimy grape, pulpy brain chordate of the sexual drama.

185

Mugwump, misanthrope, curmudgeon, maxigrump,
everyone get fucked, go hell, jump up ass, fuck off,
mentally convict, execute, no commutation, midnight governor, fry the sonofabitch, think I give a
shit, I want men dead, scythed like lemon grass,
leave standing women, my cock's great enough
for all, semen gushes from like a flood of bibles
rushing women wonderward overawed, satisfied,
my god-rod, greater than the sum of males pathetic at offices and power lunches, mercifully crush
with superiority these ineffectual worms and millipedes swarming under rocks, all spoils mine,
an infinite slavish wifery of writers, caregivers,
academics, artists, nurses, and maids worshipping my rocket and incomparable virtuosity, I
fulfill every woman save those who die of shame
from my rejection, Hercules, Achilles, Odysseus, Ajax, Zeus, cut same cloth I, condemn
rivals to non-existence with spear and clod, unlikely I, repulsive of lipomas and toenail grunge.

186

I failed—poet, husband, father, lover, employee, mind, god-fearer—failure became cynicism, cynicism judgementalism, judgementalism self-loathing, a toxic inwardly-sucking blow, ash-lungs resulted and ash-lungs do not conveniently re-grow, but this shall be final spewage of crap poem in a toxic succession of guilt-saturated incendiaries, hatcheted souls require cessation, from today forward I shall join audience of the talented, gasping every metaphor, finger-pressing lid, squealing every denouement, flourishing applause, I wallowed in Neanderthal viscera, introjected plunging, hubris, gut stew, mistook psychoanalysis for poetry believing blunt suffering triumphal, I am sixty, a Dodo, squawked slap-footed tearing throat on spite, the brilliant eagles shriek a fierceness I considered cowardice, I applaud Jorie, W.S., Maxine, Donald, the Pentax crowd sterile and invisible, miscalculation eats me, fantasies worm me, resentment cores my beautiful shell cratered to condemnation, my daughter excommunicated me whom I annihilated, I'm adjunct independent parasite without benefits leeching a fourth wife, I'm filled with schadenfreude, let they who possess genius transcend, I'm stiff-necked, petty, mean, hard, I'm rage engorged, yes, let this be my final word in verse: rage.

187

This phrase sees, this one clucks tongue in outrage, this one indiscriminately pees, this one digests, this one cleanses blood, this one blows gale across wire into moan or hum, this one sucks jet fuel, this one squeezes off waste material like a fist, this one demands adulation, this phrase runs rigid up shapeless trees, this one mushrooms inside bomb, this one lubricated rotates, this one blows deoxygenated air out tube which revitalizes in this one, this column spins out itself graceful nebulas, this one stitchless wraps, this one grows bone-hard over tenderness, this one twitches, wriggles, this smooth one slips over all like a kid glove which transforms into a metal grate, this one knows who pushed him out and plans its revenge, this one worships its invincible self, this one manufactures charisma, this unassuming little phrase murders God with an oyster shucker, this one's a soft hemisphere, this one's a dual hemisphere with a hole between, this one erupts sour sallow clots extraneous to engorgement, this one folds lower extremity over a pencil eraser, perpetual peristalsis pushes downward through this one moving the material, this one shuts, this one heals, this one pops, this one peels, this one sheds, this one seals, this one wets, this one congeals, this one ruptures into a bruise, this one measures itself and divides, this one hears voices of greatness and strives, strives, yet all lie dead before their creator, mocking and accusing.

188

I crack open my father's mouth as I crack open mine,
ruby, breath-stink, "stand up straight" it screams, "foot-
dragger," "big shot," "get haircut," fumes unleash, foul
reek, yellow teeth, bite-blisters, it tightens, stretches—
a lipless rubber band—I rush mirror, attack myself,
"lard ass" I scream, "pig," "piece of shit," his cranium
fills my cranium, two angry skulls, identical noses,
bug eyes glaring, "ass in gear, buster," "smell coffee,"
I stick my fist through to scramble his brain, burst yolk
eye, I stick my hand in a whole raw fish, fish puppet,
"looser," I scream, "fucker," silvery shimmer, hand
up guts, big turbo, fish mittens, fingers in fins, I work
mouth, masturbate with fish, I strive to yank out
mouth the full body net my father, a bloody wire,
arms slide out arms, crushed-love criticism, legs
slide through legs, scorpions, worms, castigations
wrapped with pseudo care, "toughen up," "stiff lip,"
"triumph," "persevere," "down without fight," tor-
so like mail—you've heard this before, I mimic my-
self, old hat, well, screw you, things require repetitive
recitation—torso as if medieval, a rough hewn hur-
ricane fence, guilty, blameworthy, shameful, repre-
hensible—oversensitive crybaby—inside out like 3-
D graphic, pretty daddy, grandiose, bipolar, electro-
shocked, cruel, slipping out my lining, two hard
sons-of-bitches erect, stubborn, invasive, visceral
parting at lips, lip-kissing in final exorcism, his,
mine, before collapsing, both, boneless to the floor.

189

Dear god, speak to me severally, all of you—rain, mountain, love, sex, mist, corn, God of forgiveness, loving-kindness, speak floods and productivity, when crops vaulted like insurrectionists and loaves magical mounds tumbled out ovens girls and boys, dear God speak in numbers beyond imagining, in Hebrew, Aramaic, Spanish, Catalan, speak in animal through dreams, trances, nibble my fingers, sip knees, drink me like tidal pool, coconut, cactus swords, say you I loathe, detest, abhor, adore like a brilliant lizard, reptile, amphibian, javelina swilling bog, I cradle while you, pompous clod, tromp and stuff chops with lobster and pot pie, idiot, lunatic, mislived, I pipe-clean aortic veins and align front end, accident awaits, disaster lurks, shithead, but I speak pantheistically, God of footsoles, ottoman, sclerosis, dystrophy, bedsores and rigor mortis, protect, direct, shield, my buffoonery, gluttony, misanthropy, upon mahogany pray, dear omnipotent talk to me in numbers, zebra, wildebeest, oscillate my ears, for I am beyond kite, creamsickle, and sewer frog, I am toothpoor, tepid, mediocre, failed, stiff-necked, defensive, antiauthoritarian, dear Mitosis, girdle my cells, bag me like marbles, melt me in crucible into thick glass lighthouse luminous in mud, shove fire under skin, humility, guide me through humanity in familiar canals, suffer me their squalls, typhoons, cleaving wounds, dead, dead, I am already dead.

190

I'm fascinated with the concept of slitting my wrists, jabbing a steak knife straight through and gushing into a tub and I don't need your crap, "go ahead, I don't care, who gives a shit, this isn't poetry, it's therapy, kill yourself or write poetry but stop whining, shithead," well, fuck you, I'll write what I want and call it what I want, who made you Vendler, Bloom, those two parasites, I'm obsessed with knives and suicide, clichéd carving knives and razor blades, knives to slash throat or slice steak fat, grasping kitchen knife to dice onions freaks, I go berserk, slaughtering the dog, the lackadaisical cat draped over sofa, thrusting it through palate, murdering overworked wife, throwback to prehistoric rage, cellular hostility, paranoid-schizophrenia perhaps, I fantasize killing hate by killing self, bursting heart inside heart, curtailing inevitable inhumanity, unbearable shame, and who are you to consign this to prose or diarrhea or hypergraphia, you and your prudery and ultra-conservatism, your outraging pedantry, it's bloody, messy, disgusting, cowardly, reddening bathwater, skin flaps like raincoat, the primeval scream, the bitterness, the futile regret, the cruelty wormed into the finder's apple, it fucks up everyone in selfish torrent, well Helen and Harold, there you have it, a brain dead entrepreneur shocking poetry back to life with suicidal fantasies, throwing the switch, yeow, I am block of colorless lard shot with insucked veins, lipless, eyeless, drained of piss and platelet, topped by mismanaged hair, in a preformed one-piece plastic laminate tub filled with luke, formerly fixated on death, cocks, shit, power, fornication, perfectionism, and God, and flatlined, or practically so.

191

My lover's lips are razor blades, her breasts Molotov cocktails, her hands two wads of wire with flesh bits caught on barbs, nails blown outward to maim or kill describes my lover's hair, my lover's hips are rock drill blasting granite slabs, my lover's gams two tall glass shards, throat a falcon's claws, oh, when my lover sings what doesn't receive a back full of shotgun pellets, those two wings of poetic vision, my lover's feet, grenades with pins just pulled, her brain is a thousand snapping turtles, each clamped to a twig, her buttocks could back down Sherman's canon and minnie ball brigade, scattering them back to Slocum, her heart is pure double bubble gum, six wads molded together into a science fiction blob, no better or worse than yours or mine, when we couple atop the palace bed in the sulphurous lime-stone cave looked on by subterranean albino scorpions, winged rats, and horror cats, after the clawing slashing bashing melee of scant saliva-and-speed-filled seconds she crawls away, a twisted bloody eviscerated slaughter of a thing dragging its death limbs through the night.

192

Humility and its corollaries pathos and rupture, saith the Lord,
Jesus was an idiot—I ejected him for irrelevance, stupidity, he's
a wastrel, foolish tramp trashing his talents on bums and whores,
I instructed elitism, superiority while floral dreams surrounded
his head, sissy, pushover, the whole bloody trial and crucifixion—
it's almost comical—I meticulously orchestrated for this baptism
escape routes through which to found an invincible military, I
hoped for savagery but received a whipped retreating blood-
less twit clasping pantywaist for comfort, think what prodig-
ious skirt he could have cowered behind had I married, dis-
appointment, quitter, humility and its corollaries pathos and rup-
ture, I repeat, smashed on his receding chin, I've a mind to
dismantle the little shit and kick him to the ash heap but for
sadism, I delight in his diminishment and the multitudinous
lunatic duplicates prostrating themselves complete with dang-
ling crucifix to this Milquetoast! I would beat him senseless
if he weren't abed sucking his big toe, autistically rocking,
I pour a Smirnoff, lean back, and pity the peewit, always
ran from the ball and adored musicals, got his homo head
wrapped in a thorn bush, and now like a bad fucking penny
he's back contrite for pot pie and cream puffs, I spit on him,
I slapsalt his wounds, I drag him out the mansion door and
blow it shut, embarrassment, drowned rat, he's not my son.

193

I'm profane, I say motherfucker, asshole, sonofabitch, shithead, fuck off, goddamn, piece of shit, bitch, cunt, slut, gash, capitalist, shove it up your butt, go fuck yourself, I'm tourettes, I grunt, sniff, grimace, shrug, twist, shriek, bark, echo, I give you what for, I shoot the finger, I'm OCD inspecting every centimeter of toilet paper for the slightest smear, wiping myself bloody, lock checker, dental flosser, urinator, snack gobbler, insatiable masturbator, profane and disgusting, rage-aholic, self mutilator, nose picker, bruisey self-beater, host of unwanted psychopath, hypergraphiac, who could love this walking freak, two heads, three legs, dwarf king, amphibian man, hermaphrodite ogling prime cuts like a billionaire, who's middle-thickening, ignored, street slinging, mad, always mad, like a circus freak, defensive and cast, let us pray, no let us denounce, no let us indict public divisiveness, isolate unsavory creatures, god is my shepherd, saltpeter these people, longboxes, I am leering lasciviousness, women's toes shock me like a dentist's drill, wincing excruciation, I weep by the road, throw bums out, solitary confinement, down with nonpeople, game show champion racking up winnings without a rabbit or soul, profane and profligate shooting jism into his grand canyon, kill the bastards, one two three heave, just this script of self-incrimination and in some Metropolis Lutheran Hospital's storage facility a plaster impression of my teeth.

194

Just fuck the man, you're a klipspringer, a steenbok with loins, forelocks, reproductive apparatus, instinct, screw meticulous squeamishness, that flimsy surface cellophane wrapping greed and drive, the primeval godless multiple growling for loam, power's magma charring bones underneath hell, and you in pink and blue garbage playing coy with rage, blood soak these ribbons in copulative immersion, fuck the man, who gives an adulterous shit, you crave his muscled cock, his worship, your crushed nipples deep in throat, fuck on ripped out pages of the bible, Ephesians, Corinthians, Luke, John, spew them with urine and female come, excrement and sweat, that black roaring pinpoint, volcano, god unspeakable, black as shit or coal beneath guts and marrow, beyond earth or consciousness, the homicidal clutch twisting up shiest, and you with your beauty bars and exfoliation, your precious Saran Wrap, your lungs insuck, heart chambers bruise, glands swell and sweat, tongue thickens to glue in his appearance, crawl under him gape, cleave primal pit, giraffe, wildebeest, hare, human.

195

She's asleep, I'm painting her body with nail polish, smear, flourish, dot, streak, eyes, beak, no endearments, a hip abstraction, she's deep sleeping, exhausted, stressed, she slumbers through this minor sensation, dark red pigment designed to rivet eyes to feet, to crazy-make, engines of seduction, seahorse, bird, zip lines, this my power, tattoo, defile, assert over inert will red fascism, red omnipotence, my wakeful hands possessing the reclining nude, the moribund, I own her like I own a custom Ford, what control the conscious over the unconscious, streaming above, manipulating, dipping in, effortlessly, at will, polish smoothly applied as god applies fear and stuttering, I draw bull's eye, tic tac toe, cracked heart arrow-ripped, cupid's madness down valleys of ass, up spine furrow, the vial half full, I cannot desist, peel back sheet to naked feet and dot the toes, terrorist, insurrectionist, I figure-eight ankle to heel, there! and there! she's a blossoming tree blotting sky, I scratch fence with nail, etch initials, mar undiscovered dirty rafter, alter all, staple crossbeam of wooden table, Thor, Apollo, Yahweh, Woton, incompetent twit, wordslaughterer, misfit, perhaps she lies awake, perhaps she feels brush stroke across flank, perhaps she keeps eyelids shut like a dozing horse in a luminous field, perhaps the world pretends to sleep in a comprehending state of grace while her scrawny citizens before extinction cover her flesh with their ridiculous signatures.

196

And that was that, I love those words, and that was that, cockatoo died, and that was that, made F, and that was that, not attending, and that was that, eat the sprouts, and that was that, sometimes nasty, you're going to mass, and that was that, no to Bowdoin and that was that, not marrying Sal, and that was that, end of story, they're amputating, buried not cremated, and that was that, we're deteriorating, you're not getting traps, put on the tux, and that was that, and that was that, goddammit fucking sonofabitch, non-negotiable, it's in the lymph, surgery, war, and that was that, thirteen million, we're watching Parr, bubonic decimated, a meteorite, they bit the freaking apple, crucified, roasted her leg, ate, survived, that's that, alcoholic like dad, got butt to class, attended, passed, went to state, Bus. Ed. dusted off hands, sued, won, custody of Jake, nobody pulled wool, they drank *en mass* the cool-aid, families clasped, others yammered, popped off eight rounds, lethal, then self, she insisted, delivered, gave it up, that was that, he burst in, declared himself womanizer, hedonist, deceiver, suicidal, desperate, bolted, never returned.

197

The Brain revives like a movie monster, we shout, we thought they killed it with tanks and bombers in the stubble field to which it retreated terrified, capitulated, it throbs, oozes, shoots malignancy like a gland, disgusting creature nerving vulgarity, pullulating, it violated a minor on a red pony, its many-veined erection devoured women like gum bears, lethal alien shocks alive, a resurrection, screeches like bats, scientist confers with president, priests, general, politician, orders lockdown, floodlights hit it like surgery, giant scrotum accumulating, how annihilate, monstrosities of grotesquerie rise behind it, nauseating monuments, split chord wood of female thighs, fire roasted males, villages frozen in enzyme, shameless disconnected organ eating alive or violating the insignificant plankton of bipeds strained through acids into hell, lover rammed through lover, wife gorishly splashing husband, oil tankers spiraling soundlessly down, the thing in drag with multiple penises, impervious to ordnance, MIT neurophysicist and heroine over whom it vomits green bile, hypothalamus, medulla oblongata, basal ganglia swallowing the hydrogen bloom like a lude, the entire discotheque decimated in full swing, crushing perfectly decent people.

198

Obscenities cleanse like mineral bath, obscenities hurled
through lecture hall, sanctuary, obscenity splitting capitol
dome, obscenity-shouter filth-liberated, tainted blood,
solid waste, purified, absolved, he who throws Jesus
down port-o-potty delivers self to rectory, he cursing
Mother's lavender-sachet cunt plied and pumped by
a thousand Johns, frankincense of filthy swine shitting
museum, grunting, peeing, chewing mummies, and
she who liberated them granted non-malignant lungs,
spongy pumps with which to suck sheets of sparking,
vulgarities arise! dance the pristinities, the clean fact-
ories of frocks and gloves, hospitals and wedding
gown, foul with dirty tongue, finger, and thumb, caut-
erize spring air crisping the sun like a horse's thigh
over which mongrels puncture each other's throats,
claws ripped out like hazelnuts, burn clean worship-
pers, too, like so many Christs scraped free and
smooth, and loose on all skunks, pigs, goats, and mice,
but most of all befoul thyself, shit upon thy own
face and squeeze through fingers the expunged meal
of groats and chops upon your venal perfection, flaw-
less ewe, god's unblemished, pure beyond uttering,
beautiful as the colorless, undifferentiated, virgin void.

199

A woman's voice emanates from the room in which I sit, "I know," she said, meaning what? that she knows I am desperate, lonely, or does she know something about me I won't for years, about how I will unravel or die, or that she knows how but cannot prevent the plummet, and her "I know" blurted in futility, as when mother admits her son is dumb though he believes himself outstanding, no one accompanies me, it is dusk, I am intermittently writing and dozing, perhaps it was a dream in which I heard the woman say, "I know," when in fact I said it sleepily to myself, a prophecy of some future I intuit such as my failure as father or writer irreversibly approaching and I said resignedly "I know," as I am obscure and underemployed and my wife's devotion falters as she requires financial and emotional security, not depression and cynicism, "I know," she spoke from behind where door meets hall as if she floated furtive in twilight, as if she were God in Her omniscience, and I repeated consciously, "I know," after she said "I know" because I have always been aware and cannot stop it from happening.

200

Because I demand to be worshipped like God, because I permit no man to conquer women whom I find desirable, because I strive to slaughter rivals for sexual spoils, because I am the finest writer alive, because I am immortal, inestimable, and Olympian surpassing all, sparing none humiliating acknowledgment, überman among mortals, because only I throw male charisma forging slaves from lead, concubines from loam, wives from clay—magistrate and magi—blonde flesh sprouting silken flutes through which I sip exquisite wine, because the sphere my physical power, full and round, eclipses the body of all humanity smelted into one unimpressive sun, darkening and possessing it like lozenge under tongue, my hands brilliant and ridged beyond Bernini's ridiculous tools, because I breathe mother's purple plum and slew father on the table of blood, a triumphant yolk-red eye rising like God through hazy sky and required required required, because I wrap like phylacteries about my arms chariot's leather lashes and fly through filthy streets overrun with butchers, mutton eaters, and prostitutes plying wares like brick-headed mongrels drooling for gob, that is why I have failed, am failing, and shall fail.

201

Everything I say he repeats, everything I say he repeats, he said, I feel lousy, I feel lousy, he said, I never understood how to love, I never understood how to love, he said, I am angry, egotistical, cruel and objectifying, I am angry, egotistical, cruel and objectifying, he said, feet, vagina, hair, thighs, feet, vagina, hair, thighs, he said, atheism, atheism, he said, godlessness, godlessness, he said, married to mother, married to mother, he said, defensive, defensive, he said, ever-present male enemies assault me while ubiquitous females salve the wound, ever-present male enemies assault me while ubiquitous females salve the wound, he said, he mimics verbatim, I need a drink, I need a drink, he said, I need a fuck, I need a fuck, he said, I need a confessor, absolution, a cleansing, I need a confessor, absolution, a cleansing, he said, fuck you, fuck you, he said, I'm shooting you the finger, I'm shooting you the finger, he said, I mean it, I mean it, he said, go fuck yourself, go fuck yourself, he said, I'm a rage-filled psychopathological addict, I'm a rage-filled psychopathological addict, he said, I masturbate to Internet porn, I masturbate to Internet porn, he said, I shoot into a hand towel, I shoot into a hand towel, he said, and ashamed bury it in dirty clothes, and ashamed bury it in dirty clothes, he said, to be instantly washed, to be instantly washed, he said, evidence, evidence, he said, I'm in the vortex of another lousy relationship, I'm in the vortex of another lousy relationship, he said, squabbling, pushing, regressing, squabbling, pushing, regressing, he said, never be satisfied, never be satisfied, he said, yea, walk, valley, shadow, death, yea, walk, valley, shadow, death, he said, I don't care, I don't care, he said, I mean it, I mean it, he said, I'm done with all this crap, I'm done with all this crap, he said, goodbye, goodbye, he said.

202

The momentous event is upon us, women deliver pythons and porcupines, men shit cockroaches onto animal guts burst from inner explosion, pets vomit tadpoles which seek the female anus, babies muscled like bull terriers shoot from tracheotomies bullets at adult males, oceans turn to excrement and reservoirs to slaughtered poultry, and from world's four corners god releases the grotesqueries: cellist, quarterback, professor, priest, each with innumerable omnivorous heads and the thousand uncontrollable sphincters, and the people flee with swaddled neonates, photo albums, pills under a black crustaceous sun, copulation everywhere, blowing and getting blown, drunk on everclear, guts hanging out like overstuffed hampers, faces fused to spleens, women finger fuck themselves on liquefying beds, men receive spontaneous episiotomies releasing sackfuls, moon weeps chemical weapons, each perpetrating a holocaust, Superman speeds into a fly swatter, and god slides open the manhole of hell: throat slashers, spree killers, cannibals, racketeers corn hole children and C-section girls, and down slides Jesus parting the gnats like an insecticide-slathered hiker, admitting none, excepting no one, naked, emaciated, psychologically damaged, sad, half erect like frankfurter, the savior, the sower, shooting new fireball forests from fingers, bees invading oceans of clover, and the worshippers laden with death mass on the river bank like double mastectomies after the scalpel, messiah in sandals drifting across desert flinging plasma and apples, and here is where ends, a crucifixion sucking through itself off this sere white ball the swarming plague of an entire population of monsters and fools.

203

Executions: sawed-off to face; snake fed down throat; poison spiked toddy; baby inside cellophane; forced mercury ingestion; threaded down nostril tube connected to faucet; slashed trachea; shoved off cliff; knife in gut; kerosene doused, flared match; hammer bludgeoned skull; friendly fire; electric drillbit through cranium; strychnine-laced candy; bled upside down from slaughterhouse hook; lashed to trucks floored in opposite directions; basement cardiac surgery; pistol rigged to flush handle; hosed down woman lashed to a tree at sixty below; pumping ink into a poet's scrotum, locking him in prison with the penis his only pen.

204

I love the women I beat, their faces bowls from which I
drink and to whom I protest—depleted in T-shirt—tender
love, hovered over, worshiping lips and milky flesh,
frazzled, devoured by deity, gnawed bone, cup face
like pottery, baby, please, you're my world, open-hand-
ed, gristly, frustrated, annihilated, love blooms like
rosy welt, pleading, heart a crushed cardboard box,
appeal to sympathy, lap-headed, stage performer, make-
up, costume, props, protagonist, lover, climax, snif-
fles, Kleenex, audience cough breaking magic, I em-
brace knees like a buoy, disgraced, remorseful, love
the women I batter like sensitive wounds verging on
happiness, bruised eyes in November, Klieg lights
illuminating pores and pain, face stings, the absinthe
sweet, the catharsis of attachment after strangulation.

205

Extract and examine human uterus. resembles nothing. forty grams, five centimeters. purple hunk designed for specialized function. unattractive. disgusting. reminds of psychopathic murder or bomb aftermath. math. useless severed from neighboring, something for wolves. could shove in fetus but wouldn't take devoid of miracle. severed from net what use? medical school. anatomy lab. freak show curiosity. museum. under extreme conditions would eat or cuddle it, and had it vagina might penetrate it. men are capable. not removed, however, from the crux of woman which requires no liver. heart. appendix. spleen. doesn't require anus. perhaps handles on either side. man wants leverage. could eat meat opposite it, and fried potatoes. have wondered whether one can determine from severed uterus its donor's race—amusing conjecture. some could not identify uterus confusing it with exotic dishes such as monkey or roach, others poke and imagine possum. useless disembodied thing, sticky, rotting, in indifferent space. liberated by monster. it is, I am told, an aphrodisiac, available to men of certain persuasion. like garlic on mutton rub it on penis to drive prudes mad.

206

Whom should you loathe if not yourself, and one must loathe somebody, virtuoso describes others but you are shit, mediocrity, alien in the family photograph eternally self-immolating—fraud, fuck-up, fake, fool—curse yourself, cut yourself, bash inferior brain against wall after another catastrophic misadventure, extraneous irrelevant idiot, neither embraced nor expunged, merely tolerated by the exceptional, unimaginable to question the meticulous ingeniousness of others whose pinnacles shed you like a cloud and whose brilliance bleaches you like a skull: disappointment, embarrassment, Bozo.

207

Insignificant, trivial, meaningless, vapid: everything not it. it the sole importance. it rules corporation. it wages war. it fuels political egotism. it swishes silk across terrazzo. it researches biochemistry, launches into space. it welds steel that becomes cities. is creature's heart and hunger. devours ribs. it battles cancer. it sucks air through turbines. it snorts lines of language like cocaine. it hits dopamine like a hammerhead bait. die for it. beg for it. confess for it. balance on soles for it. wrap head and pray for it. pray to Jesus. drive ninety for it. acquire junk for it. imprison it in teardrops. loathe daddy, despise mother. impale it on dinner fork. paint the Guernica for it. paint the Raft of Medusa. it eats money and money serves. money squirms. people vomit money on yachts for it. people swill drambuie, raise cockatoos, blow preservatives into animal heads. under severe pressure it pinks urine. people swing from rafters by neck from it or duck-quack in barren rooms. it supercharges spit through consonants and stiffens leg bones with sudden flexion. knit battleships for it. detonate scoreboards. master flugelhorn. it eats cheese through eyedropper and weighs what its height in paperclips weighs. dance the funky chicken. without it rot gut, ten car smashup, acid reflux, brick bowels, cytocryology in Midwestern city. with it you leave, six gun smoking, Masterson, Holiday, Earp heart-gushing on street, garbage trucks flip away swatted, torpedoes fired from skintight U-Boat incinerate enemy battleships, your brain night-burst from biochemistry lab eats The Varsity meatloaf crowd, devours male planetarium patrons, bowls down Bijou blockheads en route to the statehouse chocked with idiots, dripping man-gore while hypnotizing girls into worshiping Gods. with it you smoke, dash, curl, stream, pogo to cypress peaks and blow in breeze like the Resplendent Quetzal, and never die.

208

Give me preference and I'll win it for you, you'll have it wrapped and labeled like a center cut, if I must circle—wit or grit—this bloody planet, your clawed protectorate, give me command and watch me destroy, I'll deliver throats, rubies, testicles, souls, fetch bodies with beautiful debris, your Apollo, African cat, "bring me love," I'll spear my heart like a grouper, serve it in steaks and cubes while simultaneously resurrecting my pulsing pump, dual aortic tubes feeding midnight bliss, nerves of spun glass, "bring me constancy," I'll procure devotion in Timbuktu, the selfless gusts inside onyx delivered on an oryx, circles within circles of soda and spermatozoa, stirred, not shaken, for I am claws, fangs, stealth, genius, lethal as dart, gentle swab, "brilliance, please," and I blow torch crayons into the Whitney, atomic tangerine, razzle dazzle rose, flung, dripped, drizzled into orbs, obedience, subjugation, "bring potency, insemination, aggression, erection," and I transfuse ox into veins, drink rhino piss mixed with nitrogen flakes, eat a living condor spleen wrapped in bison and, sporting hides and flight plumes, scream to you reeking of cottonmouth venom and river muck with a scrotum full of rockets and a ramrod cock poised to shoot into you god's tadpoles packed with billion seed bursting into voltage and Spring circuitry for I am champion and civil war canon blasting you to caverns of liquid red jewels and bronze-turquoise pools swirled like dolphins round the glistening full-moon, electric and dripping, "bring me zero, nothing, negative space, that unnameable absence, neither vacuum, cavity, nor black hole, which is everything's essence, fuse, life force, detonation," and I drink my juices, eat my digits, toes, appendages, appendix, finally stretch mouth backward over forehead and disappear save for an inside-out gut on the floor which implodes with onanism like a bloated white dwarf off-gassing the fumes of grandiosity and dead possibilities.

209

The dependable ecstasies no longer satisfy: food, sex, love, power, poetry, prayer, nothing engods, mouse under cabinet splashing blood against heart walls, nose twitching for oblivion to fill out skin, nothing, flat, highs sliding, and I needing refined, higher grade, purity brighter than white, multiple simultaneous partners fused into one explosive orgasmic tide, tie off arm and shoot naked women like speedball; poetry sickens, art of prima donnas soaking faces in egg-milk until they resemble pot pie, calling it courage, squeamish civility of conformity, gulag of cutesy, give me entrails that I may wrap myself in shawl of bowel, liver, blood, balls, god's reeking mansion sweeping me into Pan's hermaphroditic room, transcendence, foetal, magnificent; the coitus interruptus of gustatory thrill, table centerpiece, I want mouth bomb created by exquisite explosives assembled in Lucifer's smoldering kitchen, mangoes blowing tops off heads, kumquats previously orbiting Mars, aperitif blanketed with Jesus's jism, a candle snuffer suffocates ambition's flame flickering for god's nonexistent air, smoke encased brittle black wick, daddy cannot nor holy ghost escape, therefore, washing to shore, hair plastered, legs sucked back, flat as flounder, raging incrementally less, I resign, like my parents and theirs before them, occasionally flicking stinger or flare, fantasizing fullness, overplus, satiation, fat, conditions necessitated by central control and its brick-like gray impenetrable compaction.

210

Suicide being wisdom's pinnacle, I offer my neck to radial saw, a swift and sudden beatitude, sanctifying and canonizing this inchoate saint, blade splatters flesh but not soul reserved for servitude to the King, already parting from putrid and hideous robe I grow luminescent, swimming upward through lice and barracuda, past sabbaths and anxieties like flashlight beam sweeping cove, abandoning the flesh-wrapped ladder of relationship and multiplication, promotion and inflation of the grotesquerie of board meeting table and podium stand, beyond demand of physical perfection with vanity's opening thighs minting gladiators like furnaces, squat and beastly, the incomparable violence of sumptuous suicide, bathwater blessed with blood, brain-splattered bed, asphyxiated capillaries, grisly, yet transcendent, unassailable by the cannibal masses clotted in stadiums and lecture halls, suicide holy, the smallest bit of which, like the Eucharist, transfigures sinners into asphodels, I ram neck into circular blade in workshop witnessed by nails and sawdust piles, at this instant—now—become super-beautiful: evanescent, ever-present, invisible, calm, photons and phosphorescence, wisdom's culmination; mourners of the dead, mourn thyself.

One cannot help but exclaim "what an adorable little Shikse!" Jewish men worship blonde sharp-nosed Christian women, fuck blind their insatiable occipital lust with black hair-whorls, reviling atavism of Jewish flesh, repugnancy of mother-incest and the terror of Israel, consider Kelsey's life-companion: erotic platinum kitten, lubricants oozing, game for anything and doubtless spontaneous, curled over cock like a come-machine, lips pink and parted, enamored of Clinique and Este Lauder, a behind-the-eyes devil releasing from ancient coffins demons and diablos, ramifications and commandments be damned, one cannot help but exclaim "how unbelievably devastating," upon entering the Catholic babe, uncrucified, unstigmatized, drooling and alive, Christ some dusty lunatic delivered into bastardy on a reptile-scorpion floor through loins of the delusional adulteress, oh well, and there it is, the second coming referring more to nastiness than millenniums, the fucked-up guilt-smashed Semite full of black menstrual blood and feminine napkin horror seeking the cleanser of Christian blondes, pale nipples and cloud-light pubic hair, shama yisrael adonoi elohenu adonoi, ditto certain exotic products—Ferrari, Breguet–blonde goddesses, ooh la-la, mothers disgusted them into self-loathing escapees-through-fractures where Jesus's ecstasies free them from horrific afflictions.

212

Humans love to fuck, they ache, weep, suffer, scream, shoot down causeways in shitty cars to assignations, half-dressed, tight, high, or rich, crooning to CD, flicking ashes or tic-tac boxes, racing east-west, north-south, crisscrossing like a disturbed child's chalkboard scrawl, love genitals, pubic bush, removal of pants, unhook, unzip, scream of silk on thigh, toes in ecstasy, the naughtiness, nastiness, anal, vaginal, blow jobs, 69, bondage, fantasy games, adultery, infidelity, and pseudo masochism, haunches, dog style, masked, costumed, the deprived, ugly, lonely, terrified crumble in mascara, abandoned in bistros or stood up, diddle themselves, in mid-fifties commit suicide or binge to oblivion, while the lucky ply with viagra and gyrate to ninety their hideous wrinkled hag as if she were paradise, people die to fornicate, aromas relinquished in airport embraces, closed eyes savoring the soon-to-be snapped by cold distances, poignancies of goodbye mitigated by amazing conquests, broad experienced girths rubbing perfectly, tight orgasmic women cracking hearts like walnuts, motels blessed beyond Bethlehem, marijuana, cocaine, booze-enhanced curdling, mom and dad images repulse daughter but they get it extra-maritally and from each other, arrogant youth has no conception of middle age fucking, old shriveled dicks stiffening granite hard and twice delivered cunts gripping like soft fists absolving fogies like epson salts, and so it goes, lit grid, highway system, fortresses, facades, Chevrolets, elevators, offices, foyers, hallways, stomachs, lungs, intestines, bladders contributing to hot functioning triangulations and gravities, heads bobbing like cabbages or kelp bulbs in a boiling sea, scanning the waves for devastation.

213

I commit the virtue of lying, I righteously exploit gullibility, I disseminate falsity about accomplishments, assert I survived parotidectomy, that my parents terrorized, that I am squeamish over blood, I insist roadkill instructs and excrement enthralls, I employ electronics to mislead, computers facilitate aggrandizement, I decry atheism, I consign lust to unctuousness and heretics to sewerpit, lying castrates the monster and eliminates clutter in vistas—people genuflect to me, softened before the conquering lie, I defeated OCD with Herculean tenacity, what could be more utilitarian than the bald faced lie in the milieu of mediocrity, don't shout turpitude, I shall never inherit, and am therefore deprived, unstable momentarily, I stand ascendant on stilts of deception, like the Pope and politicians, like CEOs and the professorate, see pterodactyl me unfold wings above the hammering sea, the pathetic masses of integrity—children and the fleshy puppets of probity pathetically squirming for respect among their coterie, while the ingenuous, the uncynical, the selfless progeny of honor ski radiantly to glory on the groomed slopes of mendacity.

214

Look, man, what do you want, I'm no god, you expect halcyon meditations and you get self-loathing crap, shitty psychodrama scribbled by a parent-loathing masochist, monomaniacally spewing self-aggrandizing hate, if you'd rather, to get your money's worth, then I love the fucking tree in its seasonal manifestations outside my window where I fling soulful epiphanous luminosities such as "break into blossom" optimism, there, happy? go have a pizza and Diet Coke, swallow a Nikon and ascend to the pinnacle, meanwhile I fantasize stealing into my childhood home in early dawn, the monsters asleep on respective planks, and committing double homicide, first Popsy in hospital PJs, sour smelling with chamber pot, lipless mouth dribbling reek, by a single gunblast to head waking Mother in her chiffon nightie who will momentarily thrill that I have come to ravage her until she notices my frozen face and weapon dangling lethal revenge, let the neighbor discover—who hasn't seen them for weeks—the grizzly final serenity of two grotesque adversaries married sixty years too long, I'll confess and get capital punishment, but this is fantasy and I love that goddamn spruce and wish you an edifying reading experience, I'm going now, I have to pee and meet myself somewhere in this catastrophe of a world for soup and sugar, one last thing: young I electrified toads on lawn mower spark plugs, laughing at their squirm and bubbling emissions, I'm good at this sort of thing and know exactly what I'm doing.

215

"Shove it up your ass," I like to say, "Oh, shove it up your ass," or "shove it up your goddamn ass, fucking jerk," or "why don't you go shove it up your ass," "up yours," or "cram it up your butt," "stuff it up your butt," "fuck off, shove it up your ass," "asshole," "fucker," "bastard," "big shot," "get out my face," or conversely, "jump up my ass," "butthole," "shove it up your ass," "fuck you, up your ass, assbutt," "you big fucking ass," "go fuck yourself," "shove it up your goddamn fucking piece of shit ass," I shoot him the finger, "fuck you," "no, fuck you, no, fuck you," "prick," "piece of garbage," "fuckbutt," "trash," "blow it out your ass," "assbreath," "go blow it out," "why don't you blow it out your piece of crap ass," "filthy piece of shit," "shithead," "shove it up your ass," sounds like business, like beer and business, "sheister," I love the phrase, "fuck off," "bite my butt," "eat yourself," "eat my dick," "take a flying leap," "shove it up your ass," "shove up ass," "dickwad," "skank," "sewer rat," "up the ass, blowhard," "turd," I swing round, a look of indignation, incredulity, "shove it up your ass," and quit the room, "lunatic," "fuck yourself in the butt," "eat shit," "go to hell, do not pass go, insert in ass," I'm crippled with it, liberated, empowered, glutted to gills, rich in blood, egg and egg sac, fertile, alive, birthgiving, "shove it up your ass," "cram it," genius, defender of the cause, champion, hero, take no prisoners, lion, a public storm of beauty and incomparable elegance.

216

Once again I praise devouring stomach, elimination cycle, throat
and enzyme, slaughter and frenzy, ribs, potatoes, bacon, toast, I
marvel efficiency, tearing, grinding, pushing through slippery
expandable tubes, peristalsis, sphincter, ravages and renewals,
poultry, plants, fish hatcheries, mastication, swallowing, proces-
sing, eliminating, working and money-making, clashing cutlery,
jaw hinges and reproduction, suckling baby cooing and raging—
Napoleon in Huggies—I continue the rhapsody of animate life-
form, beautiful eater lashed by gut to conference call, committee
room, cashwrap, power tool, the thunderous growl shifting and
gnashing, collapsing the acid-spasming vat, god's beautiful bag,
Rachmaninoff, Mozart, Bach, Michelangelo, I love the inevi-
table, working to satiate, satiating to work, the interminable cycle,
mouths that philosophize, pontificate, preach, parted for pasta,
excellent tongues wine stained, sophisticated lips greasy with
fat, magician's wire hoop and oval of satisfaction, once again
encomium of viscera, pliable stout bitter mean propelling to
scraps on killing floor, snout, hoof, ear, beak, skyscraper, brok-
erage, antique shop, firm, management of malnourished children
and adults, furnace outraged, furiously roaring, and there will
be boots and uniforms, power suits and heels, lubricants and
pistons, dismissals and citations, suicide on the trashy river bank.

217

Dogs don't seem to comprehend cruelty, when abused return like fly-back ball whining camaraderie, ignorant, burn with cigarette and crawl back to couch nosing affection, take black lab, bone-headed loyalist, mimics, returns, sits, wags, withstands shouts, kicks, jabs, door slams, slavishly lopes back, no concept of perturb, sturdy tail convulsing, believes adored, expects reassurance, lunatic, soldier, patriot, numbskull, walk? dinner? kindness? affection? would spurt last ounce for master, altruist, blindmind, here shithead, here fuckface, here bananabrain and he jumps exuberantly, companion, protectorate, alert for strangers, knee high lookout, doesn't comprehend kick, cuff and keeps protecting, biscuit? bone? fetch? stick river-thrown, drop at feet, stick river-thrown, drop at feet, indispensable, essential, lobotomized slave, one-dimensional, lumbering chub bucket solid as table, one laughs, were he but soldier with artillery, taking incoming, blowing apart, singing America, France, or Herzegovina, singing and dive bombing, were he but troop, warrior, foot soldier, army, incinerated, shocked, drilled, tortured, sodomized, blown apart, drowned, still fighting, fighting, brisket and loin, chanting anthem, dumb reflex, frat boy or footballer, I slap and after momentary wince he sidles, automation, underfed he heralds, soul-eyed, adoring, scarfs dinner like fresh kill, guards bed, shits outside, polite and palatable, revoltless still as I hammer nail through forehead into the center of his brain.

218

Because I love I invent love, nobody has loved before and none will love after, my ecstasy unique in annals of happiness, I caress my lover who glows beyond brilliance, I stroke, she thickens with readiness, we warble and kiss knowing none could comprehend such deliciousness, males have never experienced this stiffness nor women such vaginal flood, ignorant slurpers and asinine fools dumb to true penetration and fusions of air through orgasmic lungs, reduced to imagine thrust and moan, to conceive in the soul such masterful seeds only god can appreciate, I stand alone, the greatest inventor, luminous beyond luminosity, incomparable, when I die love's fire shall perish leaving behind the cold sourceless socket.

219

I dislike establishment poets, rarely read them, they numb, apply prodigious intellect upon trivia—potpourri, shirt, cow, June first—apparently adore themselves for never confess homicide, grandiosity, never slash off tongue and stuff it up ass, one would think they levitated, they gag, insipid, self-aggrandizing bores, radical conservatives to fear and avoid, line 10 nod, line 20 slide off chair streaking spit, give me cynic, addict, narcissist, imp, self-immolator, the creep over this civility, there's one now: professor, gourmand, flower gardener, cape, water-colorist immersed in foliage, frauds to a T, experiencing them is experiencing mummies pushing blood, my poet laureates focusing everywhere but in, stone fence, barn owl, show host in mirrors, I destroyed my son, seduced heartlessly, I'm a cold hostile bum, I lick filth off concrete and gnaw love's bones, my thigh's an encyclopedia of delectable hell, my guts pass through god's anus.

220

Numerous possibilities present on techniques of murder, bullet to head, heart, or chord, the well many-thrust blade, bashed skull, suffocation, immolation, drowning, poison, heroin, snake, shoving off cliff, strangulation, industrial machinery, vehicular, hanging, cult sacrifice, one needs stop a vital function, blood flow or breath, severing trachea or excavating wrist, war a separate issue involving white phosphorous, agent orange, napalm, torture, but we must bracket our subject round peacetime destruction, psychopath, cuckold, vengeful worker, rapist, pederast, hit man, paranoid schizophrenic, the dispassionate random attack, one practices on animals, ice pick through dog-chest, cat matter on fireplace tool, perfecting accuracy of thrust or swing, fencing champ, the confidence building measure of tossing up parakeet and smashing with bat, female-the-weaker may destroy in sleep male-the-stronger, this fair and requiring no practice on lorikeet, the chemist or well-informed can slip mickey, the anesthesiologist fornicates with lethal weapons, as does surgeon, one could force alcohol into victim until nervous system ruptures, exotically speaking, removing one's heart in satanic ritual, cannibalism, Jack Ripper slitting, burying alive, an inexhaustible list worthy an encyclopedist, what one could do, for instance, with glass and rage, with insignificance, with festering littleness, I'm off in search of rashers and eggs and leave you with this hideous quivering abandoned neonate.

221

Insignificant cretin, cipher, faintly malodorous, breath
and clothing, perfume of pillowcase, news-dabbler
reeking homicide, tax hike, tooth-rotting politics, pulp
of body, deadwood of leg, embalming fluid disk jockey, coffin vinyl seat, suddenly bang! bang again!
artery gapes mouth, gut craves, God, madness, imperative, power, ecstasy, fist, you want It, continuously, uncontrollably, obsessed by light, tormented by
night, phone number, email, locked on rail, rice
thick delusions, glutenous carbs stuffing mind, iron
galvanizes, irreplaceable solid iron, brain racing
past irrelevancies, mundanities to the monster,
the oblivion, head gears mashing out omnipotence,
imperturbability, superman among lunatics, It
wraps fingers into clavicle, rips you through grate,
It grinds and whips, pumps against living flesh,
gouges out dominance, capacity, It's nudity among
plums where you were once droll factotum, hypocrite, glob of spit stuck to fantasy going nowhere.

222

Let us pray, then, for everybody needs prayer, let us bow heads and pray that fornication striketh us full blow in head, that fornication arrive in sweat and foul breath, lubricants and testicle wallop for thou art desperate in life's desertification, let thy face fall in palms and weep for cunt and sweet male meat stiff and upthrust to hit thy swollen clit, glossolalia for absolution, water thy cars, soap thy cacti, break and beseech for carnal dip, add money, let us pray that cash flow from clientele to thee, inexhaustible rivers of coin from magi's sleeve into thy registers, hallelujah, petition almighty on scraped knees for turkey, stuffing, for petrol, for prescription, for art supply, flagellate, thrash, cut thy thigh in Jesus-cut and shake out wine that Bowdoin shall accept daughter of loin and son of seed, and that coke shall not devour brain nor eat soul, masturbate and if man with match torch thy seed and if woman with file scrape thy cunt opening door for Satan to leave that thy shall receive absolution, pray then for Godliness, immortality, incorruptibility in a sour world replete of losers, idiots, fatsos, cripples, retards, fools, pray for frog-leaps over imperfection, for favoritism and indemnity, for in effect, mass annihilation of rivals that they shall usurp not glory nor everyday and consumable spoils in a constantly regenerating bowl, and splice thy serpent tongue in reverse oh thou believer that thy may dissemble undetected, that spit shall look as pearls, that the blind, dull, and mute shall perceive as gospel calumny from thy sly and give over offerings such crystal or silver pitcher, praise God the Intercessor, and finally, finally smear swath of blood from pricked pointer finger of image of Ghost that thy be white, dominant, and indestructible, slaveholder and not slave in this enslaving planet of the heretical, impure, and heathenistic, pray then thyself hard into luminosity.

223

I am in love with my daughter, she loves me, and we have husband-wife sexual relations, how gratifying to spawn from one's seed one's mate, to perfect her, she worships and obeys and we sleep side by side, often intertwined, I diapered and washed her, caressed babyflesh, blubbered her tummy, sang to her before slumber, I taught her correctitude of fondle, the masculine lap, the small tight buttocks, inevitability of the taboo kiss, the gradual familiarity with going deep, one need not venture to cliched Appalachia to find such fusion, one need only know narcissists and their children: bone structure, hands, expression, temperament, a goddess stands naked before me, untarnished, smooth, fingernails virgin-nude and graced with half moons, I suck them like crawfish until meat flows salty sweet, she takes me in her mouth unabashedly on knees like supplicant, fully realized virtuosos in flagrant disavowal of biblical law, we plan to conceive numerous offspring some of which will ratify our thrilling directive at risk of dubious eternal damnation and bring forth a nation of gods—purified, awe-inspiring, selected creatures with one blood-dark name plowing through a tainted world.

224

Pumping, I slam into a wall busting cartilage, pivot on piston thighs slam into another, swivel, dash, smash against buttress, crumpled rise, turn and full-blast sprint into another, weary, weakened continue bashing blunt thuds, I am alone, torn clothes, sober, bashing air from lungs, spurting blood, bouncing off like swinging cow, I crawl up legs, limp into and slide down wall, incapacitated, I want more force, but pulpy drag into something indifferent and steep, I push, butt, ram, broken teeth, blurred vision but fantasize thrust, throb, anger, rage, cinder block, granite, crave more God, hardened sexlessness, lock resolute military jaw but sink flaccid in my own red pudding, condemned and illuminated.

225

I go searching for Satan. I do not find Satan in human fecal matter. I wade sewers: nothing. I examine fired pistol muzzle, again nothing. I lick urinals, nada. Churches are devoid. Human sweat, zip. Male ejaculate, ditto. I believe in my brilliance when I stick head in vagina: tightening noose. Dust and filth behind bureaus. Surely, I reason, Satan permeates war: brains, intestines, etcetera. Rapist does not explode Satan into victim. I plunge in dump, haunt board room, spy on adultery, nothing, nothing. Brainstorm, I crawl inside a nuclear mushroom: clean, pure scientific genius. I slit open water moccasin, the Pope spills out. Inside the manger centipedes, roaches. Bewildered I analyze baby, eyes, folds, fragrance, toes, tooshie, scrotum: zero. Something inexplicable overwhelms, captures, sucks me through portals and doorways into a fire-lit, comforting, familiar room.

226

Everything misses the point which is always elsewhere, unattainable, not achieved sensually, point needle tip tiny, love is not the point, nor copulation nor baby blues, I think point does not reside in river or tree, I doubt will greet it in fiction, Trevi Fountain will not bathe it, does it lurk in vehicular mutilation, is not, I suspect, death, repels the identifying finger, it slips away in dark or light, I thought I glimpsed it knifing through mirror but could reach no verification, once I slammed my jar over nothing, perhaps point resides in sunken ship, I frisk my and lover's pockets I but come up zip, inside grand complication watch? microscope? brain CAT scan, it is not at cola, athletic club, zoo, does it appear on tab of acid, ride coat of squirrel? should focus on what haven't searched: weightlessness, arctic floe, the microsecond atom spits, millions watch The Pope in clean white surplice might it be? nah, impossible, well, excuse me, time for Internet pornography.

227

I'm not sure, I have no idea, how do you expect me, evidence
eludes, what magical powers you ascribe, it's a laugh, you
think I possess crystalizations, I have nothing to add, mystifi-
cation, bewildered stares, I dunno, shrugged shoulders, I sur-
render, I wander moronically, abstractedly grinning, knap-
sack full of pens, an impenetrable brain cloud, stubbly, bag-
gy, you expect me—fat-fingered lunatic in tattered—to know,
I'm not prophet nor tabulator, your questions tumble down
hole, numbers cascading toward an inconceivable sum, cor-
ner economist, actuary, full professor, synthesizing genius,
I am bone-headed as a cur, do you think me calculator, dead-
eyed, sober, announcing the coefficient, I am explorer jab-
bing flags in dung, spitting and sopping, oblivious, bleary-
minded, complications stymie, what am I, who you, what
is this, I dream patches, you want totalities, find wonder-
man who knows hammers, that's him with the coldeye, I be-
queath you my wife, my photographs, my yo-yo collection,
my library of prima donnas, I have done these things: slit
a pig's bladder, eaten a pound of fingernails, swallowed
a sewing needle, crucified a frog, but have never made
one decision regarding anything crucial which mattered.

228

Starvation terrifies so I stuff, emptiness eviscerates so I fuck, intimacy horrifies so I clamp shut, I despise yammer and so retract, failure comforts so I fail, I abhor cities so I swing fists madly, gasoline suffocates so I cough clots, tedium asphyxiates so I hunt the emerald egg, flesh is dunder so I pin down, dissect woman, random violence stultifies so I stage suicide, books are wedding gowns on which I spill hot mayonnaise, books oppress so drip salsa, god damned matrimony so I mail myself in Tony Bahama to Maribu or Clobberdam, children slice eyes so I slide down a gleaming blade, walls are houses I punch holes in, daddy operates on my spleen like Mengele, mother freezes, falls off shaft like a genital wart, insomnia electrocutes so I wrap an inner tube about my head, obesity horrifies so I smash a banana against clenched teeth, resembles the exploded cigar, dogs infuriate so I lash them to rotating wheel and throw biscuits at their skulls, friendships epitomize hypocrisy so I stitch a medal through one's chest and tie it off at neck, love brutalizes so I love indiscriminately, like a kid in a sand lot shooting grackles and laughing wildly.

229

Dear god, give me love, give me money, give me ecstasy, destroy nobody dear to me, zap me famous, keep me disease free, vanquish rivals, help son beat addiction, restore me to athletic capability, spread before me horizons and free will, eliminate OCD, strike my lawn green, dear God, a little something for ennui, the chasm, the appetite, dear Ghost, kick divinity or marzipan onto this casket that I may rise and walk like entrepreneur with destination, transform me hard and big for I am neither, nor of girth, give me girth, oh God of Hosts, clog the channels of bicker between intimate and me, plug them ego-free that peace prevail within our truce, introduce reason to our communication, drops from Euphrates, perhaps, too, time to suck my progenitors to your illimitable womb, piles of money for Mom to stuff in heaven's box, fill his cancer with fatality that it may sweep Daddy unto you where businessmen succeed like cotton candy, dance him home with a kiss from his bride and appreciative kids, make me brilliant and unimpeachable with an oft-visited shrine before my acolytes, make me godlike but a mere lacolith, naturally, beside mountainous You, bless my wife with that extraterrestrial grace reserved for cliff dwellers and ferryboat masters, oh Sweet Divine, Healer of Wounds, brace my nostrils with crystalline air, cold and exhilarating, that I may pump a billion asters into the atmosphere, You make such slaves of beautiful feet.

230

Finally, one comes to nothing. One's life comes to nothing. One's love comes to nothing. One's work comes to nothing. One's world comes to nothing. One has amounted to nothing. One looks about: scissors, nail file, loose leaf paper. One counts to five, then ten, then fifteen. One does not even have the energy to hate one's self. One's femur stretches horizontally with vertebra supported by chair. Finally, one understands. The rendezvous. The assignations. The vibrating steering wheel. The momentary triumphs. The genitals and ownership. The cooing and braggadocio. Someone emptied the drier of one's breast. The gaping hole yawns for clothes. Lips close round tine of tuna. One acknowledges but does not adore one's children. One's daughter has toes and brain but does not inspire empathy. Like shoe leather upon concrete. Finally, one no longer cares about accusation of mirrors, bathroom scales, weigh and gaze, gaze and weigh. Alcoholism. Drug addiction. Food addiction. Promiscuity. Proceed and indulge. Slice your arm. Profanity: fuck. shit. cunt. shove it up your butt. Whore. Let fly the verbiage. Could the death chambers matter? The crematoriums? The slaughter? The sword wielders and spear hurlers? Give us another frankfurter and pray for a base hit. Finally, the trap door opens, the rope pays, the noose catches. Animals painted on a tin carousel blur before one's hidden eyes.

231

I'm not satiated, I want more, give me another, I'm empty, it was delicious but not sufficient, I need it again, I'm bereft without it, I know I just had it but it tumbled into a void, set me up, hit me again, I feel disappointed, pit sick, like nothing's arrived, pile this one, heaps and gobs, I'm sorrowful, crushed having just one, furious and stultified, my hand craves the source, the infinite source, dishing it up, I'm tainted, diseased, get away, I'm cruel, obese, my scream is my gut, my scream my flame, I eat you down to tallow and shriek more, more, build me decadence, a sky-high volcano of heart-palpitating stuff, pistachio green, strawberry pink, vanilla bean yellow and heap the goop, love me if you must with your temperate cup, I'll go till I erupt and erupting know bottomlessness, what fucked me as a child double fucked me as a man, blades at the bottom chop round and round, not unlike some others who unleash their own interminable howl deep as Ursa Major and high as Johnny Madness, sweetie pie, doll baby, construct me one more big as a bathtub with ladder and kick, and plant a flag at its peak, that I get so sick all that remains is the mattress and self-hatred.

232

I fasten with bolts iron casement round me, impenetrable, I step into iron legs, latch iron boots, I affix iron helmet over skull, finally clamping iron gloves, no shithead comic book hero annihilating villains for adolescents, I clunk through rooms loveless, half inch thick plate flattening intimacy like silly putty, I am machine, car smasher, crushing emotion like a junker, who could touch me, not nurturer, not child bearer, not executive, I sleep in full metal jacket, one wraps one's legs around a bank vault in liftless passion, there have been casualties, she wants to peel my armor like peach to sting me with love, but opts for lead plum, who understood the cost of perfection, so many soldiers marrying mud, I eat through a blow-torched square, wiping sharp edge with cloth napkin, see through slits, shit through a deadlocked door, "monster," she screams, "freak," bathed in histrionics, weeping like a leaf, disillusioned, shocked, "I am so dumb," "idiot, idiot," "why didn't I listen," I register nothing, "psychopath," "misogynist," "egotist," she levels, again nothing, no one can enter this indestructible shield with warm pulsing care, all break like a bit, behind lids clamped tight pinpoint light flickers on brain's gray slate.

233

Dearest and most wonderful supreme progenitor as I twist outward into light, grant me a massive easily stiffened cock, creative superiority preferably in art, Crockett-like stature, wit, precision, amiability, that intangible pheromonic quality which nails skeptics, bestow me with constitutional vigor, an indefatigable musculature, lungs like Seabiscuit's, a gorgeous vascularity, dear most benevolent exalted, forge me with anvil and sparks a lesser god, a prince whose hips spark like heaven, I am now but conical, flaccid, filth-streaked, pinched and puny, sliding toward finitude, make me phenom, specimen extraordinaire, brilliant at Borsendorfer and Slazanger, with Mediterranean skin and South Pacific eyes, Mother shall be beatified and Daddy enshrined as extraterrestrial vehicles chosen to beget this monumental child, what a little chigger I am now, soft-skulled suckler, boneless and gummy, jolt me with testosterone, testarossa, sequoia sap that I may outstrip the asinine pack of feeders and writhers; lo, it is fabulous, bursting out the fold, stung and stinging, The Astringency, The Ascension, ladies, gents, bow before your virtuoso with quivering lips, clamped navel, suctioned nose, hung upside down by feet and slapped, more powerful in mere arrival than the collective human horde.

234

Quickens the heart when son bashes dad, one loves family savagery, broken knuckles, bruised ribs, wife in the mix, punched, shoved, who doesn't love it when consanguineous blood flies from mouth, animal wail winched from gut, profanities blunt and truncated, torsos in pugilistic thrust, ox-hided, solid, wild-brained, how we love sacred desecration, the broken taboo of son popping dad, dad's retaliation, mother sucked into the muck, machine going at itself, the thrill of choked trachea, clawed flesh, inheritances, jealousy, primordial wounds, snapped bitterness, fuck you, piece of shit, ungrateful monster, hurling the cur, what more gratifying than brother-sister-father collision among pork chop and streak fry, related spermatozoa shouting and punching, don't pretend appall at this orchestra seat to dramatis personae, the Giavongelos, the Nowickis, and you at thrall, Mr. Verana in temporary insanity blows away Larry, daughter's bullet severs father's small, pageantry greater than football heroics, pushing seat belt restrained toddlers through lake slush, incidents in the night, and we electrically gleeful like switch thrown klieg lights, involuntarily stiffened, yolk broken across the sky, viscous red unfertilized egg stubborn and indifferent, overflowing fissures and cracks, dyspeptically eddying and snagging outward, illuminating the uncontrollable appetite.

235

Two steel balls attempt to kiss, "kiss!" commands God, but spheroids mechanically bang against each other, "kiss!" barks God and slashes mouths with brilliant sword, mouths meet, slashes hinges, mouths open and clank, God with fiery awl punches in eyes, mouths with a bang of interest crawl, God miscalculates and sticks legs on foreheads, then angrily scrapes away mouths, eyes, and legs, spheres clink together, roll round each other searching, stop and wonder, other projects have long since distracted God, when last seen our prototypes lay in bed together weary, featureless, and without interest.

236

I have nothing to say, pithy thoughts elude, something or other, some day, perhaps tomorrow, mind blank, I roam it, echoing warehouse, swept, locked, for rent, I meditate closed eyes, stare intently at something, but nothing appears, I try wrenching a topic of importance, something urgent like extermination or glut but mind rejects inauthenticities, I am space devoid, nerves to brain bunched and cut, the illimitable blank, even the perception of blank ungraspable, nor can I attempt the academic exercise of poetic bloat as even this inanity darts like minnow, so I give you abyss, rimlessness, I am not therefore this or that, I do not feel therefore X or Y, this symbolizes the death of nothing nor a birth, nor can it be tectonic for you, something has cut receiver from transmitter giving us an intermission from data, a spell or cavern of fabulous gas, that formless primordial cloud of nothingness underlying the transmission of vision.

237

Infant smashes against wall, who hurled him, what happened, rage-smash-death, he wouldn't stop, it's monstrous, someone delivered, someone fathered, someone purchased pablum, babies die, like this, without bleeding, internal contusions, flash, white rage, frustrated, tattered, alone, worn thin, arcing motion, neck snaps, thud, broken sack, mother appears, unflapped husband sits on couch, hands folded, explanation, justification, cliches "snapped," "can get through this," "love you, baby," "all I've got," candid discussion, sex, sheet covers baby, all quiet, apartment, cranium, universe, what does one do with a dead baby, disposal not an issue, it's prying neighbors, family, report an intruder, a murder, muddy the evidence, were asleep, didn't hear, apoplexy, shock, what manner of psychopath, not a clue, cops could never prove, stove head, sever member, remove fingers, random cult sacrifice, gang initiation, Satanism, I'm not like that, would never, blow over, com'on sugar plum, don't let destroy, survive, eating us alive, slaves, I cracked, I hated, grotesque devastating monster, sooner or, anyway, later, get the saw, the newspaper, let's get on with it.

238

Nihilist, at age sixty I start smoking and tippling, from lifetime sobriety and righteous denunciations I entice vice, with Winston dangling, I greet prostitute and sodomize, I lie, devour tortes, ignore athletic sanctuary, refuse colonoscopy, struck match is god, vodka expiation, I savor onion blossom and sticking prick in multiple mouths, until now pasta represented evil and the elliptical trainer immortality, fuck elliptical trainer, fuck dumbbells, fuck gravitron, light up and clink the highball glass, I anticipate peeing on a naked woman and oblivion-fornication, I awake at noon to a disheveled room and the goddamn house needs stain, goddamn house with its goddamn neighbors, I break my comb, violence repulses but what about the dominatrix, me as whipped ridden donkey, I jack off like a maniac regardless the judgmental ghosts, and imagine fourteen old year flesh, conquering virgin territory, I admit to jealousy, envy, hatred, sloth, homicidal fantasies, feelings of worthlessness and grandiosity, I admit atheism, a tinge of racism, I admit self-loathing and annihilating lust for adolescents, I clutter ash trays at phone sex and nauseate my aging guts with Smirnoff's and wonder where to score cocaine, drugs my next Parthenon, ecstasy, meth, swept in rushing strophes of insanity, whom have I imagined I was these abstemious years, four square, lacquered oak, Prometheus? Superman? Maserati? I have no meta-ontology, erosion of face, mouth-cracks, time for monkeys, rats, leeches, crabs, debauched, sleepless, suicidal, murderous crackling tip of fire and the splitting and ramming of genitals in boozy unselfconscious empurpled gluttony.

239

Go ahead, steal behind, split my skull with an axe, roar
cathartically, exorcized, examine your hands, yes, they,
papery but utilitarian when the moment arrived, animal
versus animal, not homicide but survival, axe, skull,
means, will, a reasonable combination under circum-
stance: anger compressed to critical pitch vibrating to
exactitude, perfectionism ruins, in despairing position
facing window I shall avert, splatter brains against chair,
I have bequeathed you all and prefer extinction, you
not physically strong but the accumulated momentum
of swung steel will prevail, finally the cessation of
my maladies, paranoia, acrimony, grandiosity, pride,
the predilection to interrupt, will run like cracked egg,
basement contains the implement, extract it like a
nugget, steal upstairs, enter my study in which you
know back faces door—I will intuit your presence
but not stir—and stove in my skull, plead self-defense
which marriage imposes with its dual pathologies
spit together, dust off hands, exhale, nap, arise from
the nightmare of magnification, tonight, in chair, fac-
ing my monitor, head in hands in attitude of despair,
eyes pressed shut by another crisis, neck exposed, I
await with anticipation the culminative shave releas-
ing us from the pestilential crustacean of bitterness,
I do not wish to survive the writing of this poem.

240

Men desire beautiful women, movie stars in slippered feet, luminescent hair, hands designed to make men come, women who mimic ripening virgins with mischievous smiles, softened faces tilted upward with moisturized lips, reject obesity, disability, require apricot genitals molded in fawns whose breath smells lavender, mature psychiatrists prefer teens who inspire suicide, men feign love for adult but shatter them to plate glass shards—feet, breasts, cunt, knees— men love, as well, Piaget, Aston Martin, Ascot Chang, but would trash it all for a naked girl with huge aureolas, goddess worming through apple slays man who resents their wives' cotton bloomers and craggy toes, self-pitying dreamers turning to porn or Hollywood classics. not the Semite but the platinum Baptist fantasized in Dallas or Tuscaloosa, pure as ermine sucking him off or locking feet round his globe, that is that, clapper strikes iron, the good stuff, the strut and immortality, the worshiped girls, too, slither through desperate fingers, the seductive pose, the raging fire raging inside brain's permiscuous tumor, Zachery conquered one, a Rita Hayworth, a Marilyn Monroe, until jealous apoplexy at discovering infidelity, and until, further, in some stinking indeterminate men's room it all became an asinine delusion.

241

A yellow jacket stings her eye, another behind ear, another
peach of cheek, another neck, several rapidly lips, lips, lips,
sting between shielding fingers, arms and silk, a pummeling
deafening nightmare swarm, she dashes pursued by a solid
beast with swiping limb, on knees collapses like a broken
mule, then topples while stings persist, the writhe, the injection, the stinger-kiss, swollen, welted, penalized, what
her crime? thrummed aster? shaken tree? raked under sacred eaves, the unintended misstep calls down hell, the chaffed
ego and retaliation, the insulted hive avenged and satisfied, thoraxes catharticized, while she dry heaves, cowers
behind bed, fantasizes grating herself gone, sanding herself
indistinguishable—pine ball or lathed lamp—head a pumpkin,
shoulders oatmeal, he retracts, whip coiled on nail, tongue
recalled to scarlet cove, she contemplates his impressive
accuracy, his fists stingingly fast, a darkling blur, she deserves this castigating mist, slur, attack on stupidity, idiot,
cracked doll, slut, fool, these sadistic soldiers returned
to alveoli, cruel, prime me to intolerance, outlash, jealousy,
righteousness, and sudden demonstrations of furious love.

242

I consume Internet porn for inspiration, being alone I need visual stimulation, for man in woman's a lovely place, I thrill at woman prying lips, intently watch cock within, swollen labia delivering bliss, nothing's more magnificent, surely heaven consists of eternal fucking, to hell with casinos, what matters beyond lovers giving, flooding the miles of flesh with pleasure by burying six inches in another, I pretend she's sucking and that I am throwing, and I masturbate—human demands catharsis, completion, suicide, the kill, stabbing the sun, squiggly leaping strings of semen—proud of my erection and pumping onanistic fist as she prides vagina wet enough to crucify shaft with divine friction, breasts swinging on clavicle chest, man requires ownership of breasts, brands them with fiery come, stars shotgunned upon sky, to hell with gyres and horizon's anesthesiologist, sexual frustration drove them to sublimate, naked toes exterminate madness, obliterating fascism arrives the neck, goose flesh ass ends battle, when my wife returns I will push my cock between her lips, finger her, and muttering the senseless desperation, fuck her deeply, trying to die we live.

243

I hold the keyboard upside down, I type with teeth, I type behind back, I douse it with lighter fluid, flip on match, smash it against the monitor, I masturbate with pieces dangling from wires, they bang like wind chimes, I leap from chair to desk to floor flipping mop of hair, shouting, tossing undershirt into air, I smash a window pane with printer which tumbles two stories, I am hopped up, emaciated, sexy, masculine, boa-wrapped in leather hat and bangling chains, I write man goddamn fuck baby all right let it rain, I write all night baby baby get it on chicken pot pie, I write tear it down cut it up bash it strip it off, I snap my head forward, back, yeah yeah yeah yeah, orgasm, paroxysm, I crash into wall, spin, crash into another, I write screw war screw consumerism screw Judeo-Christian deity screw republicans screw conformity screw the whole fucking post industrial sewer, pray for an unstoppable comet, I suck smoke, type Nixon Hitler Exxon Haliburton Lockheed Martin nationalism and football, nihilism I shout, antiauthoritarianism, hedonism, fuuuuuuuuck it aaallll, writhe like lunatic in asylum, LSD, mescaline, peyote, tea, somersault and snake crawl on a slimy plywood plank, hey man, thank you, thank you all for coming, I wanna do one more called shot my parents dead ragtime blues, sadistic old man, avaricious mom, shoutin and lashin, baby baby baby, went me downtown, got myself gun, heyhey heyhey heyhay, stuck it under pillow for any rainy day, rainy day did come, stole in at midnight, blew them both away, hoho, hoho, hoho, blowed them both away, throw me into prison, lock me in the tank, two back-to-back life sentences 'cause I blew them both away.

244

I erect a shrine to my member: raw beets, cucumber, broccoli florets, GI Joe, baking powder submarine, beach rocks, glass shards, bow before it, moan, chant, hiss, twist, fling mustard, mount it like Magdalene, weeping Jesus, wrap green sushi grass round it, drape washrag over head, meditation room, no furniture, sitting pillow, miniature fountain, cock, penis, worship it, vespers and matins before this poppet, this love thresher, continue adding: plastic fish, needle, toothpick, spike heel, lipstick, heaping mountain honed to peak, national flag planted, om, aum, ah, hu time to add dead woman, smashed child, brown log, beautiful heap of cloaca, this shrine, add a slit pig and goat feces, I want, too, a holocaust of tumbled bodies, bones, skull holes, piled in pit, my centerpole ramrod hard, clouded in diesel fumes, this shall be God to whom every day I pray for pleasure, death, suffering, gluttony, happiness, grotesquerie, add a fat red suffocating koi.

245

The noblest act is the act of self-hatred, privately, hellishly, informing none, hating your lethargy, ineptitude, deterioration, dictatorialism, frigidity, catastrophic miscalculation, binging and deprivation, clumsiness, is spitting in your own face, internal castigator shouting idiot, loser, fucker, shit, cognizant of cowardice and the crippling consequences of destroying faith, immaterial the sin but crucial the self-flagellation in pestilential severity, split, double-spitted and automatically rejuvenating for deeper hate, here lies the secret to weightlessness, baths in Christ's punishing luminousity: dog jaws about one's spleen, battering your flesh, insomnial recriminations, this sacred psalm of self-abnegation eliminating any isotope of complacency, beauty, happiness, peace, unearthing the gangrenous truth of brutal narcissism, this our noblest act, continuously to irritate with self-manufactured acid any instinctual convalescence or spontaneous rejection of infection.

246

Words in manuscript conspire to murder me, one snatches
brick, another pipe, another jagged glass, they surround
tapping weapons to palms, what do you want? I ask, may I
assist? menacingly they glare, I'm innocent, I blurt, and
suddenly blows, I'm down, groaning, then deceased, slain
by words, these vicious fuckers, psychopaths, ignorant
sons of bitches drunk on power, unskilled at self-defense
I throw no punch, attempt civility, appeal to reason,
bastards calculated my demise, I die and resurrect in bleak
metropolis leaning against high-rise where a word gang
loiters, flicks, encircles, shoves, I smell marijuana, jabs,
punches, switchblades cut me like a slab, I spurt, buckle,
die, "narcissism," "genitals," "grandiosity," "repugnant,"
slay me in greygreen blur, again disbelieving, I applied
logic to homicide, violence solves nothing, I'm broke,
let's communicate, to which they spit, pummel face,
knock to gravel, again I resuscitate to roaring surf, littered dunes, bum, from which appears a mocking clot,
little leather-jacketed shits of words, "it," "cock," "lie,"
"impale," swarming, with midnight specials, straight
up moonlight, pop, pop, pop, and one blathers "pop,"
they collect and disappear like a winding scarf, saltwater laps as I die by hoodlum bursts, again, again repeatedly, I revive beside twisted oak, warehouse, grate,
Dairy Queen, Starbucks, packs mass, punch, bash,
slit, blast, strangle, taunt, enraged alienated euphemisms acting hot, performing the inevitable execution.

247

The whole thing goes kablooy, hypochondria torments sister; dementia creams Daddy; mortality frightens but cruelty out Mother's skin; forty years of tolerance collapse under Larry; BDD splinters me in circus mirrors; preemie lungs asphyxiate Kevin; Depakote sloshes Bradley's brain; Hep C like a rabbit nibbles cabbage of Allan's liver; genocides cook and serve severed leg; have another chilled eclair, sweaty chocolate, chewy shell; oh baby; testicles strike like factory workers, tongues fall mute; rocks clog urethra, plaque arteries; well, smasheroo; brisket, lamb, claw, stew slide off table into Magical Mystery Tour performed by nutcases at Unity Church; refugees land in black fog of dereliction and flies bite beautiful faces near McFadden's; Witcomb crawls into death's bomb shelter everything rips through: guilt, shame, dejection, despair, paralysis, rage.

248

I down bottles of Ipecac syrup and Ex-Lax bars; rage, depression, sadness, self-excoriation, dejection, despair flow out two holes, black-green rivers of farewell, fuck them, fuck them both, I'm organs in revolt, liquidating, vomiting, waves of bitterness flood over gums, anus releases dumps, purgatives my savior evacuating crimes of inadequacy, unexceptionalism, bile mixed with yolk bilges in chunks doubling me over, flesh bruise-gray, enviable the healthy in Christian forgiveness, tumble into them plush with love, nerves softly wrapped, shitting purges used Kotex while vomiting the foot, a double Vesuvius, leaning over bucket while squatting on throne, gagging and waves, alone, sphincter battered, out floods big nipples, red chasm, dead dog, xylophone chest, drum set, India Madras, up flows acrophobia, streptococcus, the boy scout sash, Mallomar cups, janitorial mop, the dictatorial buzz cut, father's rasped throat in pale wet tissue, through both orifices: cry baby, big shot, movie star, bum: every twist transformed into watery expurgation.

249

I masturbate myself bloody, not with lust but desperation, chafed circumcision smarts in head and heart like hammer-blows, I looked at porn, semen eaters, swollen labias, saw not love, only dust and prayer, old man now clinging to pulse with faded triumphs, grey dead triumphs smudged, time-eaten, great grandfather smiling in daguerreotype, and so over toilet groaning beat myself raw, hand blurry, hummingbird fast, and I come a white paste thimbleful, hard gobs, soft rocks, and scream for food, bed, death, horse, that is all, it's pork loin now and god with his collection of blunt instruments.

250

I love you is storm slammed through concave breast, is swollen ocean littered with flesh, is dotted outline where person stood, hot and sumptuous, is scattershot blown through cardboard box, tree pierced by stick of straw, he who discloses hooks a shark which tears off leg, I love you is climbing out a viper pit and plunging back in believing it fine, I love you, well, I love you is raw lambshank center bone-in bleeding on lap, he who inks these words inch-by-inch like molten lead seeping down nub betrays god, mother, self, cat, and stands upon a bomb like a cartoon dupe seconds before boom, frog dissecting self stern-to-stem bubbling from mouth formaldehyde spit, death, death, and death, I slice round head and remove skull top like casserole lid, air stings brain, flies appear, worms bury eggs in their earth, glutted, fat, soft as glue, "I," I say, "I," I stutter again, "I," I look into her face, "love you, have always, and will past claps of yesterday, unrestrainedly, retreatlessly without the back petal grin, against door grin," having thus spoken some twisted cable eye-screwed to my breast withstood an ice, nails, shale, fire, glass, and biological blast, I gleamed in morning light.

251

Addicted to Jesus, addicted to wine, addicted to sugar, addicted to sex, addicted to literature, addicted to film, addicted to Mexican food, addicted to motorcycles, addicted to shoes, addicted to speed, addicted to adulation, addicted to cats, addicted to travel, addicted to laughter, addicted to surgery ("they're going in"), addicted to war, addicted to babies, addicted to suffering, addicted to negativity, addicted to mountains, addicted to scuba, addicted to running, addicted to cleanliness, addicted to coffee, addicted to Coca Cola, addicted to contradiction, addicted to bird watching, addicted to nail polish, addicted to gambling, addicted to porn, addicted to Rachmaninoff, addicted to jazz, addicted to sports, addicted to sado-masochism, addicted to school, addicted to horses, addicted to talking, addicted to evacuation, addicted to sleeping pills, addicted to superiority, addicted to grotesquerie, addicted to nationalism, addicted to telephone, addicted to Internet dating, addicted to masturbation, addicted to power, addicted to scrupulosity, addicted to money, addicted to eating semen, addicted to dogs, addicted to helplessness, addicted to black, addicted to astrology, addicted to pilates, addicted to miniature objects, addicted to horology, addicted to facial hair, addicted to self, addicted to photography, addicted to jigsaw puzzles, addicted to appearances, addicted to banzai trees, addicted to selflessness, addicted to victimization, addicted to dental floss, addicted to the first and the last but not the middle, addicted to water purification, addicted to sky, addicted to mathematics, addicted to exotic fish, addicted to Friedrich Nietzsche, addicted to dictionaries, addicted to honesty, addicted to sharp pencils, addicted to primal rage, addicted to death and suicide, addicted to back scratchers, addicted to palm oil soap, addicted to vitamin C, addicted to cemeteries, addicted to mindful breathing, addicted to sharks, addicted to wounded sparrows, addicted to gargoyles, addicted to cowboy boots, addicted to cigarettes, addicted to religious iconography, addicted to violent weather, addicted to fire, addicted to dangerous people, addicted to punishment, addicted to adrenalin rushes, addicted to petty crime, addicted to environmentalism, addicted to angry excuses, addicted to sneaking in, addicted to vintage cars, addicted to vomiting, addicted to frigidity and inhibition, addicted to lemon twist, addicted to childbirth, addicted to Apaloosa horses, addicted to rocking chairs, addicted to dead seriousness, addicted to sin and absolution, addicted to confusion, addicted to apocalyptic thinking, addicted to perception one ruined one's child—that most of all—guilt, banishment, depression, self-nullification, addicted to preconsciousness's infinite ether.

252

I think of nobody but myself, nobody else exists, everyone reflects my image, everyone's moods subsidize my own, the world comes when I come and when I slice my thumb world bleeds, on beach I am God, book I am reading is superior, only I will die and my death denotes everything, when chemo wrenches you I suffer and require ministration, you receive my award and incur my indignity, I suffer my son's crack addiction and when he succumbs I will need attention, I milk my parents' unhappy union as a private holocaust, have seduced with it women and the mysterious irresistible alphabet, here a struggling innocence, there a delectable sin, never distant from moist panties, rushing dopamine, cradling hands, the sacrificial breast, when I am infirm and sputtering phlegm I roust lovers awake, when sickness wracks them I sprout ear plugs and blackout mask, god damn them, you do not exist beyond my relationship to time and space such as signpost or cairn, nor is your heart an exceptional instrument, I have euthanized a dog whose bark aggravated and dumped an imperfect wife for indeterminate alternatives, roaring nightmare, bullshit, horrorshow, everything stained by my vermillion soul like a sanitary napkin full of eggs and nitrogen, creation and myth, death and birthgiving, the fresh green algae-rich botany of myself washes over and oxygenates the starving universe.

253

I'm going to make you pity me, you're going to despise everything, every smile shall disgust, every lip smack, my timbre and wit, not one atom shall thrill, you will grunt repulsive, repugnant, pinch your nose, after I exit the car you will hiss like a punctured raft, my hands make you queasy, bowel habits flinch, you anticipate my absence and loathe my beliefs, when I snap down the menu you will stiffen with frigidity, you fantasize homicide or wish I would hemorrhage at gym, when I unclothe, revulsion, rotten fish, past seductions will nauseate: innocence, boyishness, meloncholy shall collide in you, I will make you pity enormously, from soul to flesh, I will suck scorn from your bugles, liquify guts and you shall pity with smirks and clucks, parodies and cacks, chalk screeches spine, a panoply, I coerce and you succumb, bruisy fugue, you shall embody familiarity's disdain, deepened as I touch my face, revolted by my smacking gums, I wish no sympathy, it is not compassion I desire for that would imply a brand of rot, it's pity, disgust, revulsion, yes, for my very love of you, you shall despise, let's face it, you shall hate me.

254

I have something cataclysmic to say, I've been stuffing it interminably, it's time, its formulation perfect through decades of rehearsal, I've been cowardly and fearful, I've imagined repercussions, blind reprisal of criminal to victim, prideful deflection over years has diminished me to marginalia, to sycophantism, but I am chest-massive, inflated, uncurled like Godzilla, instinctively messaging and compressing, hear me now, emphatic, thunderous, you will cower, incinerating invective, I am planting my feet, flexed, my chest could blunt missiles, I'm about to unleash the seven-headed monster, the glittering chariot to cowards and weaklings, I am about to light the firmament with phosphorescence intended to brand marrow, unto every human creature arrives this moment, the ultimate penetration before which all others bow, I have been undead, immaterial, unsubstantial fritterer, certain utterances give birth to glittering, ladies and gents, compatriots, I have drunk from the geyser, be patient, pregnant with myself I stand before you, certain preliminaries must be respected, you will not be disappointed.

255

I give myself the colonoscopy, clean as shell, unblemished, nothing but original sin, mucus-lined, slippery, pliable as oyster, I marvel at my person, I pull up scrotum to see bridge, fragile lip, anus underneath like ribeye, I am fascinated beyond disgust or theory, I am objective biological instrumentation, clinical anatomist, I pull forward ear to find crevasse wanting bath, crying for grace in oceans of space the undeniable face—chief narcissist of mirrors and ponds—I angle looking glass off looking glass to examine fatty sagging ass, how it must flap during sexual thrust and scrape against briefs, I am drawn to road kill: dog, skunk, coagulated guts and stop at fetid grimace-locked mass, head gashed, body spilling, pass over it jeweler's glass to detect colors in black, glistening shimmer, cavernous systems drained, gluey, I want to grab forehead shelf and peel skull, open head like a hood, packed matter spilling instinct and fear onto my fingers and furious at truth thereby revealed: I am manatee, cow, oryx, pig, slaughterer understands, soldier intuits, war architect knows, I decapitate myself to see interior neck: esophagus, trachea, carotid, spine, nerves, thyroid, blood sausage lymph—severed mouths by a madman's hand—I stretch, bend, crane, twist, lean, contort, crawl under, gawk, I love myself beyond redemption.

256

To cement her surrender smash a man, brawl on pretense and redesign a face, woman loves man to slit in air an ellipsis for her wearing sheer see-thru blue to slip through, forbear from her knowing a final stoving blow, make her respect tyrannosaurus thighs, domination, fury, smelling of whiskey but not inebriated, darkly lit bar of sexy fifths, feeling protected she will glide, slain, to Firebird kissing, studwork glinting, demand the dance of dickering hands: pet, stroke, pinch, slip, loose bobcat hell scraping castiron pit, whale on a man, pulp him like pudding, lift boot from neck one millimeter from death, there to pity and call down prayer, self-condemnation like Christ gristle and stringy in this invidious world, through impenetrable scrawl slice that sharply defined portal for woman to bask in, she's your babe like hot baked chicken slid off bone, the woman of he whom you thrashed rushes to his side, shrivels, whitens, giggles with derision, and quits the pathetic little prick which was always, frankly, too small for pleasure, about drubbing: be commanding, philosophical, and forgiving, make it cruel with total body whipping, contemplative, heavy with sweaty naked flesh hard as barked timber, make him buckle, choreographed, with split lip and blood-matted pate before your superior structure, something glistening on understated leather and breath rushing nostrils, it's war, every gesture, glance, phrase, and shift reveals the enemy.

257

I've witnessed mother's vagina innumerably, watched her pee, I could identify her nipples anywhere, I know her toe nails like I know fudgesickles, I've memorized her foot architecture, she calibrated my tumblers to her voice print, she married me, together we slaughtered dad times one-thousand in foyer, den, hallway, kitchen with imaginary knife or blunt instrument, we strangled and crunched through spine and with each massacre maniacally giggled, I know her head hair and coarse pubic bush standing up and curling toward slit, I know heels sliding across fabric and painted bullet toes, I've mapped her moles, strawberry under left globe, needle point above cunt, is this odd, sons and mothers, especially beautiful sons whom mothers who hate their husbands love, parade naked before and sit-pee in exhibitionist cube, then ease wrapping fists round soft bunny penis, nails lacquered like thunderbirds, I know rapture of mother's lips beyond lips of any thunderstruck girl, mother's divine, otherworldly, overpowering, thrilling, unzipped, cool hands round thickening shaft, slain daddy in the clothes bin, or crawling up creamy Port Aransas thighs to the labia-bulging mound, women beware the monster-coupled man, here's the truth: we stabbed Daddy thrice through neck and fornicated on the corpse, everything shone iridescent red, poor dupe always resurrecting from ash to die anew, imagine an angelic face, roebuck lashes, Louise Brooks brows, high apple cheeks, gullible chocolate eyes, bow shaped lips, the total package involving adoration, devotion, depravity, fertility, bliss.

258

What spectacular sky but who gives a shit, one has to be insane to believe nature sanctifying, sarcophagus of gut, hiking makes me wretch, I'd rather die than lake-swim, nature-distraction, nature-deflection, daffodils, gentians, irises, what crap, I'd follow any naiad up mountainous hell for a piece of ass but never for altitude itself, volcano of slaughter and digestion, infinitesimal mortal howl between cliff and cactus, nothing's external, proudly proffered red carnation's a mangled hand, shorebreak pathos, eagle fierce tenacity corrupted with disillusion to whoredom or lechery, silver veins trickle down granite face, cowslip, columbine; blindness, arrogance, ignorance, pride, hubris, power fire me, yea, but natural world's supplemental allegorical metaphorical radishes in a fantasy field, tears fall more beautifully than dead leaves, I claw the sky like gypsies, Jews, and gays clawed the gas chamber ceiling.

259

Men don't kiss, initial seduction, yes, but after, sheer pay-off, balance sheet, ROI, men don't own peripheral zones, nipple kisses freeze, sucked toe disgusts, men cold like pliers, woman might imagine she has landed Mr. Sensitive, "adores making out," but soon throat jammed cock and the flip over, mouth concrete, what to expect—bulls, badgers don't cake, they collide—action is semen, ovary, sub-epidermal net, do you think homo sapiens males give crap about ear lobes, ridiculous lacy boudoirs furnished on the myth of Sharif, crisp uniform, men tear in half, wad like rough draft, subdivide, best not to want mush is advice heftily given, limited tenderness as opposed to carnage makes the most sense to want in the bedroom.

260

You're weary of me, you're sick of rage, bitterness, animosity, you've read this far and want to wretch, pathetic, insufferable, self-absorbed, monstrous father and lover, can you imagine, megalomaniac, cat slaughterer, worshiper of own cock, and so self-loathing it winches from gut as if by creaking cable, you think of cracking roaches with shoes and their yellowy bile, dragging a string of shit, you think of miscreants clothed in newspaper, disgusting, degenerate, but this is your book report due on Thursday, your condemnation and crematorium, now he scrawls human excrement across God's face, now he decapitates a dog, now he digests his father like head cheese, you wonder when he'll hang himself with his own colon, what will you say, what analysis shall earn you A, ribs of fireworks and explosion of umbrellas, sinister ovums, many-tongued liver slurping ice cream, wriggling lies like Eisenstein's maggoty meat regarding mother's cunt, son's cocaine, dropping and crawling across floor, you might say effluvia, cloaca, miasma of trust, you might say onomatopoeia or diarrhea, indulgement and expurgation, hot split onion baked apart in clay selects you to divulge to professor or world your bloody hell, pinks of baby, blue cotton booties, gladiolas blooming, and the shimmering machine, you're weary of this, wanting damp rotting roots, copper mud, fecundity, the pungent blackberry-pulpy fingertip suck.

261

I starve my two dogs to see what transpires; first day: tail-wagging, chop-licking, enzymes anticipating, confused disappointment as I ignore bowls, lovingly I scratch, they frolic, doze, forage, stalk, older without friskiness, gray muzzle hairs, dysplasic, I haven't space for running though they worship walks, seem accepting, assuming mental lapse, dozed under coffee table and stairs, nightly feeding: upright, tails banging, yellow one expecting heaps talks, black one rears, bodies twisting, sensing moment by sunslant, arrival, sounds, looking over shoulder to pull me to Friskies, I know, I understand, performing chores I pass bowls over which they hover, greeting with soul, canine loyalty, they would kill for me, night curtains, forgiving annoyance, foraging kitchen, anticipatory postures, can still lick hand and do not reveal disgruntlement toward hunger, enjoying my cooing, perturbation by degrees, quiet all night, day 2: frantic excitement, muscle, body weight, propulsion, I take out trash accidently kicking blue feed bowl, pass pantry, pour milk over flakes, uncharacteristic yipping, finish cereal, pass pantry, dress, aware an adrenaline-fueled lethargy, drooping, one nips another, I utter reassuring note while putting them out where crouch to pee, squat to shit, absent all day so cannot recount behavior but imagine dissension, antagonism, nightly feeding: usually a cup plus biscuit: noticeable rivalry, testiness, disgruntled butting, enervation, lassitude, pork chop, salad, pintos for me, aromatic cooking, visibly discomposed, yellow one naughtily rears to counter, bad dog, I shout, rap snout, amazingly tails wag, put them out, yap, bristle, snarl at imaginary or literal danger, predictable discomposure but adoring still, roaming night rooms, hungry beseeching eyes, forgiving expressions, unconditional, day 3, morning feeding: oatmeal, cream, d'anjou pear, rushing, (early meeting), ham and cheese bag lunch, in periphery two hackled animals competing, lapping water, pass feed bowls to back door, out they flow shot from fire hose, viral behavior, snarling, snapping, twisted, acids shooting, stiff withers pushing, gnarled paws, nightly feeding: attacked each other, torn ear, puncture wound, ripped out whole almond sized nail, slightly bloody, shame, patchy, curled in crawl space baring, refuse helping hand, humiliated, I drag the yellow one, heavy sack, through powdery filth, the black one crushed into corner angry, attacking—let the games begin.

262

While petitioning god to fix my cancer I realize that god couldn't give a shit, supplication before embroidered cuffs, terrified, metasticization, malignant margins, death, I clop in sanctuaries, mendicant whose seen sufferers dangled in web of feed tubes yelping pain to deaf-as-dirt oedipal Prince, I shout fuck you! fuck it! and break at knees because without strandofhope I'm rampant tumor pinching dishes in hot pants, a wicked flip, the cheesiness abandoning disease experiments, I pray, dear crapbag heal myoepithelial carcinoma of parotid gland, vaporize clear cell banditry like a clot of crips, eraserman, emptypants, and so I twizzle into an atmosphere, Hebraically downcast unvisited, like the whole world of blockheads desperate, half-dead, or fine, scraping can't-miss numbers on a lotto card.

263

First, destroy the cat in non-mutilating fashion, poison or pentobarbital, then perform thusly: slit underside chin-to-anus, empty entrails (save liver for dinner), hose out, cure in sun, treat lining with Vasoline, then when tough and supple stretch
it over head, face forward, presto, catskin cap, how beautifully breeze parks feline fur, textures infinite, short hair to Persian, obsidian to tabby, suitable for opera, crumpets, outdoor fucking, status conferred, naturally, on specificities of grimace, how graphically is horror frozen on face? teeth bared? lips curled? pupils stunned? general extermination-aesthetics? and how in-tact the tail? wipe anus with alcohol-swabbed Q-tip, here lies "highest best use" of cat, here rests utilitarianism beyond clumping litter and plangent wails, unisex headwear like tam or cap, you must, of course amputate legs, though dangling extraordinarily exotic paws enhances if luminous or exceptionally marked, I have meditated on the efficacy of skunk, marten, or squirrel but rejected not on quality but impracticability of capture, though can imagine fantastic death mask accentuated by delicate tapering snouts, whereas, alternatively, cats are innumerable, domesticable, and trusting, so gentlemen, ladies, let us begin the re-application of the utility of cats: procure plump, perform procedure, outrig children for envy and popularity reminiscent of American pioneer, frontiersman, Crockett, pop's, mom's, daughter's, son's closet adorned
with shimmering, luxurious, practical, and plush gutted cats.

264

Sylvester smashes into frying pan, with pan-shaped face slinks to floor, stars, taps, Tweetie in cage the Angel of Innocence, mother slapshoots Sylvester with broom who careens through a window chased by his fur, Sylvester sneaks back in unable to resist fricasseed bird, loses his face to a sizzling iron, Sylvester smokes a stogie with which he ignites a fuse but Tweetie has reconfigured things, the bomb blows off Sylvester's tail, he slinks fuming and ashamed, morning, Tweetie tweets in sun ray, swings, mother's big shoes, Sylvester pantomimes sleep, then sneaks upside down on the ceiling to Tweetie's cage who twitters May Day May Day, mother spatula-bats Sylvester who lands against the grille of an onrushing Mack powering him splayed like an X-Ray to Tijuana where a bull butts him back to mother who boots him into a closet where a bowling ball tumbles onto his noggin forcing bump and planets, Sylvester crumples, Tweetie twits (she'll be coming round mountain), mother knits by a crackling fire, Sylvester dreams serving plates, Sylvester inches along a power line to devour Tweetie, Tweetie twangs wire, the vibration snaps Sylvester silly who dangles by three fingers, Tweetie pries them, "piggy, piggy, piggy" and Sylvester vanishes in a swirl, lands on a sanitation truck which crushes him between steel plates, deposits him in the dump among fish heads and chicken bones which he serves himself on a trash can lid after which he greens, leans over bridge, and falls through a steamship-chimney into the raging pit which shoots him out where he explodes like a firework, Tweetie sings, mother cleans, Sylvester screams down the sky splatting on mother's doormat, fuck this shit, he says, and with two buddies—bum and profligate—bereft of chickadees, heads to Buster's to get bombed on boilermakers and comatose on prostitutes.

265

You suck, you make me sick, you're disgusting, you're fat, go to hell, fuck you, fuck you, fuck you, looser, bitch, prick, cunt, piece of shit, lunatic, Texan, nutcase, Jew, Christian, drop dead, jump up my butt, I despise you, you ruined my life, what of it, lunatic, charlatan, whore, I never liked the way you fuck, ditto, brute, shrew, bastard, witch, get out my life, happily, parasite, block of ice, go fuck yourself you goddamn piece of misogynist garbage get out of this house leave me fucking alone I'm outa here, I'm not going anywhere it's my goddamn house don't delude yourself psycho freak passive-aggressive monster get the hell away from me, go flush your head down the toilet, better than sticking it between your legs you taste crappy, murderer, oh Jesus it's over what the hell life is over I'm cooked I give up I don't care anymore I took a chance blew it I thought you were it it's my fault all my fault fuck it all I'm dead you win I'm finished, oh baby don't be so hard on yourself you're always so bloody hard on yourself why do loathe yourself you can't accept anyone's love it's like poison anyway it's not all your fault okay honey we're both messed up, I do part of me loves myself I'm so defensive right now I feel so I feel so…annihilated like a piece of shit I didn't mean what I said all those things retaliating lashing back you know and I didn't mean what I said earlier either I know I said it but I didn't mean it I was hurt abandoned angry enraged and I lashed out at you no excuses it was childish I'm sorry I'm really…me too I'm sorry too I'm not exactly rational, forgive me, I'm raw, I suppose we both are it's all so sickening, I forgive you if you forgive me, all right of course, kiss me—again—will you fuck me I need you to fuck me here now on this floor, I guess why not you know you're everything.

266*

I do not hate Jews because they killed Christ, they did not, I hate
Jews because they're filthy, they worm into power, promote
their own, degrade the host, they stink up hospitals with miser-
ly doctors, colleges with socialists, banks with momsers, and
flaunt flaunt flaunt, a restaurant full of Jews is a sewer and
a Jewish quarter a rat's nest, Jew cunt grinds meat and fe-
male Jew fingers glint like razors, Israel festers like maggot-
y flesh oozing disease over which lime must be dumped, one
more thing, the clipped penis deludes the Jew into believing
himself purer, sequestered in pants the secret handshake,
mushroom cap of contempt and superiority, the Jew like ba-
cilli mutates against extermination and we always know
when among one, he exudes a lascivious garlicky conniv-
ance, a hairy fetid ass, this beyond the telltale Shylock
nose and savoring hands, Hitler failed to convince, The United
States eschews genocide—rats require total extermination—
and deserved suicide, answer resides in exposing this teem-
ing infiltration by proper name: Spielberg, Eisner, Levin,
Kissinger, Bronfman, Metro-Goldwyn-Meyer, Green-
span, Abrams-Wolfiwitz-Cohen, Libby, Dershowitz, Ber-
nanke, Lieberman, Bader-Ginsberg, Murdoch, Dauberstein,
Berger pontificating from palaces of power, ready like
a swollen cunt for hard fucking to crush competitors in
the service of influence and dominance, I abhor this palpi-
tating miasma of coarse black hair and breeding lust—
own, my comrades, the crawling hate inside your walls
of flesh, with our smoking rod let us cauterize this canker.

*Voice of Steve Ulrich, 1966, anti-Semite.

267

Husband and wife privately vow to outlive each other for one blissful moment of peace, finally, without a tormentor, daddy, ninety, eyes mother, eighty-six, daddy owns the edge for a pig's valve saddles bedridden mother, though dementia clouds daddy, mother hoards money and conserves energy believing every gesture self-defeats, daddy conversely exercises by cleaning house believing key to victory lies in dominating circulation, mother seethes at his relative vigor while daddy gloats at her dissipation, locked loathers hooked together like warring scorpions, mother imagining wealthy suitors such as cardiologist watches her figure with thighs resembling regurgitated pasta and feet like turnips, mascara-fattened lashes and Revere-ware hair, daddy hoping her heart explodes bull-charges her, fists doubled, shouting, usually with cause, but she has internalized Buddhist imperturbability, daddy rages, browbeats, occasionally inspiring fibrillations but she tabulates money and refuses extirpation horizontal and pillow-propped, she, alternatively, begs, Father kill him, stroke, head-on, cardiac infarction, cancer, just claim the man, I petition thee, beautiful combatants pretending comparability, daddy complains turtle-penis has retracted into pelvic-shell forcing him at wee-wee time to pry it out, foul rotting bird—feathers and beak—sticks in mother's cunt, sexual communication decades cold, only freedom fires them, mother diets and chiffon-peignoir draped rarely moves savoring actuarial advantage while daddy acknowledging handicap but always the immortalist prosecutes continuous subterfuge, great rail-splitters drive home the spike, bang, bang, bang, bang, at dinner table mother mashes egg, lightly scrambled, with fork and toast daddy bursts a second yolk, remnants of shingles rankle mother, daddy tolerates his irradiated lymphs, the usual communal sundown supper, each wrapped in hazy internal speculation, not speaking.

268

None of us added up, we failed love like one fails new year's resolution, married six times and six times fuming malcontents, women believed their victimization crying narcissist narcissist, men convicted themselves of insensitivity, the shebang rubbish and resentful kids, moneyless wallets, empty vulvas, the stage a tableau of desperation, angles, schemes, extortionist women incessantly dissatisfied and monstrous men divorced for inadequacy, streets like e-vacuating colons of the lost slicing nightdreams like fried liver, failed predators devoured by unnameable abstractions carried within like tuberculosis, painters, poets, dramatis personae never fully disengaged from sperm and egg, therefore engendering laughter like circus oddities, python-man covered in scales and countess embryo, translucent, veiny, unfinished rounded digits, wombstreaked, small as forearm, well what did we expect, blank pages, tabula rasa, infinite gestures, fat on cheese curls and anxiety, failed, too, at beauty, but who is beautiful but the lunatic in sequined boots and burgundy blouse hurled howling into the galaxies between facing mirrors, we never amounted even as hedonists vomiting umbrella drinks, weeping into hooker's tits, flushing cocaine, settling for twelve hundred naked square feet cat-clawed and cleanser-streaked, fractured between contentment and desuetude into paralytic shapeless piles of warring neutrons, and faith-fueled redemption, don't even mention it.

269

Not even porn gets me hard, I want to shove cock through a Jewish star, I think of wet dog food, of mother's pig valve, foot ridges used to slay, now not films of favorite ecstasy, blow jobs, how delicious fellatio feels, like heroin, like crack cocaine, now I'm comatose, somebody hyped Pentothal into my dick, it's misshapen like a Southern slug, naked women dizzied me, I swooned to slide off blouse, do you know how nude breasts intoxicate heterosexual men, now not even pictures of nude aureolas stir my brain, I would masturbate with ground glass, with jagged can if only dick would stand at attention like a patriot, once I vibrated like steel, like flourescent light, what malaise grips my dick, basal lobe a rotten pablano, I furiously click movie screen, two cock craving cunt swappers, sexy Nicole sucks and gets doggied, hot Euro chick nailed hard, nothing, nothing, my pants imitate the grave, I slather astroglide on puppy ear between thighs thirsting for onanism above the john, my real dog resembling Shakespeare's fool cackles at knees, who am I whose identity and source of pride, cunt-getting, has dessicated, I lie in my lap like a pool of spit, eyes stuck into, revolving, let us pray, I cannot beat meat, women fail to arouse, I am inside-out, crumpled sleeve, help me respect that which I debased, dehumanized, like pork on plate, help me embrace the merely alive from whom I no longer require that legs strain for opposite shores splitting her sex like a slashed fig for deep thrusting.

270

I fornicate with myself, I learn to enter my ass hole,
I eat myself, I come into mouth, I eat my hand
like a beefsteak, I spit out finger bones, I spit out
knuckles, I eat the flesh, swallow, digest, shit
what I do not process into fire and creativity, I
eat my feet and forearm flesh, magically I impregnate my stomach, grow big with child, deliver god, the Christ, cousins bear packages, I
am addicted and fuck myself repeatedly, alone
I drink, then lay myself like a monomaniac,
David's Star swings on neck dumb and glorious, orgy, I snap like turtle, growl, snakehiss, snarl like dog, blood soaks bed, wide
cloudy stains resembling zoology, spermatozoa
spotted, physically disgusting, caged, I backbend and bite my heels like a blind Chihuahua,
I self-flagellate with my father's belt, buckle
first, I conjure mother's dark red napkin, almost black, mouth gags, knife wound bandages, I conjure something hideous and indescribable inside daddy, I fuck myself, I eat my
hair, I twist round back facing front, bend,
lick my butt's fleshy mound, tear a piece,
swallow, squeal like Jesus of Nazareth rotating on a nail, I am sagged and not proud,
sack of grist, am old, anus resembles a bloody maw, I induce nausea, slit wrists seldom
bleed definitively, my mattress a dense placenta pie, on my bed javelina-pig-hog-dog
peeing, eating, coming, grunting, nosing
underbitten tusks in its own gushing, bristlehaired, quilled, on back scratching itch, depositing from between squat craggy cheeks a
black and iridescent green likeness of himself.

271

Experimenting with the concept of enough I eat donuts until nauseated, what constitutes enough, how large emptiness, how much required to compensate, I am not satisfied with one serving, knowing the gnaw of eternity, applies to discussion, film, literature, a hurtling—slippery—I shove into gut more than it can bear to prevent deflation, this was true for women until indifference, leaving a rubble of husks, I stand on my Pakistani rug, a furnace, bottomless and enraged, I reject narcotic for its monetary suck though appreciate how fools jam in junk, how ineffectual the single torte vibrating upon plate, or the fuck, shoved over lip into gape, tumbling small, my teeth deceptively dull like the seducer of children, when does moderation rule and surfeit disgust, I query, as I fantasize binges, embarkations into the thick unknown without destination, something horrible extends beyond crumb cake, the copulation, depression, oceans of fumes within which monsters sleep, what surrounds a poppy surrounds me, hunger bursts from pod like spore-thick air, fecundity littered with warm hard shells, dust covers artichoke and kale, do not despair, the educable achieve college degrees and everyone steers a wheel, I've no idea, unconsciousness an unconquered cake, consciousness a tiny finch, doze in chair, legs numbly crossed, flirting along edges, overflowing mouth, peace broken by an air raid siren stuck on blare.

272

I adore you but hate your presence, I hate feeding you and watching you grow, I hate your eunuch voice and ridiculous epiphanies, I hate your hairdo and fragile skull and the greedy menacing insatiable monster consuming food like a locust cloud, I hate your horrid singing and shifting identities, I hate your pestering edges of my nap and fantasize destroying you, I hate your stomach aches and strep throats and drag you to supper club anyway, stop dogging and get out, I'm busy, I'm napping, I'm smoking a break, get out, stay out, I hate my ravaged exit wound and decimated ventricle, you threw me in hospital for a month, grotesque beast, I hate spending on you, underwear, Levis, shoes, food ceaselessly, mercilessly, I hate your depthless and obvious stupidity, here's your Baby Ruth, your tapioca pudding, your Chef Boyardee fatso, have another Snowball, my Robert Goulet, Tom Selleck, I worship you, I despise your tray of colognes and cockiness, big shot, show off, you want to see bliss, here's bliss, ignorant ass, I hate your sentimental experiments with love, Sheila, Tia-Shan, Nancy Stapp, bloodless gentiles with their powder puffs, how cute moustache fuzz and cracking voice but hate every costly expansion of you from jacket size to trendy shoe, pray for your happiness and death liberating me from flesh created hell, I am god, I am goddess, you are nuisance, my daddy doted beyond comprehension, crowned me queen, I hate your bloody necessity and butch wax wave standing up like a fence and your baseball mitt, your whole goddamn sanctum of cinnamon toothpicks and thermostat mercury, childish fripperies, and platinum wetdream disgustedness, but most of all, as I've said, I hate the fact that you live.

273

Better to go unloved by one's parents, to be called monster, bum, idiot, beast, to be disinherited, best if they invoke God, "God damn good for nothing," nasty God damn loser," children worship parents while parents despise offspring the instant delivered, subterranean fact: mothers fantasize killing their infants, father resents rivalry, best the busy telephone, the blocked email address, the whole thing cracks apart like a baked briquette, invariably, women stuck on daddy become queens, men dreaming of mom frigid masturbators, every nuance of hatred—neglect to homicidal rage—nourishes the child, unloved Howard pees freely off highrise, loathed Beverly slits a chicken's throat, and parents full of warm red lube tango in Argentina, I remember razor gills slicing fingers in a fiberglass boat, and brilliant ribbonfish writhing in sun, best not loved by one's parents, best not to love, they cold warty toads, bumpy gherkins frothed in brine, each clasping something significant, composition bow, blow torch, axe haft, crystal quartz shaft, powerful.

274

One wants to rage at the ill, scream get well god dammit, one wants it over, to go to Carnival or Tamarindo, get up one shouts, what's the matter, but then one identifies egotism, lack of empathy and places hand upon brow, serves broth and slips into bed beside the afflicted for affliction abounds causing pain, nausea, diarrhea, numbness after treatment, sterility and tenacity, brain or bone, one strives to eliminate the imposition of Explorer or whsiperjet to Newfoundland or Patagonia, all that retching and incontinence, one cannot avoid messes no matter the buckets, and that bloody Knorrs chicken broth worthless as squirrel shit, perhaps pills and the monstrous drilling machine, but one goes nuts, callousness, cruelty, one wants a beautiful lesbian, sado-masochist, naked savior crocked on wine, ultimately one identifies narcissism and saunters bedside with Pampers and Ensure, always the filing of selfishness against the soul of integrity leaving behind a sticky pile of flesh, though one employs phrases like "imprisonment," "indentured slave," and eats vulgarity like overcooked groats, vengeful, victimized, luckless, profane, but one discovers for all that one is not such a monster regardless of Rio de Janeiro or Paradise Island, and delivers a faltering but superb degree of compassionate care.

275

Jew haters invade a Jewish home, Jew one blurts, another, kike, a third raids closet, another rifles cabinet, another slits curtains, they imbibe, one smashes photographs, one pockets things, one defaces walls, they yank books, overturn cases, one strips the table, scores antiques, disembowels the cat, they masturbate, one pees, another shits on carpet, one empties pantry, one smears cat on mirror, they scrawl swastikas with cat blood, one guts the couch, another defecates on the bed while another trashes the medications, they rape, stuff pockets full of jewels, execute the Jews and split, deep six the Jews, push Jews into the sea, screw Jews, rape Jews, blind Hebrews, amputate cocks, pipe in rivers of shit, paint the world with Jew guts, feed pigs Jew, smash Jew spawn, goddamn fucking plague, they slurp catsup, careen through town, one receives a congratulatory blow job, one sodomizes a tight ass, one listens to heavy metal, all curl finally and sleep like blameless gods.

276

I want to write something fabulous, something inexpressibly profound, but because I cannot I am a failure, you too are a failure, we are both failures, you imagine because you make money that you succeed, but you are a failure, all fail beyond refutation, we shame our parents, we have failed and disappoint but that does not define failure, who gives a fuck what parents think, we fail ourselves, by our own standards, we slump like failures, ungodly failures manipulating gas pedals, even you bursting with semen, switching down Saab top, hair swept back are a blue-rimmed bullet hole, your inner tongue murmurs fraud when you pontificate, specialized at something but fake like the segmented wooden snake, I do not glorify myself by denigrating you, I am you, internally leaking, charlatan, buffoon, children never imagined their parents' ineptitude until likewise they became failures, how utter in this miasmic blather the word success, ram-rod it through, mockery, sneer as if you and I were great and yet I shove it into this mess—I need to write something fabulous to correspond to something pure and true, and you wanted one moment of weightlessness beyond life's nullifying monstrosities but I have failed and you have failed and we continue to fail, collapsing in each others' arms.
.

277

I'm wedged inside my mother's cunt, head sticking out, torso stuck in lips, I ride her like a kangaroo, dangling, bouncing, first I bawled, then scratched, then tried to corkscrew out, but kegel-fisted she chewed me down till growing big I wept, half born, extruding but squeezed nonetheless and fucking girls as if complete, "why can't you love me," they plead, "what's wrong with me," "bastard," "fucker," "ego-maniac," "get out," and I worm wriggle in her cunt like a Moray eel in its rock, I satisfy mother when my penis stiffens and rub my nape against her clit until she shrieks which, sweating, gives me pleasure and I, too, come, like a maniac, grown comfortable inside this mouth, sometimes struggle, but like finger in a Chinese puzzle work in deeper until only eyes protrude from this hairy fist, one would think—don't believe it—that her eighty-seven year old groin would finally spit out its purple chunk but at sixty I cannot twist one inch and am weak from trying like bull dragging banderillas, and have quit, that is me in the unendurable loneliness between women stuffing myself with hot fudge sundaes and devouring novels, plotting to conquer another woman while being conquered, a double holocaust.

278

It's okay, that ubiquitous American phrase, it's gonna to be okay, thousands of corpses, okay, we're gonna to be okay, everything's okay, cancer, o-k-a-y, ovarian, okay, all right, everything's all right, war, okay, we're okay, famine, starvation, cholera, drug addiction, look man, it's okay, we're gonna be fine, diabetes, bankruptcy, adultery, it's…don't worry, you're okay, he cradles your head, he wraps shirt round wound, she hides the computation, someone inhales water, she leaps, a suspicious shadow, can-do, okay, all right, soldier with blown-off leg, morphine, it's fine, it's okay, you're gonna be all right, legless, impotent, crematoriums, the crushed heart, oh sweetie it's okay, you're okay, I promise we'll be thumb and pointer O, three finger K, whup ass, thumbs up, meat to market, emphysema's last breath connected to cannister in hospice, here here—cradling—it's okay, it's gonna be all right, meaning life, the world, you safe in world, it's okay, smooth sailing, oxygen obstacle-free, the decapitated wife, multiple sclerosis, wiped out by fire, blew off his face, it's okay, everything's okay, you-'re gonna be all right, red sickles clump Tommy's blood.

279

Because I am extraordinary my death shall be cataclysmic, death does not attack the brilliant the way it attacks the dumb, I will die like a Ferrari or an Audemars Piguet, nobly, monumentally, the transformation of legend, you reading this stand in death's crosshairs and will drop anonymously like fox or hare, while I, the illustrious, even deceased will eternally breathe, there exist broad-chested colossuses such as I who see telescopically into hairline cracks or the next millennium, but you lower-case enmeshed in sod, clodded blind, marching in columns to your abyss, how will you survive but through me in your diminutive pants and fishing rod, hear me scream like surf over rock, I blot the sun and drizzle mist, shudder under me, I do not gain an ounce and can split a millimeter one hundred times, I feed on hammerhead and lion as well as swallow's eggs, I am centuries from dying but will form a vacuum when I fall sucking the breath of millions including dramatists, poets, presidents, and studs who gasp life back into lungs desperately and without beauty as when the bomb flashing in an instantaneous state of grace pulls in all combustibles prior to exploding fire, vapor, gas, radioactivity, and dust into the caught and choking indistinguishable masses.

280

I shut drawers, first I shut all drawers, then I switch off lights, every one, so it's drizzle gray, then I tighten every lid, jam, mayonnaise, cooking oil, burying odors, next I assassinate the pets ridding myself of responsibility, always, non-negociably, I straighten shoes, each beside mate, laces folded like casket grace, one indispensable must—all in preparation for the cataclysmic event: grind pencils in sharpener, needles with immaculate hats, then this: dust and lemon wax the massive pieces, then obligatory and predictable, piggish and meticulous, painstaking attention to self, clip and clean nails eating the waste, core nostrils like hallways of cockle, Cutex to cuticles, alcohol on balls, hand cracks most demanding, like restoring Dutch canvases, head shaved bald, anus scrubbed, every genital ravine swabbed with Q-tip, the festival approaches like four howling twisters, bruise-blue, green-black and in preparation the bath, Epsom salts, cardamom, lavender, oatmeal, steaming, deep, luxurious such that I emerge babytender, glowing, lastly, with contortionist expertise bind wrists behind back with eye-screw anchored rope, teeth-tighten over shoulder and neatly chew off slack, exposing self unmercifully on the edgeless white disk, chest fulcrumed out, face upthrust, like a succulent baked pig, awaiting with thrall and trepidation the fabulous collision.

281

I set ablaze Q-tip torches and jam them up nose and, Nazi, cremate follicles like Jews, gypsies, gays, and crips, six million olfactory receptors connected to brain exterminating persimmon, rose, lavender, pine, a charred hole where gods once sniffed; with one hand I grab my tongue, with the other drizzle acid decimating buds, obliterating taste from Creamsicle to beet, vulva to lychee nut, a napalmed village; eyes and ears are easy, guileless, uncomplicated, knitting needle thrust and yanked, from puncture oozes symphony's blood, braided, knotted, coated, clotted, crickets, violas, cataracts, disgust, four decisive aluminum thrusts into trumpet and jelly, bubbles and pudding pots releasing pucker of busted yolk achieving silence and sightlessness; now the imponderable, calculation beyond geometry, the primitive frontal lobe lobotomy, slide paint mixing knife up and under eye holes smashing up nerves between bone and brain decimating mind, flattening response; so, cloisonne-man, ceramic man, lower myself into molten bronze, emerge with a shiny solid shell dulling me to whatever loathes, loves, suffers, or knocks, and rendering me capable of nothing but subterranean, insular, low-impact tactility.

282

Miniature dog like an electric razor appears before me growling perfunctorily, unthreatening, don't bite, I exclaim, protectively, two yokels, comically he hackles sandy brown hair like a clawed cartoon pillow, down boy approaching I sing, but suddenly shifting he expands wolfishly, thick jowled, brindle, brushy, superficial still, a mangy protectorate of bedrooms and slippers, I feign trepidation beside hollyhock and elm, black flies, mosquitos, down boy, go home, trustingly, I shriek, frame skips, he flicks bigger still, bear cub, javelina, fangs drip enzyme, eyes flicker, I brake, freeze, hairless now, fur spray-painted over muscle, treacherous, vicious, not-dog, otherworldly, cavernous maw, I back-pedal, arms stiff, go home, I command, boulder now, granite topography as if sculpted by weather, columns of razors studding mountain of rage I cease in naked inadequacy, bungler, idiot with carrots and language packed rucksack, legs like tyrannosaurus it flinches to pounce on the four-wives man, artful seducer, delusional fake sucking his toes, eating his hair like pink cotton candy, object of adult-daughter hatred whose baby flesh bore his hand-shaped welter, of surgical removal of commitment procedure, the wallows and warps, sticky accusation, it's expanded to the height of a threshing machine, sprockets, belts, rods, hydraulics growl like ignited diesel fuel, I embrace full defensive stature, arms raised, chest broadened, yet reassuring chatter, like schoolgirl to kitty, nice kitty, good kitty, sweet kitty while stumbling backward into mother, I am unprotected, tender, and ready, friend, I mutter, buddy, see, I'm going away, going away, retribution my inheritance, bitterness my bread, such antiquated anger, I want to say, such antediluvian sorrow, but can ask forgiveness from neither Jesus nor brother, an irrememovable black cave dominates my final vision.

.

283

Said aliens raped her in their craft, ripped off blouse, took turns with fat translucent members, afterwards threw her into a drainage ditch, gaudy teen, crooked yellow teeth, ruined and discarded her like trash, on some fantastical shiny surface, naugahyde or vinyl between captain's deck and navigational instruments tearing hymen and virginal silk spilling ashes and stickiness, smelling of Uranus or Saturn, gouged and ripped, seemed brutal and stupid, like nose guards or left tackles reeking self-aggrandizement, anyhow some pinned her limbs while others rammed, in some vehicular inner sanctum thickly upholstered like a whorehouse bar, she rasped to cops knowingly glancing at each other and she, wild now, thrashing and yanking to dash madly like a jackal, chipped lacquered nails either bitten or scraped against rocky shoulder, they fucked her and fucked her, she gushed dark blood and they shot yellow ejaculate, Jupiter she shouted or Mars, weeds stuck in steel wool hair they teased and slapped, flipped her pennies in the school cafeteria, amusing to the popular clique, reeks of dirty linen and skin, a special needs kid with gaudy tits, foul breath, crooked toes sticking out plastic sandals, abducted and despoiled, mouth ringed with Black Cow juice and irrepressibly skulking about the lockers.

284

I tell my adult kids I love them when actually indifferent, what
decent father speaks the truth to his children? says, "son, I re-
sented your intrusion into my marriage, you destroyed it" or "I
never empathized with you," instead I ooze compassion regarding
their current ridiculous predicaments, I correspond with my
daughter who recently delivered, though I would rather read than
compose polite prevarications, "love you, thinking of you," "love
to visit," who is she, anyway, some by-product of a head-on
collision thrown through the windshield of a womb I'm required
to adore, she emails occasionally which I dutifully answer with
the appropriate verbiage though peripherally interested, I have
never seen my granddaughter, but should fate coincidently take
near I would bounce her on knee and praise precociousness,
while internally gnashing some critical issue involving ambi-
tion, injustice, or dissociation, my children disappointed, then
callous toward their bastard dad barely cognizant of their hum-
anity, at pot luck I exude conviviality, soles crunching gravel,
at the company dinner I lean in, listen beside new rabbit cork-
screw, "fascinating," "amazing," I tell my daughter, not with
dry ice swirling out chest but with chilled diffidence, "smart
thinking," I praise my son who lays out a radical path toward
sobriety, "damn fine," I reaffirm, with profound detachment,
the boy hangs up, I imagine, with a high degree of affirmation.

285

Something he covets suspends mid-air before him, the materialization of longing, yes, that's it, he exclaims, precisely, all else curls back from this brilliance like plowed clay, I have desired this my entire life, like cavity desires gold, and now it appears solid, attainable, filling the void, how long I have prayed for this perfection, he reveals, in this disappointing world and awakened mournful, bolts tightened to bluntness, a naked blunt machine draped in plant products cleverly dyed, never until now has the hope of completion floated so close, it breathes down neck, colostrum sweet, soft pullulation, not like pear for brutal plucking, but a fragile thing, skittish, easily vanishing in discomposure, I shall employ my wiliest art, my Mesmeric talent to this is non-negotiable presence, gesture, innuendo, inflection, suggestion, the hypnotist's penetration of spellbound innocents, finally the end of false conquests, the slashing through and disposal of insignificance has lead to this incalculable treasure, and, he pledges resolutely, I shall possess it, it shall be mine, as is my breast's hammer, my appendix and esophagus, I shall introduce irresistible tension along crucial surfaces, the hypnotic brow, magical spaces, the well-orchestrated reserve, classical boyishness requiring ministration, the mysterious wield, the aesthetic magnetism of power fused with ease until willingly into the beautiful trap it slips eradicating my despair.

286

While I masturbated in the chair in which I write these words my tabby attacked the mouse my dick, its head darting and vanishing from fist, taunting, teasing, cat from table pounced pricking the purple circumcision, instinct-prey, the mouse head bleeding, cat arch-back leaping to rip cock's throat, tear its guts, I was desperate to fuck an Internet porn chick sucking off a man, panties round ankles, he on couch, she kneeling, and nearing my climax Napoleon struck, I usually come reservedly, mouth muffled by lover's pillow, but when he ripped my slit for the first time I howled bloody ecstasy tearing down God and heaven.

287

Comfortable with the concept of total loss I masturbate into toilet, a branding sizzle, wax initial sealing envelope, flat smacking, kicked backward onto floor where I lie, pants down, comatose, dust bunnies, hairline cracks, granules, now I croak god damn fuck it all and emit slit-water like tiny packages, dick shriveled like a powdered barrister, midnight, broke, unemployed, loveless, spit-strung with faith a slum Cadillac, house fly harasses, and lover's lips sting like two kissing wasps, wings whirring, and I afloor banged bloody with ennui, a lukewarm casing, gazing into a lampless dank, disgusted-lover expunged, attacked, exiled, comfortable with the concept of dereliction, orphaned by two titanic narcissists, quartet marriages like a tub of tapioca, and masturbated, head against rug, half groan, half sneer, satiric of opportunity, cinema-man, language-man, encuastic-boy, nothing but spasm, scrotum, semen, and spit, sister baked in a pan of jumbo puffers and impracticable, my playing card wives whisked through each other, by God, by Christ, and two ridiculous children rolled out my howitzer like harlequins, surrendered I say to the lemon scented oil of indecent decency, catlick, dogrub, plum weave, palms together with swindling preachers, well let us catechize, the paper-thin pap of wrapping papacy, stars and wizard hats, fuck this shit, the resurrection downward, loss, lightening, the pecuniary blunder, taste of bitter fission at the nadir of crevices, birthdays a scoop and slice of clay, comfortable, easeful in my house high hay, nibbled by The Vagaries untethered from their chains approaching my clover like bulls or oxen lugubriously lumbering.

288

I shove Daddy into Mother's cunt, climb in after, sew her shut, Mother crawls into Tridacna Gigas—the giant clam—which clamps shut, me inside Daddy inside cunt inside clam inside amniotic sea, finally serene, eating each bit by bit, the Massman clan's inevitable reincarnation, Daddy stuffed into sticky emission, I in Daddy sucking my thumb, evolution's staggering incomprehension, the Gigas perambulatingly pulsing, Pop of the fascist perfectionist brain meting out pain, smashed into wife's corporeal refrigerator, Mother split pitless thing elegant of the enameled nail, and now this violence, shoving one into another into another into another, inaccessible fuckers finally engloved, fool inside sadist inside narcissist inside gut, digesting pieces, dissolving into each others' torturer, finally digesting nemesis inside nemesis while being collectively digested.

289

In the final tableau innumerable arrows penetrate him, the first, whistling, pierces right thigh, next shatters groin, more ensue, then hoards produce a hail of arrows, spiny human cactus staggers under sweeping clouds, archers howl, target drags clacking quills, defiant still, rages at sky, rages at sun, rages at God, fate, mud, at flies, the liberation imminent, his she-viper screaming, mansion flaming, steed disgorging clotted blood, Constable on knees, stomach, dusty lump, dead of arrows and retribution, they rape, loot—jade, gold, lapis, jewels—daughter violated, disemboweled, spaniels skewered, finally charred rubble, killing field, male child fed his severed balls, rebellion-massacre, in the final tableau: fornication, inebriation, plunder, pillage, vomit, bacchanal, celebratory treacheries with furtive daggers, masturbation into corpses' caves, crackling fat, pseudo homage, pig-gutting, contortionists, sodomy and pederasty, exhibitionist-defecation onto faces of celebrants, snake flayers, sword swallowers, and, from thick wiry bushes of blacked-out victors, grunting and farting on the courtyard floor, intermittent spontaneous shooting yellow fountains

290

He thinks she worships him; she loathes him; she's fed up, food smacker, energy sucker, saggy-lobed fucker, cannot believe she married this lummox and constantly secretes availability fluids—saliva and sex fluids—she's game, hot squirmer under champions, beaver a blond mitten for freezing hands, wit like a raptor, he's glum and lopsided *ad nauseam*, he thinks she adores him because she comes squealing and stir fries vegetables, dupe, idiot, everything he is repulses, his very timbre the soul's eraser, money and creme de menthe, aphrodesial green, and the great broad hard meat of financiers, she would rather produce her pancreas than take the Colonial Williamsburg vacation, predictability, boredom, death, living room, kitchen, living room, kitchen, he's fascinating on politics and ancient philosophy, Socrates, Heraclitus, his ponderous must-covered skull the antithesis of Cobalt leaping waves, fantasizes untraceable poison or a highway mishap, living room, kitchen, den, kitchen, life as palindrome, on one head two profiles facing inward smashing against themselves, well, as I said, he thinks she loves him and that stainless appliances anchor and secure wild urges in himself and her, a sharp gleaming corner like a granite palisade, and the stars twirl candid features, the cat curls on the windowsill, the bed accepts what humans give it, he bends to kiss her, repent, repent for the end is near.

291

I laugh satirically, shove her thirteen year old face into my sixty year old chest, triumph, twist her hair like spun silver, spill it like cash, she kisses, nuzzles, licks, rose fresh, rose pink, baby's breath, resurrectingly sweet, immortality, and I intoxicated, pole stiff, finger her cunt, luminous bush standing and innocent, Sweet Tart feet I bite and lick, cocaine rushing blood, hitting heart like an accelerator, push her head to my shaft, she takes it, math and biology, Red Pony book report, thirteen years fresh, bandy-legged, taper-heeled, skin scarcely containing blood, and I letch, fucker of hundreds, 4X married, addicted, beard soiled with miscreancy, nipples like blackberries, nibble, bite, pull, release, delight like chime no child could grasp, struck deep and down in sea, rage, death, despair, urgency, blindness, intestines, spleen beyond Big Chief and glitter pen, this squirming child I toss, drag, haul, split, and shoot sparks into, cinders exploding a silken mass, the nebula, men hate their mothers and fuck children on cusps of maturity, wanting "it," wanting him to crack innocence on the rock of clit, their prying fingers, smearing mons veneris against hips, crawling atop, snail trail, the weeping, bleeding, oozing slit stretching wide and deep, oblivion, chlorophyll, collision of green with winter, creme de menthe, chrysalis and bloom, buttercup, crushed, pollen drips from lips.

292

Oh yea, yea, *oh yea,* yea, *wanna bet,* damn right, *okay then its a bet,* okay bet, *you're gonna lose,* you're gonna lose, *idiot,* dope, *fool,* moron, *oh yea,* yea, *who says so,* I say so, *oh yea,* yea, *well you aint got a chance,* oh yea, *yea,* peckerwood, *dick breath,* fuck head, *dip shit,* oh yea, *yea,* you fuck your mother, *oh yea,* yea, *well you fuck your dog,* well you fuck your sister, *oh yea,* yea, *leave her out of it sombitch,* your sister your sister your sister sucks big black dicks, *fuck you,* fuck you, *oh yea,* yea, *you ain't even got a sister,* you ain't even got a father, *well fuck you,* fuck you, *leave my father out of it what do you know nothing piece of crap,* I know you aint got one your mother's a whore that's what I know piece of crap yourself, *oh yea,* yea, *shove it up your ass and you've got a tiny dick aint worth shit Sally told me,* well Sally's a big fat liar and a fuckin' cunt, *well she told me your dick aint worth shit and had to finger herself that you're a joke,* you're the joke joker big joker whose mother fucks jews dogs and pigs, *eat me,* eat me, *eat me fucker,* no eat me fucker, *jew,* spick, *nigger bait,* ass hole, *piece a shit,* dumb ass donkey fucker, *oh yea,* yea, *shove it where the sun never shines,* I'll shove it where I want, *you'll shove it where I want,* make me, *make me make you,* I'll make you when I'm ready, *oh yea,* yea, *well I'll break your face,* sure thing, *you don't believe me,* you don't believe me, *don't mock me you little pussy,* don't mock me you little pussy, *oh yea,* yea, *well I'll feed your balls to a dog,* least I got balls unlike you who's got tapioca, *think you're funny,* funnier then you, *ha ha, ha ha,* you're crusin' for a brusin', *you and what army,* these ten knuckles is what army, *knucklehead you mean,* wise guy huh I'll show you wisenheimer, *ooooh I'm shakin,* fuck you, *fuck you,* oh yea, *yea,* piece of trash, *sticks and stones,* hey jewboy why do jews have big noses cause air is free, *ho ho ho,* don't ho ho me you little wormass tub a lard comebucket, *twat,* who you callin' a twat, *you you twat,* well fuck you, *no fuck you,* no fuck you, *oh yea,* yea, *oh yea,* yea, *oh yea,* yea, *I'm gonna pop you,* well I'm gonna pop you, *com'on,* you com'on, *whatsamatter scared,* I aint scared of nothin, *oh yea,* yea, *here chick chick chick here chick chick chick chicken shit yella belly fuck off,* oh yea I'll show you call me chicken chicken chicken gizzard chicken neck chicken butt, *oh yea,* fuckin' yea, *you wanna fuckin' fight you little wimp, douche bag, dickwad kike* com'on try me barf head double shit numb nuts I'll stomp your freakin' balls into jelly and feed em to you on toast, *oh yea,* yea, *oh yea,* yea, *oh yea,* yea.

293

I need a god, I become a champ at something and worship my worshipers, they slobber and gawk, I am therefore my own god, we loop back on each other, closed system, but it crumbles; I genuflect at altars of tobacco and alcohol, euphoria, black out, oratory at sloppy table, room rotates and lands at package store, erotic bottles, by externalizing God I attain maturity, can focus on a fixed point toward perfection, but it flattens into woman; cunt, ecstasy, tits, toes, throaty voice, lubrication, groans, kisses and collision before which I kneel, psalm of psalms, cock and fire, stiffen and come, earthen hymns from heart's blood like magma, reverential eyes closed in ecstasy, fallopians and eggs, orifice and catatonia, untransmutable God until it clawed and twisted, a flesh-like thing petulant, bellicose, pugnacious, priggish though not horrific and bursts the word; devoid of meat, loin and rib, spirit only, abstract, immaterial like an emanation, formless tiles of mosaic God wider than sky, than universe, before which finally gratified I pray, palms together at the church of beams, catharsis-rays, let us then murder pride, sloth, avarice, lust, illusion of self with its jutting bone, heel, and thrust, its grizzly filth of want and heave, let us scoop out our pulp and levitate in word, the true glory until, boiled yeast, knotting like a sour gut, and here does gristle pull pillars to rubble though one spews the word in hubric trust, besotted on dreams; finally puking mewling palpitating thing, fresh mint, innocence, eyes like ponds, baby, angel, swaddled, suckling, unadulterated, soft spot throbbing like an opened chest, bawling at obstacles, interested in pure comfort to which naked I succumb in domicile, weak-kneed, half-stricken-half-risen within eggshell finish walls, swallowed by domesticity, marveled beside cradle, wept inside with revelation, humility, sustenance, arrival, fire, kneeling, toes doubled, cave crisply cracking, yes, perhaps the baby.

294

That's a laugh, laughing head off, I could laugh forever, Jesus fucking funniest thing I ever, sides splitting, thighs stinging, oh brother, I'll remember that, paroxysms, hysterics, now see what you've done, hiccups, god, god, god, stop, you're killing, you're bloody annihilating, cut it out I said, gonna bust a gut, something's snapping, if you could bottle that, stomach hurts, enough, how long can this persist? how freakin', gotta get out, I'm dying, hear that, hear that, oh man, you oughta be on tv, in pain, can't take anymore, where's the door, if you don't stop I'm, okay, where's the bloody, still hiccuping, gonna vomit, oh Jesus not again, gonna be sick, where's the head, porcelain bus, keep this up I'm not responsible, can't you see, I'm doubled, jelly, cease, desist, god damn, just regurgitated tomato sauce, whaddya want from me, okay, uncle, you're king, decimator, now shut up, cookies I tell ya, I'm erupting, over the edge, on knees, it's no good now, even if I leave, never stop laughing, laugh myself to death, that's what I'll do, laugh myself fucking deceased, it's already started, I'm dying I tell ya, perishing in chasing echos of laughter.

295

I invent a machine extracts fat from flesh, a processor: computer, magneto, alternating scalpels, switches, speeds, monolithic cube, stand in drain pan, embrace like table, bent over and forward, arms in grooves, with fingertip flip switch: clashing blades, sewing needles, slurping, suction, syncopation, synchronization, inexpressible trustworthiness, precision incisions masterfully stitched, utilize gauze, two weeks' bed rest, nonstrenuous activity, gradually reintroduce solids, salve wounds with soapy water, antiseptic liberally, refresh bandages, proven success with cottage cheese, saddle bags, forearm waddle, double neck, results will vary but all will receive noticeable reductions, guarantee two-size downward adjustment, sterilize before re-use, replace needles, refill tubes, empty fat collecting trays, you may experience nausea, constipation, sweating, vomiting, depression, fatigue, hemorrhaging, tremens, you will experience elevated self-esteem, confidence, giddiness, deep satisfaction, relief, rejuvenation, don't be shocked by extemporaneous public breathlessness, magnetism will occur, thrilling propositions, I invent The CruciFixer which disabuses fat from corporeality, blemish from sensuality, desuetude from energy, dowdiness from youth, and unlocks the most unimaginable potentialities.

296

I wish I could do that or something approximating that, something in the same ballpark, as they say, you understand, someone demonstrates, just when you feel omnipotent, the true potential of the thing, virtuosity like a whistling arrow, and your pride sinks, you the rubber tip, the suction cup, and you thought you starched your father's back, redoubled heads, "but" is the word, always "but" qualifying significance, the asininity of it, you have the T-shirt, the logo baseball cap, but suddenly appears splitting air toward god the genius, leaving you stuck in glue, I wish I could do something even remotely related, a Stradivarius sort of thing, hanging the bell-vibration of perfection in the air.

297

I beg to interrupt here, if I may, please allow me to interject at this crucial juncture, I have relevance to add, experientially based, trenchant, attention please, let me clear my throat, felicitations all, this could re-direct discussion, thread it through unexpected eye, please, I have direct and incontrovertible experience, as well as compelling circumstantial evidence suggesting a contrary teleology, where is my napkin, ah yes, here, I clink crystal with knife handle—that international and civilized bell—one and all, ladies, gents, colleagues, friends, even those whose politics I oppose, if I may possess the floor at this austere occasion of our mutual admiration, this merging of souls, congenially, as it were, my heart veritably palpitates with import, how will you receive this collectively, as a body, an august board, this game-changing introspection, here, in this establishment, at this unpropitious celebration, well, frankly, if another had not broached it I would never… but she has, turning formidable heads, Rothschild and Kennedy, and Astor Caperton, nettles snag against our grain, please, if you will, before in one consensual spasm we release the congratulatory annihilating tongue of homogenous consent, allow me this triumphal or catastrophic stroke, silence please, let us admit as a deliberative court the possibility of miscalculation, hear this borne in being's every pith and pore, put down your forks, I am ready to begin.

298

I learn that Hitler was a necrophiliac, meaning he demanded all people die at his feet, cities too, Paris, Antwerp, Moscow, London, buildings, sculptures, infrastructure, every wall and piling, buttress and embankment, goat and lorikeet, required holocaustal devastation stretch before him gasping for second genesis, and from ground zero a rapid new world, beautiful and shining, rises along the edges of an outwardly spreading ring, like a nuclear holocaust in reverse, a Nazi planet useless for crematoriums and Zyklon gas, hallucinatory green trees and brilliant toilets, crisp officials getting glamorous pussy on desks, and without deformity, and I think of the ratlike functionary stuck in sewer cubicle blowing his paycheck on lotto stubs and booze, scratch cards and grease fries, mortality-sloppy, atherosclerotic clot throwing swine, darting through tragic traffic en route to appointments, and think maybe the necrophiliac…well, just maybe…understood the trashy underbelly of man and the beauty of mass extermination including Christ killers and kimono clad queers which are clots of sewage in disguise, it may require pyramids of skulls and mountains of shoes, as depicted in Night and Fog, a hellish epoch of pyres and burial sites, nauseating to pacifists, but finally a decriminalized society safe from desperate bastards packing heat and kilos or forehead-bone low horrid migrations debasing the very foundation of a superior physics, like a termite plague gnawing flawless timber.

299

Everything sloppy, sloppy the word, belly slopping over belt, desk dishevelled, cockeyed tchotchkes, tumblers strewn, bills invoices receipts wads sticky notes spoon glue-stic, and beyond unmotivation into paralysis, trash cans erupt plastic bags, socks everywhere, filth, dirty feet, stubble, and I without whit, shiny sheet unkempt, sloppy all, and sluggish, nearing descent and downslide, up and over like a trick engine, yards of computer wires explode out tower, tangled, knotted like wadded shirt, the end of well-being, the beginning of dissociation, the thing finally pushless, pasty, inert, though churning stomach, enzyme baths, grinders and rippers yellowly glistening in lamp-light, one must not, cannot, must lash muscle to lobe and slave-pull tonnage of granite block by rope, by God, by gruel, by rape and wrath, one must not pulp, part supports pumping whole, oh but Christ, crushes of bathers glistening and barelegged scissored by sun into crispy chips, frantic dashing, throngs and hordes, glutted eateries, multiplying street corners, frenzied thrill rides, how can wet sluggish formless sand discerning necessity march forward with so much Sisyphus at hand, so much Godzilla vs.Mothra and I weary paleontologist, classroom worn like slippery pima, critically distant, Fluvoxamine plowed into ratiocination rows and frankly exhausted given societal and chromosomal psychoses well, still and all, this moldy cheddar, this smouldering sloppiness, oily pillowcase, slid, sagged, slung, flung, supersettled like eyebrow dust, amidst unwrapped peeling, fidgeting, sausage-fingered, torpor-swollen.

300

He throws himself far as he can, inches, solid thud in
dirt, lift, heft, heave, thud, one does not far throw moun-
tain, winded, lungs yanking airless fists, overhead the
usual (contrail, beak, vapor, sun), below the throwing
drama, money money money, failure, one blows life's
exam and thickens into soft solid lead which does
not creekwater travel, molding, curling, bending, no,
cubical broadsided lead bureau large, can scarcely
haul himself up in petrification, as though drugged
sluggish with psychotropics, Depakote or Trazadone,
Fluvoxamine locomotes about veins, connecting rods,
etc., and throws himself, exerting, far as possible,
inches, and thunderously blunts earth, meaning love,
yes love, he loves phenomenally like an old bull chew-
ing tufts, Ferdinand, with nose ring, love the old
wet nose, of the lollygag red tongue, lashes & all,
one throws one's self for this, like scoop of mud,
some, a nice cud-ball which whistles down air to
the back of always, oh one adored strategic behav-
ior, thermodynamics, astrophysics, one penetrated
biomedical engineering and hurled one's self strato-
spherically, but, he, I, just millimeters like a piano
forte or bunker, faux cripple on the world's other
side sloshing molten philosophy and diacriticals
into a hardening diesel block thrown half an inch
into eternity, vibrating some, before a lover's toes.

301

For thirty years' service they award me a frog with leopard markings, I name it Strindberg and construct an indoor habitat with waterfall fern fronds slate pavers dried flies, nights Strindberg croaks accusations, hack dreamer fake amateur bitter slob, side-to-side in bed autistically I rock, Strindberg persists, tenacious, ungrateful, inconsiderate, Strindberg raw machine, Satan's spawn fizzing glop which I cannot crush, cold clammy squat nosing water, charlatan, twit, leopard judge in silver sheen digesting invertebrates, head aflame addicted to granite erupts complete sentences, you comical moron confusing competence with megalomania, ineptitude with abjection, believes bull shit of destiny, superiority, steamed and pressed, good god what an idiot, dumbkoff, hadn't a prayer nor are you brilliant, shelve it, loveless as an injection who imagines himself indispensible, I drag calf's liver through catchup and slurp, favorite meal, onions caramelized, pond swallows produce executioner's tongue, disingenuous puffer aware of his scam, bombastic mediocre wimp, false prophet, self-castigator.

302

I operate alone, a cartilage-nerve grotto, and want no chums
their idiotic cutseyness, dark jungle drum, huntsman, animal,
pink fern fronds, deadly red trap pulsing, boyishly, sucking
down nursers, motherers, beer caves, wet tabled, shiny, urin-
ous, torque of literature, enfold of poetry, helpless vulvas
swallow image, sufferers curled like pintos, serious slip side-
ways seams cracks alone apparitional alone into sanctum,
chiffon, silk, perfume, toepaint, female smells Cutex cotton,
fuse, bang, pupils leaking onto nipples, nopples of me, love
swoll, coupling, prowl lean and slithe without crust of chor-
tleheads, bleating pigsnouts scrawling up the air, see her
guide my long smashed finger into her, my smashed de-
formity and moan, moan, coon, hound, I always, always,
smooth warm milk caressing, enswirling, baths of milk
along nude contours, mounds, hips, heavy white dream
lain in, cream poured hair, lying in bowl of heated milk
produced from my wrists, eroticist, Mr. Bataille of the
intellectual class, nothing more crucial than penetrating
flesh, I pour myself round shivering curves, amber eyes
tripling night, like the Catholic confessing sins slide
my tongue through swollen lips, the slayed and the slain.

303

One spends one's life, one must of course, total devotion, absolute divinity, worship and sacrifice, altar, fire if fire, one enslaves one's and piles, hill perhaps, mountain maybe, ants, grains, unimportant expirations, throw them in and keep building, increments, increments, layer, layer, chip away they say, stiff upper lip, boot straps, never die saying, everyone else snorkeling, sailing, but subject total energy, grinding off prints, backache, hemorrhoids, brain rag, but what else with the grunting onslaught weakling-trampling, mush and human paste glowing like toxic waste, one extends and distends, devil-labor, pacing out crushing hooves, tidal, head afire with, uncompromising, superbeautiful, with indisputability, well, flesh of the thing, fibula through calf, wholly given like a manna loaf, muscular forearms, the metaphysical apron, lead, asbestos, firewalling always, cradle to dust in service excellence, scraped off nipples, chin, aforesaid prints, glockenspielist, surgeon, horologist, engineer, grinding on night grit elbow to nub, explosives technologist, sutures and wounds, well, one life invests, whole bolt, or naught and naught anyway often, soften the blow with zoloft or coke, microscope, sternum spreader, dead center lathe, mallet and rail, wheels on rods indefatigably pumping, or drilling unimpeded through zero gravity space a perfect hollow streak like a fired human bullet, effortlessly, to terminal implosion.

304

In the meantime pagans rampage, cunnilingus, fellatio, orgies,
inebriation, gluttony, golden calf, human sacrifice, murder,
one bearded jackal auctions his daughter while rubber lady
stretches herself into a massive vagina, the clangor rising
atomic, sodomy-bleat, kid-slaughter, noose-creak, vomit-
sputter, while peakwise solid energy singes and sunburns
Pop-Pop crazing his eyes and walloping breast in a little
private ceremony involving autokinesis, ventriloquism,
automatic writing, astral projection, and hyperreality, Pop
turning blue to shocked to radioactive praising alike pos-
tules and elasticity, staggers, loses footing with such
cumbersome rocks, tumbles bleeding knee, regains, the
usual overburdened mountaineer comedy while, as stated,
below like ants rudimentary musicians whip the masses
like curdled cream, between God and hedonism a gaseous
bloom, clear hostility, burnt-robed Daddy and come
smeared Baby on bubble's outer edges, piss on it,
no other, vain, honor thy, false wit, pull penis from
pants and piss on it, better yet, defile with defecation,
squat and shit this alphabet, then tickle her till she
shrieks, naked orbs, well, I mean, blasphemy, so
many gaping naked hungry organs, ecstasy nodes,
mouths, orifices, lips, flesh, pressing the sky, rub-
bing, banging, longing like a root-intwisted brick and
Father drunk on eternity descending into this pit.

305

Stomach hurts, stuffed with wheat thins, bananas, I've
eaten faithlessness and anger, stomach converts dough-
balls into dry putty, cannot excrete, I eat punishment
and retribution, stomach rife with crocodiles, I devour
but rarely enjoy love, stomach eats heartlessness like
the national anthem, now it squeezes box-cars stuffed
with corpses, I drink Pepto-Bismol, I dissolve Borax
in hot emetic but do not imbibe, stomach's fist snatches
gummy bears through mouth, mischievousness's big
molars, I reject the suppository as ache expands to in-
somnia, I scarf woman's scalp and toe nails through
licked chops, and hair in lovely clumps chased with
Revlon, I do not eat crucified men nor athletes, nor
jurors in polished seats, unceasingly through marital
dissolutions, bankruptcy, suicide attempts it turns
industrial blades, it eats cancer and acute psychosis
and cries for pumping, I shove in chino slacks and
phenobarbital, atheism and politicians, once from lips
of death-bed friend happiness burbled, green with
phlegm like a bog monster, insignificant as a plug, my
duodenum demanded tragedy, celery, cat claws, ham,
I need Tums, Mylanta, Rolaids, and God-Lax and
am sour with gas, but ingest fish teeth, spine bits, rat-
gut, and Wednesdays the sperm covered Eucharist.

306

Do you think, do you imagine, don't make me laugh, what a ridiculous, I mean really, what joke, you, you must be out of your, bonkers, us? we? are you kidding? with our distinguished, reputation, notices, announcements, the very best, one glance was enough, dilettante, interloper, shoddy impersonator, curiosity is all, amusement, idle distraction, and you honestly, in your filthy rebellion imagining yourself, what, Sacher-Masoch, de Sade, Rimbaud, Bataille, outlaw lawlessness, filthy manifesto, and you think we would, lunatic, nutcase, arrogant nonentity, inflation to the nth, my good man look about, cathedral, fearful, reverential, capacious, we pulp in our steel machine poseurs, hacks, amateurs, idiots, knew immediately from your jutting, tinsel eyes, hesitancy, the betraying works of your, doltish wooden responses, to overuse a word, clueless, dumb lost dog pushing to nowhere, voidishly trotting, flatness of eyes, wax paper sheen, vague reflex, intelligent enough not to comprehend your disability, we are, look at us man—jawline, superstature, eye-dazzle, luminosity—selected, an uber-species, whereas you and ilk incorrigibly average, futile, though I may say acceptable, but to expostulate, to propound that you could ever is to bash your head against the inestimable.

307

I don't want to be friend, anyone's friend, distrust, suspect, you and rage, blindness, and stupidity, jealousy and greed, brutal confections of puppetry, oozing eyes needle pierced, torrents of alcohol inflamed brain and rampant defensiveness, stay back fucker with your teenager head, idolatry and liquid cash flowing in veins like gasoline, I slide bolt and read Schwartz-Bart, Yevteshekno, leave my family alone, headlights and lead pipes, steering wheels and zip guns, I too am integument and testicles, intestines, and ganglia, pulpy bug under your crusher, I cower in earth scar with wife and child under dirt and leaves, three throbbing morsels, as you thrash by clutching slaughter like scripture, bullets of terror freezing through my blood, hooligans, rapscallions, god's minion-butchers, begone, disappear, leave me sit in chair and read testimonials and acervations, gunpowder baby, hack master, automaton, schizoid on viscera.

308

Clown death, Bozo death, red ball nose and bulb shoes, clown accouterments, a harnessed stubborn ass braying behind, a Bergmanesque landscape, pyres, plagues, harlequins, knights, bawdy love, Clarabel clopping, giggle guffaw, in ring with bears, sweat-streaked grease, tangerine hair, in clangs fire engine, braang, braang, death falls on butt, bounces up, dashes, caught in ladder, run run run to keep up, spotlight drums facial pores, cymbal, death rolls to stop, dashing under trapeze, a shitting elephant elicits hilarity, oh god that's rich, death hops like a broken cricket round the half naked bareback beauty, glittering white horse wearing king's crown, plumes, sequined tail, naked thighs, death throws a pail of shredded paper water at a child who flinches, laughs licking a bright red sphere, audience erupts, canon-man arcing to net after the pow! resounding, death upended bounces trampoline to canon-man who spiders off net to riotous applause, death pantomimes, producing a big yellow bat which he bonks upon birdman to birdman aplomb, oh well, miniature chromium motorcycles interweave Kadiddlehopper, lace him up like a worn out boot, he shoots the water gun daisy, produces mallet, puts up dukes, one grabs his pantwaist while legs beat him nowhere, teeth, tongues, waddles, hats, in rushes cuckold, pederast, terrorist, geek shooting firehose wildly, wet begets wet, ass in ague ecstasy kicks away followed by leash, the tent, the whole bloody tent wilds like shadowy gang rapists, one two three four aching for a turn, chip of lapis death as if hauled on wire flies through a rent, newly sprouted wings, dancing bear Hey-Zeus in tutu and Danskin tank whirls out a flap like a stumblebum drunk and trikes away down Haywire Ave., anticlimactically amidst a muddy trampled field—needles, Tampax, diapers, fetuses, empties, and puke —it ends.

309

Singing, I spin, briefcase belling like a gown, shiny patent
leathers, I swing round lamp post, on-off curb, I chirp, tweed-
le, cheep, whistle, coat tail flying, I tap, scoop apple, slam
down bill, Chevalier, Kelly, hopscotch through kids' chalk-
stick grid, hands gripping handle like a hammer throw I
whirl round attaché—kettles, trumpets—arms outstretched,
folders, pens, calculator, notebook, lunch snapped inside
brassy leather, company, firm, skip-to-lou through rot
iron gate, sepulchral sculpture, pretzel cart, jig and jag,
zig and zag, backward, forward, neck protruding, head
bouncing through crowd, between, left, right, rear, bobbing,
disembodied, arias, bellows, diaphragm finale, tonsils
inhaling all, commuters, apartment houses, department
stores, halls, la-la la-la la-la La, be embraced millions!
lucky boy, clicking, heart's mirrors flashing, break into
jig, flinging sequins, waters part, I could soar like a sheet
of breeze-lifted paper, instead I stop, planting both feet
on makeshift boardwalk, jackhammer, diesel, excavator,
dump truck, legs vibrating, balls tingling, everything
alive, it's a turn down day and I dig it, ribbons through
my head like cake icing flowers, nobody's dead, nobody
clobbered, Mr. Blue Sky, we're so pleased, up there wait-
in', oh I have slipped the surly bonds of earth, loosen
tie, open shirt collar, coat slung over, and rumbling the
skeleton arrives the gusher blowing the whole thing
in its impact, explosion, profusion, and wallop, to bits.

310

I'm unparalleled, I'm God, I'm messiah and savior, I'm damn good, I'm a worthless piece of shit, moron, idiot, I'm fucking amazing, I'm nonpareil, I'm superman, I'm trash, compost, mediocre, banal, genius, virtuoso, I'm incomparable, I'm peerless and without blemish, flawless and without stain, I'm angel, archangel, Host incapable of error, I'm bungler, bum, goodfornothing, I'm toilet, piss on me, I'm an execrable abortion, smear shit on me, disregard the hideous creature hulking before you, oaf, I'm inestimable and priceless, beautiful beyond comprehension, glowing, Abraham, Isaac, and Jacob, Jesus of bulrushes, approach me with awe for I am terrifying and omnipotent, an obscenity, leprous bastard, defecate on me, cremate me, dispatch me to the chambers, I the resurrection, supremacy, bow before your King, your coward, your fool, cover me in spit, donkey, ass, failure, bonehead, automaton, doofus, glorious olympian laurel-wreathed, indefatigable biathlete, hairless streamlined missile dissolved into the universe like a pastel tablet, infinitude, pure compact sugar burst by prayer, your guru rinpoche, Padmasambhava, inimitable holy entity whose very digits glow, bowed head halo and levitated above conformity's quotidian crush, sea-of-faces herd, but I am loser, buffoon, inattentive careless impatient dolt ruining everything, unworthy of your fingernail dirt.

311

I herewith pronounce you the next generation of killers, we gorged our gut on Zylkon 2, sulphur mustard, white phosphorous, nuclear fission, now it's you, exterminators, petit-criminals, hypocrites, Gods with unspeakable high technologies, some will murder primarily babies, others families, others, beautifully hammering, populations, Cosimo, Nathan, Abraham, Abigail of cloud puff pubis and creamy heel, I hereby decree with these graduation certificates extraordinary potential, we sated, slaked, tore, defecated until sore and exhausted, grotesque bloated roadside corpses, skulls pyramidal, a spill of brilliance like glittering jewels, we supped on liver and fucked on lungs, split with laughter, let it be said we blasted our world, now you *en mass* with millennial appurtenances, unimaginable buttons, futuristic machines, lust-buzzed heads spun here by masters: Cunningham, Constantin, Hungerford, Massman, your professorate of antiquated ideas, spiral outward small systematic nuclei and committees into ganglia, basal paste, alveoli, reproductive tar submitting in unprecedented speed liquefaction and perishment, genetics, psychopharmacology, particle physics, cybernetics, make the fatuous billion cheeks into death masks, go forth, loved ones, with new efficiency, and kill.

312

I drink until black out, alcohol saturated cortex struggles
for verticality, finally topples like Orwell's elephant,
suffering, horny, empty-handed, no cunt to fuck, keys lost,
upon dank concrete, I never vomit, gut eruptionless, what
happened, groped, pawed, yodeled, peed, phoned sluts,
tumbled, oh fuck, I remember weed, at my ancient pubic
age chasing coeds, look ma no hands, fool, blockhead,
village idiot, oh but such skin, such vagina, and me pour-
ing down Beefeaters at McFadden's, can I buy you one,
so beautiful, unbelievable hair, sinking to bluntfish, cold
bodied herbivores submarining my hips, so, plastered,
town a sick casino swallowing coins and clanging, oh
shit, oh shit, what about you, you, surely you, and slam-
ming whathaveyou, shots, pitchers, pints, dregs, look-
ing for someplace to slip my finger, a back seat, any-
where, fucked up and blacked out on dank concrete,
apartment foyer, a great big glass dome of a night,
and I licking residue, numb, not singing, desperate for
sex, field or vacant lot, hard, sharp, warm, gazing
up, scraping, grunting like a gaseous fish, old as bloat-
ed Ajax divorced by the sun and spit down here to
strike matches and thrash for a shitty piece of ass.

313

Beheaded twitching slaughtered beasts dangle from hooks pouring gore into drain, we fuck underneath, sustaining clots and thick red sashes, on slimy concrete we sixty-nine, I feel like God half down her throat, and strive through cunt to penetrate divinity, cattle swing, decapitated heads erupting drool, eyes glaring, I flip her onto knees, hike rump, take her from behind, thrusting deep into lips, stomachs, intestines, glands, bowels, cream-red clump, bone white lube, grease, eyelash, snout, stun gun, knife, hose, tray, and she and I writhing in blood-paradise, naked, smeared, my mother's trick valve like an agitating washer throwing out blood, my asinine father drunk on megalomania and sick-o dreams, hardly a knuckle on scabrous hands, cows, semen, panting, kiss, fingerpainted hips, industrial concrete abattoir, death bunker, orgy of meat, fuck on gore, fuck on clot, fuck on gut, cheap clean apricot sheets stinking of Sears disgust, Odysseus, Sinbad, Shazaam coming to boil, I find length of rope, I tie her up, ankles to wrists, naked, nude, exposed, rag over mouth, dribble the snot of freshly killed creature and take her atop a mountain of guts and gore and hell.

314

God dwells in partially digested food, vomit God, fully digested is too late, slid and drifted away, capture God in toilet bowl, see, smell God, flush God into sewer, God a burrito pool, pasta bits enzyme and acid shiny, pecans packed in Karo, God cannot exist in bundt on plate or tray of double stuff, like alchemy requires hydrochloric, spit, secretion in human gnash, this illusive proof in throw up, is throw up, ram down two fingers hunched over Toto and see Deity, sheer religion, Christ's face, and there warps a hymn, benediction, saving grace, the only God in church is the one bulemic erupts in the women's, locked, near empty offices smelling of leather, on knees, strawberry pancakes, links, margarine scoops, yellow-green Jesus, finally, in First Garden of Gethsemane, Ipecac works, 3% hydrogen peroxide, table salt and tepid, close eyes in deepest prayer, patent leather, pink dress, come to me, materialize, reveal Thy face, enfold me in Thy chunks, I confess, spare me, I am sinner, out nose, too, like rope, once it enters bowels as waste it's hell, hate, shame, brown murder, God transformed into useless fecal matter, filthy pipes, reek, rage, raw sewage.

315

I lay on carpet and spread legs so that she can see my erection from base where it joins rectum, all this she takes into mouth, blood, flesh, nerve endings, veins pumped stiff with urge, she kneels and kisses hair taking me in, on the flat of forearm and elbow jack, head thrust back, I arc my body raising cock to pinnacle—rocket, missile—which fills her throat, she cups balls and lifts me like a bowl and I belong to her whom I trust not to bite me off and spit it like botulism, not to dismember in spontaneous betrayal or mangle between grinders, I fear the psychotic break, preternatural hate, but this is heroin, god, oblivion numbing self-hate and the shame inspired mutilation wish, she jams me down like a satyress, I could, pre-empting, strangle her under candlelight, with superior muscle throw her backwards without cinematography or musical score, monstrously, but this is nirvana, spit, shaft, slip, drip, plum-red head glowing like a bomb, the human organism terrifies, low slung cruel, slaughter in dirt and deep thicket, I imagine every shot spermatozoan a poison-tipped arrow.

316

Wielding a cigarette with a needle sticking out the ash, an
intruder chases my wife who runs naked through unfamiliar
rooms, seizing he jabs the needle into her neck, drugs and
rapes pumping violently with rage, perceiving eyes in paralyzed body my wife watches helplessly, alert but voiceless,
a comatose patient receiving malpractice surgery, watches and cannot scream—vaginal lips squeeze the awful prick
whipping, jamming, shooting jism, hairy genitals like monstrous tonsils banging her ass, those alien wallpapered
rooms reminiscent of her childhood Victorian long ago
sold to aliens, this needle-bearing cigarette a most diabolical machine, injecting rape victim with novocaine,
like dental patient gums, for the witnessing travesty, filled
with sperm my wife staggers through pitiless rooms, ruined, to pillows and comforter in a faraway place frothed
with ocean unzipping and zipping warm sand in sun,
pebbles clicking over themselves in infinite profusion,
feet sinking in darkgreen pools, horrid dream, wants to
spit and wash the arrows from her slit, women take what
jams their cunt, behind dumpsters, in minivans, on dirt
roads, in dormitories and operating rooms, staggering
through crops, hallways, dead fathers, churches, episiotomies, needle sticking through burning torch and running naked through unknown rooms smack into the
solid chest of rapist, murderer, comedian, idiot, or god.

317

I return as a raving hag in the adjoining room, rasping, "kill Jews," "cremate Jews," three A.M., wringing hands, one eye gouged, rotted teeth, gut churning greasy food, lamp blaring, you perceive under crack my shadow pacing, flimsy wall between, you scant inches away conceiving, as planned, a child, pre-conscious protected zygote, I could murder everyone, I return a wigged-slipped witch screaming nigger, kike, exterminate, deep six, and you beyond the wall create a boy, I reincarnate as the anti-Christ bulldozing people I have killed with cyanide, anthrax, fire, knives, into pit, I hex-woman, Styx-fish, pythoness, and you vermin eating glue and shitting little balls of shit, pestilence, plague, blight, infestation, I perform the mandatory procedures: incineration, sterilization, gas chamber, smallpox, preserving freaks in alcohol as proof for God, previously literati, professor, abstract artist, chef, book shop afficionado, public library nut, I have returned corrected, adjusted, cleaned up, perfected.

318

Simultaneously I fuck a woman and kill a man whose
stab wounds drool, I devour manicotti and masturbate
which stimulates ferocity, I teach students Whitman
while my urine pools about their shoes, I clip toe-
nails while stuffing bedsheet down my father's throat,
oil soaked, thin, slickery, simultaneously I crack
my neck and sipping Beefeater strangle Mary Magda-
lene, popping, lolling, sin, hair, paralyzed Joseph
looking on like wimp, the things we do simultan-
eously, licking ice cream and vomiting beans on
Gandhi's feet, doubled, green, strawberry, alone,
hot wind cutting skin, glass-sharp wind, digging
into purse for change while sawing off Harry's hand,
heart and lung, tongue and law, twin exfoliations,
I perform cobra while stalking Connie with rabbit's
blood, a birthday clown stuck in fumes, well, and
what, here I pray—tifilin, yarmulka, penis in pants,
moles, age spots, spinal cage, Rock, Redeemer,
Father, King, atonement-driven in this holy mo-
ment starving for jamcakes in velvet temple packed
with penitents murmuring love, while onto my
feet a victim's bowels spill down my twisting fist.

Prayers

319

What shall we say before Thee, who art on high, and what
shall we recount unto Thee, who dwellest in the heavens?
Dost Thou not know all things, both the hidden and the
revealed? Thou knowest the secrets of eternity and the
hidden thoughts of every living being, therefore, I am, if
Thou knowest my darkest horror thoughts, if Thou knowest my misanthropic fantasies, if Thou knowest tapioca
concupiscence, if Thou knowest the red, the black, therefore I am, if Thou seeeth my brain pitchfork and asbestos hide enveloped in flame, O, O, if Thou, indeed,
noticeth inside underpants my rousing penis spit lube,
a leaky clutch, weeping, weeping, if Thou catcheth me
at toilet with photo of Cindy beating under spongy
ridge poor ramrod raw, I mean, if Thou knowest, O dear
God, of my slaughtered multitude: lithe on natal plum,
warty in swamp, and chirping in razor grass, cannonaded, impaled, electrocuted, and fried, why recount
should I when Thou already knowest my vilest ineptitude involving the neonate slick in amniotica, then
plastic of drawers, then dungaree down, shot full of
snow in a drywall cube taking it up ass for another
hit, my homo sapiens' snout blood red of him, nosing the wound, well, O what shall we say before
Thee who knoweth our punctured, our loathed, our miserably loved, our slushy intransigence, and who diveth with my deepest marlin heart, the spool of line
smoking, to the darkest ocean cleft, unto Thee we
are but skinless nipple, porous membrane, damask
dangling by pins, pierced by light, glowingly opaque,
human wafer lemoned in the yellow crisp of shame.

320

We have turned aside from Thy commandments and from the beneficent ordinances, and it has not availed us, Thou art righteous in all that has befallen us, for Thou dost justice, but we have wrought evil, therefore I am destitute with fornication for I have fornicated with wonton beasts, heavy of teat, Styxian milk, grease lips sucking me as of the lamprey and wrapped about like the squid pressing me to brand with smoke, garlicky fish, dirty foot wenches, married whores, frustrated marginalized teenagers so wet lube sheets down thighs, by lower case god, I evil, I have, blind runny eye, feeling along walls, I am desiccated of alcohol, stumbling, peeing, a dead bee, husk of rotted cells, swigging, dissolute, grabbing gin, ginned up and fucking both slut and hand, at filthy glitter mirror bartender line-up tequila whisky who gives a fuck, prop of existentialist legitimizing book, *Nausea*, I have turned aside, commandments, not availed, wrought bad, for I am horrid of abandonment, abandoned thumbsucker bawling, red thumb at driveway, projectile saltwater, nononononononono but did, yes, busting prison, unstuck from mistake, corroded I do, gunked, grit, gone, horrid I say in all befallen, unavailed of Thee, abandoned woman with afterbirth like a cocksucker by god, Ford, Michigan from terrifying Texas, concrete, bye bye and bye choking down sputt, four tens ago, benificent ordinances like dead fish in a dynamited cove, purity, chastity, truth, generosity, selflessness, pale bloated chub and I frothing like a dog craving pouches, Thou dost justice frying my bone and crisping like a wick I of the Pleiades and county dump fluttering like chicken paper and smudge of catchup, it has not availed, and grunt I char and dystrophy and funk and sclerosis and pustules and testicular and demon and jab unawake.

321

Our God and God of our fathers, pardon our transgressions,
remove our guilt, and blot out our iniquities on this day of
Atonement, as Thou hast promised, peel up my skin like
contact paper and soap raw the filthiness, amen, twist
Palmolive down my throat, shoot shaved flakes up my
urethra for I am iniquitous, abominable father-loather,
mother fucker, dump Borax into brain and acid in eyes
for lascivious licentious tastes, I carved with tongue
my initials on slut-cunt and stiffed on winged dragon
my impressionable son, dear merciful Dad pardon, this
blasphemer, idolator, piece of shit, secret exterminator
of rip-bodied males their flexion of superiority, company men and caramel mouthed fools sucking their
tongues, Thou hast promised like my birthday cake
wedge, for I am dregs and rotted fig turning water, shoot
voltage down your thumb like soul cauterization, recreate miscreant, foul fucker, cheater, abortionist, prig,
bitter borsht, atonement, atonement, this my day, my
amaryllis flower a cast iron ball bashing champions
and calling down walls of imaginary blood, Oh Father,
God of fathers, my Father, my great grandfather's Father, God of history's surcease, first human father, absolution, grace, raise this craven loser to the apex of your
scepter flanked by eagle's wings radiating inscription.

322

We sanctify Thy name on earth, as the heavens glorify Thee on high; and in the words of the prophet we say: Holy, holy, holy is the Lord of hosts; the whole world is full of His glory, reminded of Darrow intertwined round Kong's knuckles, how he worshiped that girl, platinum luminescent fairy to his ogredom, firefly glittering sky, oh god he ached, sweetie pie, honey bunch, babycakes, repulsive blunt nose and jackhammers, black vinyl chest, patchy naked ass, harboring gooey caramel heart melting for her amongst hot grit of entertainment eaters, milquetoasts, and dolts, reminded of lummoxes clomping about blonde clit, wrist corsages and Cold Duck, holy holy holy, this tight little thing, full of glory, and suicidally beautiful Kongs slaughtered on wheel, Ephemera in his frightful fist fleetingly as he swung the needle gushing righteousness from lips, and in the words, Lord of hosts, the whole world full, tumbling and bashing parapets receding from blonde Goddess screaming to Denham asphalts, congregants clutching balls and tits against the excremental quake smashing faith while upon narrow balconies mockery in twit furthering his dead sanctification.

323

For He satisfieth the longing heart and filleth the hungry with good. Oh, that men would praise the Lord for His goodness and for His kindness to the children of men, oh that men would praise the Lord for his kindness to the children of men, Oh that men would Lord kindness children, etcetera, for he stuffeth gut with bread-paste and sealeth heart with love-grout, joy-glue, for He, and Oh that men would hymn pure and gloriously within echo chamber and without among grey squirrel and red, for He satisfieth and filleth little hungry runts runny of sewer water diarrhea and those who eat twigs, yea, and the desiccated pump and how He eventually in rotation stuffeth with weird happy paste screwed through blue tube called redemption through love, or resurrection in come, hallelujah, Lord praise would men that, and add eternally, for we are children of men who in turn mewled who themselves drooled and babbled for strained peas through blackness and floods back to naughty Eve and her effeminate fool, a fucking row row rowboat round, crickets, bonfire, blow of sparks, well, praise His kindness to we shuttlecock pieces batted across epochs, Gerard, Gunther, Hortense, Peter in various raiment, beef au jus, pompano en papillote, bowties in carbonara, illuminated hosannas, bananas flombeau, a deep liquid metal swallows narcissists.

324

Hear O Israel! the Lord Thy God, the Lord is One,
and simply I go bonkers, giggling at devastation,
masturbating into dirty laundry, plotting my father's
extinction, the thing orgasmically exploding, grave
of sand, and then, monstrously, throwing in mom,
they watching sand shoveled in and possibly
shouting the grunt they christened my name, futilely
upward toward my shape, Hear O Israel, and I
cut myself, demand an answer, roaring obsceni-
ties smash banana against my clenched teeth,
that's not she under sheets, she never sleeps
like that, Little Red Hood inside wolf's gut? guilty
adulterers? boxed burglar Jack? anyway, Hear,
I open, O, I surround, Israel, I swallow the whole
goddamn pie, Lord, stomach ache, God, vomit,
Lord, second wave, One, I cry obesity shame,
watchword of my faith, frogs, horned toad, wala-
bee, and goat, I disgust—not me, my work—pro-
fessor Wilcox at State U who eschews, eschews,
how flat the serpent makes itself, through cracks,
under door, the cereal box, weddings, etcetera,
needle scratching record, wince, sin, hiccup,
repeat, again, again, O hear, is One, eloheinu
adonai, the mice are stuffed with joy, let us
live, my life to live, the silence, winter light.

325

Open unto us, O God, the gates of mercy before the closing of the gates, ere the day is done. The day vanishes. The sun is setting; let us enter Thy gates. And we crash upon Thy massive castle gatewall in a solid wave, spewing upward and smashing back into the damned mass, halted against Thine clenched jaw, crescendo of trapped man, we attack each other in frenzied Sabbath, bitten, biting, clawed, a feeding seam, open onto this slimy morass of stomachs and tongues, merciful gates O God before we rot on hell's concrete, day vanishes, omnipotent one, sun rags hang on trees' dark limbs, crack Thy grin of powder blue and pink admitting the rectitudinous, the repentant, the a-shamed, shove in them another year of cheese steak and fries, Thine Supreme Father a rival's head dangles from its hair in my mouth, death grimace fixed, shocked torn off, my back bite-punctured, at Thine gatewall pleading leniency, yes seduced, deceived, fucked a pig, coveted, stripped fat, stuffed, off ribs, but contrite, minuscule in contrition, a bled white satyr in a dirty corner, humble this cataclysmic vanishing day receding into graininess, prostrate now among the cheaters, bozos, shitheads, losers, and fools, I die to exclaim, "alas, it creaks!"

326

And they that shall be of Thee shall build the old waste places, Thou shalt raise up the foundations of many generations; and Thou shalt be called: the rebuilder of the ruins, the restorer of paths to dwell in, as in mansions raised on shit more beautiful than rice wherein absolution exists in gleaming pantries washed in gold light, I rebuild myself on ruins into stiff canvas sail ice-encased but billowing, billowing, let us pray that upon waste's vault whole societies of vegetative silk, celery love, radish empathy, corn congeniality, boyish exultation in neckerchief and khaki shorts fresh as lakesheen who shall ripen, split, and bring forth hives, faces in cells inseminating faces restoring nuclear irradiated paths interpenetrating winter, rebuilder, restorer who swallowed a church of marzipan and hatpins, hammering up a world, pray, foundations, generations, waste, ruins, dwell, oh well, we of thee shall spit rivets into fuselages, tongue-drill steel, saw lumber with knees screaming out synagogues into which we drift heart full of psalm, architects of the gong, oh they're beautiful, all of them so beautiful, painfully beautiful and here am I on ruins constructing, on feces constructing cities in the sky for god, for god, for god's sake, oh my bloody god.

327

Thine everlasting arms, oh Lord, uphold all creation. Thou art our unfailing help. Darkness does not conceal Thee from the eye of faith, nor do forces of destruction obscure Thy presence. Above the fury of men and the raging of the tempests standeth Thou, Rock and Redeemer, hatred blunts light, rage blots faith, despair gnaws joy but Thou colossal thighs, Thou pectoral mound uphold all, even Thy sinners, Peter cannot, Ginger cannot, Valencia cannot upon their strings support Thy unimaginable spangle, numberless smear across incomprehension, not even McGillicuddy's cast iron rib can support such magnificence, we crush like pestle-ground lumps powdering spine and skull, Lord alone of squeezing genie claw bursts whom we love through pressure and plague, his indestructible muscle swinging us like crates of perishables, fragile plums, bruised cassavas, boneless babes, man's measly preoccupation with power and sex, vat-snakes eating each other in holiday strophes and perpetuating the vat by laying eggs, this aloft on sturdy shoulders, angry love and facile dreams, permanent as the spattered black dome and blue cloisonne sky are impervious to the little nubs and crevasses below.

328

On this Sabbath of Remembrance, when we recall Amalek, and all the foes who have ever threatened our existence, let us dwell on the power of faith and devotion which has preserved us to this hour, preferential for our excellence in epochs of mediocrity, recall Mordecai, Judah Maccabee, Jerub-Baal, and diminutive David, Jepthah, too, with his speedy oath rankling adversaries, on this recalling drooling butchers I name You faith and rolling devotion shelving my Nietzschean wedge for hymns, we beseech Thee O Lord, preserve us now, for enemies abound clutching scimitars, nimshas, rapiers, and swords, my bolt is prayer, I need not lock, Father, Protector, up to this red velvet voluptuous hour of gleaming solemnity and throughout the years let us remember Amalek, Ramses, and Adolph, three exquisitely cut jewels set in animal dung, and their associates, and the nails of prayer which has to this preserved hour, spackle, mortar, mashed flesh, paste of tongue, oh Stalin, oh Ahashureus, disheartened, discouraged, forlorn upon knees we dwell in dubious bask, my unpersecuted father, ankles' papery-skin peeling like birch, raging in bed, unexecuted mother dripping egg from numb in Christ's Body, Texas, power faith popping off lips like costume pearls, magicians and props, seven-eight-nine-ten, a surreal production, bubbling toads observed from bridge, each burp a hymn, manfully, undaunted, steadfast, clean; God, King, performance, delectation.

329

We beseech Thee, O Lord, save us now. We beseech thee O
Lord, make us now prosper. O Lord, answer us on the day
that we call. God of all spirits, save us now for the skinless
pit monster, dripping, approaches, enzymes and razors,
tendons and stomach, the netherworld exterminator brain-
less as stone scrapes us like cherries, red flows, oh Lord
now, today, for Satan abounds about our beds, red pri-
mordial bonehead killer, pig snout, boar bones, bear
paws, panther pulse, bull back, efficient as the axe, bruise
blue, wet boulder, O Host, O King, Isaac's a dropped
turd, acids break down Jacob, Abraham buttered Jep-
thah, Mary bird-mashed, wad of blood, we Thee be-
seech with shaky nerves, hypothermia, shock prostra-
tion, wrapped in silver sanctuary blankets for nerves
transmit pain, brain vitamin laps, heart rides the pony,
to salivate tender fleshed we before incubus exits mists
of blood, so love us love us love us like you love
sweet babies and marmalade, creativity and repose,
starsmear and lax, before—in the million-appendaged
hell bastard's masticating bottomless gut—extinction.

330

O Thou who dost reveal Thyself in endless ways, deepen within
us the sense of Thy presence in the world and in the sanctuary of
our hearts for labyrinths wind through us inhabited by aardvarks,
disclose Thy whereabouts in serpent's eyes, fisher's fangs, scorpion's sac, for Thou art vistaless, without horizon, but endless
spark dancing upon All's magneto, but deepen, plunge the infinite black lightyears within human heartfist, diving longbodied like inner illuminated gossamer thread through splattering red, your universe multiplied by billions, if Thou fail the
plutostructure erupts volcanics of collision, each of us explodes in various addictions, coitus, mainline, slug, cakecity, pithed barbiturates, volatile and violent as teenage
gangs, sanctuary world presence Thy, powder us in your passage with guttural colors, silver coal, shredded red, ground
glass green, that we may bubble soak and sup on bone-in
love tenders, O Savior which endlessly dost, ensanctuaried,
stop our noxious burrowers, decay-tunnels with a single
throb, here among bees! here within oats! here on tongue
buds! omnipresent and nowhere, chimeric, borealic,
weightless road grader, go deep inside molecule of each
cell's soul, and deeper through nuclei into other dimensions where blood rushes back through Christ's palms
and Pontius threads back into his father's balls, so deep
that presence shall be felt like one filling with concrete
after wrapping his mouth around a cement mixer chute.

331

Thou bestoweth lovingkindness on all Thy children. Thou rememberest the devotion of the fathers, and, in love, bringest redemption to their descendants for the sake of Thy name, But if child's father is undevout such as fornicator, murderer, or idolator, Thou destroyeth in revenge the child by smoke, deformity, or infection, little Wilhelm with pediatric leukodystrophy and daring Darlene with Glioblastoma Multiforme, exploding hearts and veins for paternal-dereliction, but those whose propogators supported God freight, warm caramel laden, pumping weight through clover meadow, humility field, gratitude river, in love bestowed, in lovingkindness poured, soft and slow…who is like unto Thee O, mysterious Thy ways, Ozzie drools in banging wheelchair whose dad seduced male adolescents, Melanie clangs in leg brace whose smashed papa embezzeled millions, one spills ink, one kills squid, one whips flanks, all grit teeth, Thou bestowest, Thou deliverest, Thou rememberest, of devout parentage at scroll and chalice, facet and nail, disk and chop, O little gherkin, pink pinkie lass, babycakes, puss, pass, pass, through this cave door into sumptuousness, longevity, stamina, flotation, why was I so cruel to cats.

332

God and Father, we have entered Thy Sanctuary on this Sabbath to hallow thy name and to offer unto Thee prayers of thanksgiving. The week of toil has ended, the day of rest has come, for simultaneously I am glad and bitter, a psychological smash-up between rest and labor, a life-shock so horrific I vacate Saturday's sofa, to deliver, perched upon pew, gratitude for respite, my murderous toil, my rehabilitating weekend drive, my wet mug on polished wood, while I in holy place glide open heart's ark releasing thanksgiving in jasmine waves, Sabbath, hallow, ended, prayer, tongue thickening like tapioca pudding, brulee turbonado, enter, bow head, in humility stoop, hello, yontif, nice to see, no suicide, one natural cause, one terminal, this toilsome, this laborious, this intractable, enter, sit, pray, purge, shove earthward perennial bulb that it may effloresce in the grease concerns, law emporiums, sterility houses, the parts departments where clowns gash noses and rag down machines, bless souls, entered Thy solemnity, plush, leaded, polished, hard, thanksgave prefatory to a rigid babe and roasted fat, toil doth both preserve and kill, I pray Thee on my breathing day—perforated, fungal, psoriac, cold—grant me 6-colon-1, rest to toil, that I may multiply hallow and praise, six-mouthed, fly-eyed, honeycombed with love, Father God Thy I am grizzly infantryman dragging across Your threshold his blown-up soul.

333

When storms of oppression beat down upon us and fires of persecution threaten to devour us, spread over us the tabernacle of Thy peace, and fortify our spirits with faith in Thee, the Guardian of Israel who sleepeth not nor slumbereth, for birdlings we, frail fearful wanting pectoral wing, muscular mushrooming shield to beat back hail and freeze fire of fear, showbread, golden lampstand, incense ark, that, tabernacle covering like raven wing, strung with force and elasticity, rustling fan of fortification, indestructible rotunda off which holocausts bounce like baby cats, saving us for reproduction, productivity, the indefensible tedium of intimacy, saving us nonetheless in Your sleepless vigilance, inject G into our spirits, flagging, withering, wilting on bone like rotting plums or snap beans, fortify fruit with faith in Thee, Omnivorous One, wolf us into Thy warming gut, Thy packed enveloping dirigible, Guardian, Prince, Protector, Knight when fire hails and malefactors creak inferno doors, suffused need You not, secure again no, nonsensical expanding, so, unslumbering Thee when shrinking, freezing, contracting, gnawing cover me with Thy raven's, cackling, cawing enraged at ravaging, damn, and damn, You scream, bloody crow and fan over we, we breakable, shreddable, expirational material souls, awaiting Thy rigid unbudgeable flexed plate of manhole.

334

The Lord is my shepherd, I shall not want. He maketh me
lie down in green pastures. He leadeth me beside still waters. He restoreth my soul which continually windowpane
shatters like lamb's blood, he restoreth me who eats his
cuticles and fingernails, munching tufts I lie beside babbling eddies a swaddled child in Lord's sweet breath,
unworried in health and love, rich of happiness, graceful under wandering cloudhorses and sun, there a valley wreathed in shadow healing lymphoma, hepatitis,
dementia, and poverty, the crib-dead revive and the
down-trodden eat sweet yellow pistils, He guideth meram to grassy knoll, multiplication through copulation,
wet, slick, hind legs, and inseminated the rest of peace,
robe folds trail Who waves a staff rippling the flock
like wind water to crystal zones where superabundance
rounds the ragged soul, pink tongues loll, and eyes
close like gladiolas, want shall I not among my flock
of sentimentalists, pacifists, consensualists, altruists,
and lovers with heavy wet vaginal walls, calories,
and song, shall follow forever Wilkenson Sword
shaved, Mennen skin-braced, and Ultra Brite brushed
this Mesmerist into the spiritual glade where finally
even earthly love peels off man like a decal or film of filth.

335

And now ere we part, let us call to mind those who have finished their earthly course and who have been gathered to the eternal home. Though vanished from bodily sight, they have not ceased to be; they abide in the shadow of the Most High, in Cloud Palace abide Thy Fatherliness not in nighttime floodlit football, pop pads and cleated turf, nor Pontiac love, but in ubiquity, universality, passing through lead, through paint into grain and stud, occupying interdimensional ghosts who've dropped their earthly gowns like happy brides on carpeted floors, hushed with heat, floating round like light itself, that was I, ruffled brocaded satiny thing, half rhinoceros, half pile of fingernails, I Princess Abortion manipulating subjects like a queen, now gathered to home eternal in godful space drifting through everything, call-mind-vanished-sight: vanity, fear, pander, deceit, waltz off this pew to your plop of pot roast and new potatoes, cadaverous schemes of flesh and profit like the bloated corpse of a dredged swimmer, I see in your blood the radioactive orange sludge indifference to the vanished, son to mother, husband to wife finally dead and shadowed under Most High, the Prince's loss, having recalled the bodiless oafs part this varnished holiness for seedy whore speakeasy wet panties garbage whiskey debauchery.

336

Therefore, hast Thou, O Father, in Thy love appointed for us a day of rest, that in Thy presence we may regain that freedom of the soul which comes through obedience to Thy Commandments, in Thy love Thou hast, from greed and toil reprieved, embezzlers, extortionists, cheaters, enviers, blasphemous hurlers of "god damn" and "Jesus fucking Christ" wage slaves and desk jockeys performing for pay, commuted from hell this day, we worship Him in soul-resurrection scooping pith of selves like baked squash in prostrate thanksgiving, we kindle, cough, cling, and disappear this Sabbath gift, and obey obey restoring law, for in exchange protects, preserves, and pleases He, soapishly, sliding up our guts heavenly Dove washing previous corrosion's heart, liver, and anal crud or marking bet-hedger with a bloody X whose tubular lies climb the organ's glittering pipes, but we pious imbued with fuel ride freedom like a sail to wholesale jewels, discount appliances, scrap metal, vending machines, meat processing, video arcade, and plumbing sales and service.

337

O Lord, keep my tongue from evil and my lips from
speaking guile that I may be guided into Your house
through purity, innocence, and cleanness of spirit,
for snakes crawl my tongue and scorpions my heart,
I conceal the profane and beseech Your strength
to stop my mouth with mud or concrete who obiter-
ates neighbor, "asshole," "idiot," "nutcase," "buf-
foon," who decimates professions, "broker," "ad-
vertiser," "pundit," "pope," who exterminates pom-
posity, fatuousness, elitism, cowardice, O Lord,
I sting myself and am bitten, I protrude my chest,
strike, smite, blow, rent me open spilling my sin
or expiate me stuffing in love like cream in a
puff, I am Your servant, convert me to benevo-
lence, disposition sunny, though I smear toward
the critical (like squall on a window) tearing holes
in the fabric, bone head, numbskull, and sim-
ilar appellations aggrandizing myself in a barrage
of invective, O Lord, give me pith, wack, stick,
and brit, tongue-fortitude, spin sugar between my
lips, wonderful thanks, liberation blue, magnifi-
cent orb, that I ride the huge invisible bubble to
the Outskirts of Love where my skin pops open
like a baked hot pepper from which I crawl half-
born in the mansion of nakedness and fragility.

338

We thank Thee for the life which in Thy goodness Thou hadst given and in Thy wisdom Thou hadst taken. Make us know Thy ways that in our love we may triumph over grief and despair for even life of worm Thy wisdom taketh, that number each needle and hair and designs packrat's death under garbage bin stuffed with peel and bone, teach Thy inscrutable which flares clear fuel jet from blood: sobriety, humanitarianism, dependability, hygiene, frugality, legion majesties, nexus of honesty, camel's hump humility, that grief's maw does not encave nor despair's encyclopedic brain, I am Thy dying gladly, thankfully of liver or pancreatic or mammalian, however, when praising Your love, gold or lead, sharp or dull, Your love My sustenance, pendulously swinging, O dear bloody goddamn Lord I am villain, suicide, blackguard, astronaut, psychopathic spiritual bedlamite who begs continuance and appreciates demise, ways know Thy, I know them: just, punctual, reliable, precise, swift, intractable, and we praise the coin soul, the chub, the chalice of wine, the Omnipotent way-wise, this our joy, to smash lead against blood, ash against lung, dung to tongue.

339

To you, who mourn the loss of loved ones, let there come the
comfort of the hope that, though the dust returns to the earth as
it was, the spirit returns to God who gave it, death being
anti-extinction thrusting spirit furtherward into vaporized
consciousness from decomposing fuel which recontributes
its clod to Earth's biomass, but the incorporeal glorious
in silver and clear travels everywill like dream within
dream ever-expanding which is magnificence returned to
King whose heart encompasses fourteen planets and whose
arms embrace galaxies, I do not ridicule this encrustation
which dissolves, spreads, interpenetrates becomes hope's
comfort as we grieve Elaine, Viv, Sophie, Ned who have
departed triumphant from chloroform flesh disrobing
tedium, spasms, invasions, insults, and flame-return to
their soft granulations under sizzling sphere and snow-
pack by revolutions and degrees, despair not mourners of
Jessica who dropped reproductive and digestive track in-
to the biohazard disposal box for she dissolves into grand-
eur beyond flesh, definitively delivered from the flatten-
ing bag into the omnipresent supereternal illuminated tit.

340

Thy rod and Thy staff, they comfort us, for insolence demands retribution and disorientation the fence, naughtiness requires smoking smite, welts in shape of gluttony's hand buckling on back like burnt wood, for every evil act parallels contrition rejoicing in failure of falsehood, impishness demands cleaved flesh as comfort, he who punishes gains loyalty—castration, torture, caning, chains—locking us in beautiful cells, there to shepherd with crook to halcyon fields and clear water for the tongue, Thy rod for willfulness, Thy staff for obedience, instruments of happiness to the soul of man, one sturdy nut-colored club for bashing skulls, one fine-grained amber staff for discouraging floods and ushering souls, let it be known they comfort us who are blunt crude sinful bastards without heart's joy or throat's grace.

341

O God of holiness, Thou knowest that we are but flesh, and in our weakness often yield to selfish indulgence. Create in us a pure heart, and a steadfast spirit renew Thou within us, steadfastness that vanquishes gluttony, lust, deception, sloth, the full envy spectrum disorder, an extra-strength steadfastness toward Thee, like shot arrows spinning through the fat of homicidal wrath and cockeyed pride, becoming pure shaft of spirit, yes, Thou knowest, Thou madest these pustules and jacks, these purses of need, stomachs, labias, penises, spleen, inadequate infantile irretrievable brain trapped in its Brunswick bowling ball sphere covered with hair, every cell a self indulgent prick stuffed with coke, sugar, smoke, genius, pork, gunpowder, and quake, weakness-packets in the trillions per specimen, renew Thou within us the headlight of spirit guiding us incorruptible through its staggering shaft, corrosion-free, clean, smooth as lubricant, slid.

342

On this Sabbath of Repentance, O our God, open our hearts to
its solemn call to turn from the vanities of life and consider our
destiny in the light of Thine eternal truth, as one who plunges
through narcissism reaches love, self-abasement, joy on
this day may we bathe greed in river of selflessness, ven-
geance in soapy forgiveness, O God of Souls, on this Re-
pentance Day cut into flesh whips of humility, cut forearms
and thighs, vaginas and penis tips as we have loathed
and possessed and loosed snakes from throat to beguile
and wreck, dear O our God and Sabbath has arrived like
a snowshoe hare, feed us Borax, Lysol, Drano, Dove to pre-
pare for its coat, cauterize guts on this Purification Day,
for corrosion clogs our veins, cauliflower hard, and works
in grain, oh yes, I have fornicated with wenches, embez-
zled cocaine, worshiped stags, bitten flesh, god damned
incessantly, and shot up pride like distilled dope, I must
scrape begging knees on gravel, crawl through shards
of glass to Your scrolls, Your Countenance, Your Dou-
ble Bowl, to consider destinies of blood-covered ice, froz-
en veins, ice pierced eyes draining tears, destinies of fate
on this solemn call to turn, wash me whole from my
maze, unclothed, filthy, dishonest, ingenuine, and cruel.

343

We come into Thy House, O Lord, to voice the longings of our
hearts in prayer. In the pressure of daily living, we often forget
Thee, and stifle the nobler impulses of our nature, the daily
abattoir, holocaust, and destitution industry; firm, corpor-
ation, agency, dealership, criminals slaughtering nobility
in the bunker of selves, the daily brawl for supremecy, ac-
quisition, seduction, desperation-fucking, bankruptcy, dumb
obedience in which prong punctures soul, God fading like
a cedar in fog, stuck in morass, country club liaisons, re-
lationship manipulations, we come into Thy House O Lord
with newly circumcised scalps to quicken heart's longing,
O Dear One surrounded by gravel pits, blast zones, tailing
ponds, we pour rats to red resonance booming outward
cleansing soul, pulsing prayer, forgotten Thee so thorough-
ly we thrashed, beguiled, swindled, and consigned as an
internalized rhapsody to everyday world, automatic and
bland, One, One, the million brilliancies, the imaginative
infinity in microscopic miracles: illuminate! we pray Thee
in unison on broken feet, when he died he knew everything.

344

Like the stars by day, our beloved dead are not seen with mortal eyes, but they shine on in the untroubled firmament of endless time. Let us be thankful for the companionship that continues in love that is stronger than death and spans the gulf of the grave, for the bereaved eat loneliness like empty fortune cookies and clasp in hands but knots of air on which to climb from pit of flaming ice onto street of spires and revolving doors, thankful then for the itch of amputated love whose flesh of air we scratch at night beneath roofs of twinkling stars which live by night and span by day the gulf of graves which swallow mere calcium, gelatin, and hair—the absorption mask of love—one doesn't love integument, jaw lubricant, blood, for companionship, yes, that stretches unbroken through the wastes of time beyond even the mourner's ash, flows eternal in endless moil like a bullet fired in weightless space, seen not mortally our beloved eyes but firmament, and so we love beyond the scrape in comfort wrapped, untroubled by flex, hex, or reflux, in faith's grasp that death survives, but dead forever the death of love.

345

And He shall judge between many peoples, and shall decide concerning mighty nations afar off; and they shall beat their swords into ploughshares, and their spears into pruning hooks nation shall not lift up sword against nation, armories shall transform into universities, battleships into hospitals, no bomb shall whistle down tube of air that does not explode into birds, tanks shall morph into columbines, Humvees into tourist trolleys, afar off mighty nations: United States, Germany, China, Japan He sternly shall legislate pudding, jelly, porridge, pie, they shall feed skeletons and dig spuds from howitzer casing, on forgiveness knees, weeping blood and self- flagellating before tribunals of the poor, ploughshares, pruning hooks, forage harvesters, grain threshers, and thees' knees shall tremble before Almighty Lord whose face is laser, razor, and rage, Earth apalm an embarrassed living ball warm, pulsing, combed by a seven-bladed tilling machine.

346

As I review my conduct during the months that are passed, I am deeply conscious of my shortcomings. Often righteousness called to me in vain and I yielded to selfishness, anger, and pride for I am stubborn and bitter on life and wish fellow humans ill, I double fists, hiss underbreath at the inferior, who are all, insipid minds fixated on cash and body mass, properties and view corridors, I stubbed my thumb in righteousness's eye and waltzed away like Astair, I God, I Omnipotent, I pray to Myself for salvation, my shortcomings mere paddies, vaguely fertile and cloying paddies, nothingmore, and like a legal villain I embraced cynicism, contempt, callousness, loft, I wished extinction upon mother, global financial collapse, and tides of grief over a catastrophic national event: a presidential assassination or high value hijacking, I am he popping out the blur of a worldwide brawl in sheeny tux, unscathed, Dom Perignon on arm one and on arm number two a hot wet babe molded into sandaled Sarah whose blood and brain possess an insatiable and irreconcilable blindness for me.

347

Except the Lord build the house, they labor in vain that build it; except the Lord keep the city, the watchman waketh but in vain for man's constructions crumble asunder, bricks but eyebrows and mortar spittle, O megalomaniacal weaklings, pathetic beasts muscles built on dumb machines, echoes of echoes, impotent braggers pumped full of vigor at architectural tables designing the world, envelopes of tiny valves and circulation, and like hunched fists of elimination over toilet bowls, straining, except Lord build house, except Lord keep city, thoroughfares strung with voltage like tinsel, what is this: high-rise, subway, penthouse, steam, important honkers, plate glass windows swallowing gawkers: Godless metropolis of bargains and steals, lords of industry in art deco squares spearing some delusion of importance, in his or her syphilitic contorted, spinal bifidic, crab-like external manifestation of the inner world, marrow and nerve, better naked to stand on a square foot of dirt religious toward God in faith's infinite house embarrassed premonitory and perishable.

348

Like as a father pitieth his children so the Lord pitieth them that fear Him. High as the heaven is above the earth, so great is His mercy toward them that revere Him, so let us pray: shelter me, protect me, gather me to Thy buxom, O Rock, O Redeemer, for pitiable am I with female tits, protruding ears, and can of brains, I rat-scurry into walls upon Your approach, dive basement-ward, vanish spontaneously in dread of Your retributive fist or revulsion, fear Me saith Lord, I tremble as tiny under rage, whelp, wet cat, and mercy coats like amniotic rain, cellophane over naked skin, and I skip blessedly pitied past the Bull & Finch, Andiamos, and Alphaville, Him revere them toward in cricket tails arrive I at Cloud Palace, Aston Martin tie and announced as Sir Rothschild the Pitiable and I glitter in His grace because jelly-legged beneath silk fire eats my flesh, ulcers of shame, cankers of woe at lowness and reptilianism and unendurable fear.

349

Let us rejoice in the light of day, in the glory and warmth of the sun, in the reawakening of life to duty and labor, covenant of toil with columnar legs, sturdy, trustworthy, coolant of sweat gland, internal fuel combustion engine, taste-tongue, brain, rotation eyes, one-piece skin, arms designed to swing sledge, long muscle backs to crate heave, all twelve trillion coordinated cells in respiratory confirmation, efficiency machines revived by morning, bird song, warmth waves, light washing night, queues, rows, marching duty, fried eggs, porridge, meat paddies, milk, coffee spoon tinkle, peck or no peck, collars like stiff feathers, rejoicement of responsibility, organism supple, discard the sag, husk, shell, pile, scrape concrete heave-ho, blight of loafer, and bring forth skyscraper, caisson phosphorrescence mortared in sacrifice, toes dug in boots—dams, dynamos, volcanic manufacturing—lids snapped open in floodlit pods, hands resurrected from inert repose acutely self-aware no longer sand or shiny plastic doll, medulla switched on circuitry red, subterranean gratitude for blissful unconsciousness from jack box heads within every pore, manhole cover duty scrapes into place, labor stirs red ants in the blood.

350

Remember us unto life, for you are the King who delights in life, and inscribe us in the Book of Life, that Your will may prevail, O God of life, for we exist powerless among magnets, death clamps neighbors, disease slides across tiger's eye, death breathes through wires, passes through mortar, You love blower, rubbery babe, the pinkish and fragrant, You fire thrower, pumping bellows, love egg factory and fertilizer farm, vital in roosters, sourdough, or convertibles, Unto Us Remember Life, warm beach sand powdering calves glittering for reproduction, Delighter in Life, ancient blood packets still yearning for yeast and top club, smacking nodules, clapping at quarterback sneaks, jacking off to nudes or mounting some equally vitalized crone on threadbare sheets, prevail we pray Thy will, permitting salivation, peristalsis, metabolism, elimination, wiping, and bliss, chips of stiff cut-up paper continuously snow steep-edged, flickering, piling on tables, benches, beds, drifting across roads, inscription be our prayer, prevail, persevere, dear Beauteous One, we implore, at the forthcoming masquerade don't of our dance partners rip costumes off scissors.

Index by Page

I would like to go / 11	I have decided I will do this / 74
To lay a sheet of light / 12	Double double toil and trouble / 75
Gently but authoritatively / 13	Bumpkee, bumpkee, bumpkee / 76
Afterward he wondered / 15	I had an affair / 77
I want to pour children / 17	These are the grotesqueries / 78
See me slice down / 19	He wanted to seduce her / 79
And when I pulled a ribbon fish / 21	And this little piggy squealed / 80
Oh Popsy-baby / 23	Sewed two cat heads / 81
In the penis colony / 24	When the bullets zinged / 82
I've taken flight / 25	First I prepare / 83
If I could stick my tongue / 26	And the two romantic lovers / 84
Like a field of soybeans / 27	The glorious night / 85
I pluck our baby / 29	He departed without food / 86
I like the feel of cutting / 30	The whole fish skeleton / 87
Cut the tip of my finger / 32	The bird cries it way / 88
It is the epoch of corporate / 33	I reach into the liquid ball of fire / 89
My father and Irving / 34	Stopped my mouth with cement / 90
Without consciously knowing it / 35	The iron slides across the blouse / 91
What was dinner time / 36	Again the taut monofilament / 92
There might have been a hurricane / 38	Assume a keen and precise perception / 93
I down the water hard / 39	Last night sprouted / 95
Fucking the Virgin Mary / 40	Let's say your son / 96
I tell a stranger / 41	Confessions of a lunatic / 97
So I'm watching Oprah / 42	I swallowed a quarter / 98
My wife and I debate this / 44	Do not cram that stillborn / 991
The right side of me cries / 46	Dear God, thank you / 100
I don't want to appear sentimental / 47	God has a glisten red / 101
It's time for humans to lie / 48	We run backward / 102
A bursting sun unrolls / 49	And how the head responds / 103
I've stopped thinking about / 50	If I have to take this crap / 104
Tightly they backed / 53	The great massive thing / 105
Watching professional ice hockey / 54	The big puffer sucking / 106
Well, I heard about / 56	One would predict / 107
She hacks the base / 57	Money and God duke it out / 108
Half gnawed, raw black / 58	For my next, ladies & gentlemen / 109
Fish scales filling / 59	Voice of a lunatic / 110
For an aphrodisiac / 61	Razor teeth fish swim / 111
The spook on my lap / 62	Doll wrestles the wet packed / 112
Each molecule of seawater / 63	Step outside your body / 113
When the gut growled / 64	Ooh, this bed's hard / 114
I say to myself / 65	Crows scrape through / 115
I love those people / 66	Because you pleasured him / 116
Am I more like steel / 67	The borders melted / 117
I strip the raised vein / 68	Dear and most of all venerable / 118
She pours her belly / 69	What, he desires me / 119
Son has tripped / 70	Religion breaks out / 120
Left eye, right eye / 71	Against my will I rip / 121
After binging / 72	Sander takes off skin / 122
One again the bombing planes / 73	Brick began, one / 123

Tears cold stone lid / 124
Wind ripped rain blows / 125
Head burst on fire / 126
Chastisement as prayer / 127
Behind every holocaust / 128
Verbal directions are horrid / 129
Smeared across God's face / 131
I give myself an award / 132
Exploded charred heart / 133
Dear and venerable king / 134
Huey, Dewey, and Louie / 135
Gof the griffin / 136
Most amiable and loving beast / 137
Come into me and / 138
The Jesus kite / 139
He needed something huge / 140
Vulgar poet, disgusting egotist / 141
Help me say the word / 142
Today he awoke with apples / 143
I eat my nervous system / 144
I stare at you mercilessly / 145
Man distracts woman / 146
My ideal mate / 147
I break my own heart / 148
The sun will not rise / 149
I have shorn and given to you, Delilah / 150
God and I, I punch / 151
I'm not your man / 152
She adores her tiny teeth / 153
I've got five chances left / 154
I give up on the whole fucking enterprise / 155
He ceased to eat / 156
This time god, I'm / 157
The monsters bent and demented / 158
Dearest God, veal, my female genital / 159
Testimony of the best pig / 160
I step toward dissolution / 161
When they pry apart / 162
This is me, here's my face / 163
God the sissy / 164
[I want to thank you for what you did ...] / 165
Mr. Knuckles worked me over / 166
What have I done, I've murdered / 167
A window washer / 168
Today I will die for a cause / 169
I loathe myself / 170
Dear God I wish to register / 171
Hello, I'm Gordon, I'm a sex addict / 172
I flip it upside down / 173

I pretend you're a fraud / 174
Lambs and apologies / 175
Dear Mother, murder Daddy / 176
First I razor free / 177
Bugs fly off hand / 178
I masturbate to fashion photos / 179
First we plunge knife into dog / 180
I pray for myself / 181
I create God in my image / 182
Men want to fuck God, not women / 183
Men and women hate their lives / 184
Elfington practiced love / 185
Bastard seeking bastardess / 186
Poetry the poison / 187
I have never loved anyone / 188
So here you are in my room / 189
Let us pray, then / 190
It is unimportant to me / 191
I, monstrous son / 192
Fall back upon the formula / 193
Bitch, cunt, slut / 194
Today the sun births / 195
In the distance a dog / 196
I compose a shocking poem / 197
Cassanova told me / 198
The young one bathe the lapis of love / 199
I blow lizards off brick / 200
As the lord taketh I kick / 201
One learns to eat one's dog / 202
Another toothy smile / 203
I bronze my sins / 204
Three o'clock, brain aches / 205
Everybody fucking everybody / 206
I eat myself / 207
I impregnate myself / 208
Sack of shit topped with head / 209
I lay my penis on a chopping block / 210
Mugwump, misanthrope / 211
I failed—poet, husband, father / 212
This phrase sees, this one clucks / 213
I crack open my father's mouth / 214
Dear God, speak to me / 215
I'm fascinated with the concept / 216
My lover's lips are razor blades / 217
Humility and its corollaries / 218
I'm profane / 219
Just fuck the man / 220
She's asleep, I'm painting her body / 221
And that was that / 222

The brain revives like a movie… / 223
Obscenities cleanse / 224
A woman's voice emanates / 225
Because I demand to be worshipped / 226
Everything I say he repeats / 227
The momentous event is upon us / 228
Executions: sawed-off to face / 229
I love the women I beat / 230
Extract and examine human uterus / 231
Whom should you loathe if not yourself / 232
Insignificant, trivial, meaningless / 233
Give me preference / 234
The dependable ecstasies / 235
Suicide being wisdom's pinnacle / 236
One cannot help but exclaim / 237
Humans love to fuck / 238
I commit the virtue of lying / 239
Look, man, what do you want / 240
"Shove it up your ass," / 241
Once again I praise devouring… / 242
Dogs don't seem to comprehend / 243
Because I love I invent love / 244
I dislike establishment poets / 245
Numerous possibilities present / 246
Insignificant cretin / 247
Let us pray, then, for everybody needs… / 248
I am in love with my daughter / 249
Pumping, I slam / 250
I go searching for Satan / 251
Everything misses the point / 252
I'm not sure, I have no idea / 253
Starvation terrifies / 254
Dear God, give me love / 255
Finally, one comes to nothing / 256
I'm not satiated, I want more / 257
I fasten with bolts / 258
Dearest and most wonderful supreme… / 259
Quickens the heart when son… / 260
Two steel balls attempt to kiss / 261
I have nothing to say / 262
Infant smashes against wall / 263
Nihilist, at age sixty / 264
Go ahead, steal behind / 265
Men desire beautiful women / 266
A yellow jacket stings her eye / 267
I consume Internet porn / 268
I hold the keyboard upside down / 269
I erect a shrine to my member / 270
The noblest act is the act of self-hatred / 271
Words in manuscript conspire / 272
The whole thing goes kablooy / 273
I down bottles of Ipecac / 274
I masturbate myself bloody / 275
I love you is storm / 276
Addicted to Jesus / 277
I think of nobody but myself / 278
I'm going to make you pity / 279
I have nothing cataclysmic / 280
I give myself a colonoscopy / 281
To cement her surrender / 282
I've witnessed mother's vagina / 283
What spectacular sky / 284
Men don't kiss / 285
You're weary of me / 286
I starve my two dogs / 287
While petitioning God to fix my cancer / 288
First I destroy the cat / 289
Sylvester smashes into frying pan / 290
You suck, you make me sick / 291
I do not hate Jews / 292
Husband and wife privately vow / 293
None of us added up / 294
Not even porn gets me hard / 295
I fornicate with myself / 296
Experimenting with the concept… / 297
I adore you but hate your presence / 298
Better to go unloved / 299
One wants to rage at the ill / 300
Jew haters invade / 301
I want to write something fabulous / 302
I'm wedged inside my mother's cunt / 303
It's okay, that ubiquitous / 304
Because I am extraordinary / 305
I shut drawers / 306
I set ablaze Q-tip torches / 307
Miniature dog like an electric razor / 308
Said aliens raped her / 309
I tell my adult kids / 310
Something he covets suspends / 311
While I masturbated / 312
Comfortable with the concept of total… / 313
I shove Daddy into Mother's cunt / 314
In the final scene innumerable arrows / 315
He thinks she worships him / 316
I laugh satirically / 317
Oh yea, yea / 318
I need a god, I become a champ / 319
That's a laugh, laughing head off / 320

I invent a machine   / 321
I wish I could do that   / 322
I beg to interrupt   / 323
I learn that Hitler was a necrophiliac   / 324
Everything's sloppy   / 325
He throws himself   / 326
For thirty years' service   / 327
I operate alone   / 328
One spends one's life   / 329
In the meantime pagans rampage   / 330
Stomach hurts, stuffed with wheat…   / 331
Do you think, do you really   / 332
I don't want to be friend   / 333
Clown death, Bozo death   / 334
Singing, I spin   / 335
I'm unparalleled, I'm God   / 336
I herewith pronounce you   / 337
I drink until black out   / 338
Beheaded twitching slaughtered…   / 339
God dwells in partially digested   / 340
I lay on carpet and spread legs   / 341
Wielding a cigarette with a needle   / 342
I return as a raving hag   / 343
Simultaneously, I fuck a woman…   / 344
What shall we say before Thee   / 347
We have turned aside   / 348
God and God of our fathers   / 349
We sanctify Thy name on earth   / 350
For he satisfieth the longing heart   / 351
Hear oh Israel the Lord Thy God   / 352
Open unto us, O God   / 353
And they that shall be of Thee   / 354
Thine everlasting arms, oh Lord   / 355
On this Sabbath of remembrance   / 356
We beseech Thee, O Lord   / 357
O, Thou who dost reveal Thyself   / 358
Thy bestoweth loving kindness…   / 359
God and Father we have entered   / 360
When storms of oppression beat…   / 361
The Lord is my shepherd   / 362
And now ere we part   / 363
Therefore, hast Thou, O Father   / 364
O Lord, keep my tongue   / 365
We thank Thee for the life   / 366
To you who mourn the loss   / 367
Thy rod and thy staff   / 368
O God of holiness, Thy knowest   / 369
On this Sabbath of repentance   / 370
We come into Thy house, O Lord   / 371
Like the stars by day our beloved dead   / 372
And He shall judge between many…   / 373
As I review my conduct   / 374
Except the Lord build the house   / 375
Like as a father pitieth his children   / 376
Let us rejoice in the light   / 377
Remember us unto life   / 378

Index by First Line

A bursting sun unrolls   / 49
A window washer   / 168
A woman's voice emanates   / 225
A yellow jacket stings her eye   / 267
Addicted to Jesus   / 277
After binging   / 72
Afterward he wondered   / 15
Again the taut monofilament   / 92
Against my will I rip   / 121
Am I more like steel   / 67
And He shall judge between many...   / 373
And how the head responds   / 103
And now ere we part   / 363
And that was that   / 222
And the two romantic lovers   / 84
And they that shall be of Thee   / 354
And this little piggy squealed   / 80
And when I pulled a ribbon fish   / 21
Another toothy smile   / 203
As I review my conduct   / 374
As the lord taketh I kick   / 201
Assume a keen and precise perception   / 93
Bastard seeking bastardess   / 186
Because I am extraordinary   / 305
Because I demand to be worshipped   / 226
Because I love I invent love   / 244
Because you pleasured him   / 116
Beheaded twitching slaughtered...   / 339
Behind every holocaust   / 128
Better to go unloved   / 299
Bitch, cunt, slut   / 194
Brick began, one   / 123
Bugs fly off hand   / 178
Bumpkee, bumpkee, bumpkee   / 76
Cassanova told me   / 198
Chastisement as prayer   / 127
Clown death, Bozo death   / 334
Come into me and   / 138
Comfortable with the concept   / 313
Confessions of a lunatic   / 97
Crows scrape through   / 115
Cut the tip of my finger   / 32
Dear and most of all venerable   / 118
Dear and venerable king   / 134
Dear God I wish to register   / 171
Dear God, give me love   / 255
Dear God, speak to me   / 215
Dear God, thank you   / 100
Dear Mother, murder Daddy   / 176

Dearest and most wonderful supreme...   / 259
Dearest God, veal, my female genital   / 159
Do not cram that stillborn   / 991
Do you think, do you really   / 332
Dogs don't seem to comprehend   / 243
Doll wrestles the wet packed   / 112
Double double toil and trouble   / 75
Each molecule of seawater   / 63
Elfington practiced love   / 185
Everybody fucking everybody   / 206
Everything I say he repeats   / 227
Everything misses the point   / 252
Everything's sloppy   / 325
Except the Lord build the house   / 375
Executions: sawed-off to face   / 229
Experimenting with the concept...   / 297
Exploded charred heart   / 133
Extract and examine human uterus   / 231
Fall back upon the formula   / 193
Finally, one comes to nothing   / 256
First I destroy the cat   / 289
First I prepare   / 83
First I razor free   / 177
First we plunge knife into dog   / 180
Fish scales filling   / 59
For an aphrodisiac   / 61
For he satisfieth the longing heart   / 351
For my next, ladies & gentlemen   / 109
For thirty years' service   / 327
Fucking the Virgin Mary   / 40
Gently but authoritatively   / 13
Give me preference   / 234
Go ahead, steal behind   / 265
God and Father we have entered   / 360
God and God of our fathers   / 349
God and I, I punch   / 151
God dwells in partially digested   / 340
God has a glisten red   / 101
God the sissy   / 164
Gof the griffin   / 136
Half gnawed, raw black   / 58
He ceased to eat   / 156
He departed without food   / 86
He needed something huge   / 140
He thinks she worships him   / 316
He throws himself   / 326
He wanted to seduce her   / 79
Head burst on fire   / 126
Hear oh Israel the Lord Thy God   / 352

Hello, I'm Gordon, I'm a sex addict / 172
Help me say the word / 142
Huey, Dewey, and Louie / 135
Humans love to fuck / 238
Humility and its corollaries / 218
Husband and wife privately vow / 293
I adore you but hate your presence / 298
I am in love with my daughter / 249
I beg to interrupt / 323
I blow lizards off brick / 200
I break my own heart / 148
I bronze my sins / 204
I commit the virtue of lying / 239
I compose a shocking poem / 197
I consume Internet porn / 268
I crack open my father's mouth / 214
I create God in my image / 182
I dislike establishment poets / 245
I do not hate Jews / 292
I don't want to appear sentimental / 47
I don't want to be friend / 333
I down bottles of Ipecac / 274
I down the water hard / 39
I drink until black out / 338
I eat my nervous system / 144
I eat myself / 207
I erect a shrine to my member / 270
I failed—poet, husband, father / 212
I fasten with bolts / 258
I flip it upside down / 173
I fornicate with myself / 296
I give myself a colonoscopy / 281
I give myself an award / 132
I give up on the whole fucking... / 155
I go searching for Satan / 251
I had an affair / 77
I have decided I will do this / 74
I have never loved anyone / 188
I have nothing cataclysmic / 280
I have nothing to say / 262
I have shorn and given to you, Delilah / 150
I herewith pronounce you / 337
I hold the keyboard upside down / 269
I impregnate myself / 208
I invent a machine / 321
I laugh satirically / 317
I lay my penis on a chopping block / 210
I lay on carpet and spread legs / 341
I learn that Hitler was a necrophiliac / 324

I like the feel of cutting / 30
I loathe myself / 170
I love the women I beat / 230
I love those people / 66
I love you is storm / 276
I masturbate myself bloody / 275
I masturbate to fashion photos / 179
I need a god, I become a champ / 319
I operate alone / 328
I pluck our baby / 29
I pray for myself / 181
I pretend you're a fraud / 174
I reach into the liquid ball of fire / 89
I return as a raving hag / 343
I say to myself / 65
I set ablaze Q-tip torches / 307
I shove Daddy into Mother's cunt / 314
I shut drawers / 306
I stare at you mercilessly / 145
I starve my two dogs / 287
I step toward dissolution / 161
I strip the raised vein / 68
I swallowed a quarter / 98
I tell a stranger / 41
I tell my adult kids / 310
I think of nobody but myself / 278
I want to pour children / 17
[I want to thank you for what you did...] / 165
I want to write something fabulous / 302
I wish I could do that / 322
I would like to go / 11
I, monstrous son / 192
I'm wedged inside my mother's cunt / 303
I'm fascinated with the concept / 216
I'm going to make you pity / 279
I'm not satiated, I want more / 257
I'm not sure, I have no idea / 253
I'm not your man / 152
I'm profane / 219
I'm unparalleled, I'm God / 336
I've got five chances left / 154
I've stopped thinking about / 50
I've taken flight / 25
I've witnessed mother's vagina / 283
If I could stick my tongue / 26
If I have to take this crap / 104
In the distance a dog / 196
In the final scene innumerable arrows / 315
In the meantime pagans rampage / 330

In the penis colony   / 24
Infant smashes against wall   / 263
Insignificant cretin   / 247
Insignificant, trivial, meaningless   / 233
It is the epoch of corporate   / 33
It is unimportant to me   / 191
It's okay, that ubiquitous   / 304
It's time for humans to lie   / 48
Jew haters invade   / 301
Just fuck the man   / 220
Lambs and apologies   / 175
Last night sprouted   / 95
Left eye, right eye   / 71
Let us pray, then   / 190
Let us pray, then, for everybody needs…   / 248
Let us rejoice in the light   / 377
Let's say your son   / 96
Like a field of soybeans   / 27
Like as a father pitieth his children   / 376
Like the stars by day our beloved dead   / 372
Look, man, what do you want   / 240
Man distracts woman   / 146
Men and women hate their lives   / 184
Men desire beautiful women   / 266
Men don't kiss   / 285
Men want to fuck God, not women   / 183
Miniature dog like an electric razor   / 308
Money and God duke it out   / 108
Most amiable and loving beast   / 137
Mr. Knuckles worked me over   / 166
Mugwump, misanthrope   / 211
My father and Irving   / 34
My ideal mate   / 147
My lover's lips are razor blades   / 217
My wife and I debate this   / 44
Nihilist, at age sixty   / 264
None of us added up   / 294
Not even porn gets me hard   / 295
Numerous possibilities present   / 246
O God of holiness, Thy knowest   / 369
O Lord, keep my tongue   / 365
O, Thou who dost reveal Thyself   / 358
Obscenities cleanse   / 224
Oh Popsy-baby   / 23
Oh yea, yea   / 318
On this Sabbath of remembrance   / 356
On this Sabbath of repentance   / 370
Once again I praise devouring stomach   / 242
One again the bombing planes   / 73

One cannot help but exclaim   / 237
One learns to eat one's dog   / 202
One spends one's life   / 329
One wants to rage at the ill   / 300
One would predict   / 107
Ooh, this bed's hard   / 114
Open unto us, O God   / 353
Poetry the poison   / 187
Pumping, I slam   / 250
Quickens the heart when son bashes…   / 260
Razor teeth fish swim   / 111
Religion breaks out   / 120
Remember us unto life   / 378
Sack of shit topped with head   / 209
Said aliens raped her   / 309
Sander takes off skin   / 122
See me slice down   / 19
Sewed two cat heads   / 81
She adores her tiny teeth   / 153
She hacks the base   / 57
She pours her belly   / 69
She's asleep, I'm painting her body   / 221
"Shove it up your ass,"   / 241
Simultaneously, I fuck a woman…   / 344
Singing, I spin   / 335
Smeared across God's face   / 131
So here you are in my room   / 189
So I'm watching Oprah   / 42
Something he covets suspends   / 311
Son has tripped   / 70
Starvation terrifies   / 254
Step outside your body   / 113
Stomach hurts, stuffed with wheat thins   / 331
Stopped my mouth with cement   / 90
Suicide being wisdom's pinnacle   / 236
Sylvester smashes into frying pan   / 290
Tears cold stone lid   / 124
Testimony of the best pig   / 160
That's a laugh, laughing head off   / 320
The big puffer sucking   / 106
The bird cries it way   / 88
The borders melted   / 117
The brain revives like a movie monster   / 223
The dependable ecstasies   / 235
The glorious night   / 85
The great massive thing   / 105
The iron slides across the blouse   / 91
The Jesus kite   / 139
The Lord is my shepherd   / 362

The momentous event is upon us   / 228
The monsters bent and demented   / 158
The noblest act is the act of self-hatred   / 271
The right side of me cries   / 46
The spook on my lap   / 62
The sun will not rise   / 149
The whole fish skeleton   / 87
The whole thing goes kablooy   / 273
The young one bathe the lapis of love   / 199
There might have been a hurricane   / 38
Therefore, hast Thou, O Father   / 364
These are the grotesqueries   / 78
Thine everlasting arms, oh Lord   / 355
This is me, here's my face   / 163
This phrase sees, this one clucks   / 213
This time god, I'm   / 157
Three o'clock, brain aches   / 205
Thy bestoweth loving kindness on all   / 359
Thy rod and thy staff   / 368
Tightly they backed   / 53
To cement her surrender   / 282
To lay a sheet of light   / 12
To you who mourn the loss   / 367
Today he awoke with apples   / 143
Today I will die for a cause   / 169
Today the sun births   / 195
Two steel balls attempt to kiss   / 261
Verbal directions are horrid   / 129
Voice of a lunatic   / 110
Vulgar poet, disgusting egotist   / 141
Watching professional ice hockey   / 54
We beseech Thee, O Lord   / 357
We come into Thy house, O Lord   / 371
We have turned aside   / 348
We run backward   / 102
We sanctify Thy name on earth   / 350
We thank Thee for the life   / 366
Well, I heard about   / 56
What have I done, I've murdered   / 167
What shall we say before Thee   / 347
What spectacular sky   / 284
What was dinner time   / 36
What, he desires me   / 119
When storms of oppression beat down   / 361
When the bullets zinged   / 82
When the gut growled   / 64
When they pry apart   / 162
While I masturbated   / 312
While petitioning God to fix my cancer   / 288
Whom should you loathe if not yourself   / 232
Wielding a cigarette with a needle   / 342
Wind ripped rain blows   / 125
Without consciously knowing it   / 35
Words in manuscript conspire   / 272
You suck, you make me sick   / 291
You're weary of me   / 286

photo by Patricia Corley

Gordon Massman

was born in 1949, in Corpus Christi, Texas, and attended the University of Texas—Austin, and the University of Alaska—Fairbanks. For twenty-five years he acquired scholarly and trade books in the social sciences and humanities for various scholarly and commercial publishers including The University of Wisconsin Press and Westview Press. He now teaches writing and literature at The Massachusetts College of Liberal Arts in North Adams, Massachusetts, and lives in Plainfield, Massachusetts.

About NYQ Books™

NYQ Books™ was established in 2009 as an imprint of The New York Quarterly Foundation, Inc. Its mission is to augment the *New York Quarterly* poetry magazine by providing an additional venue for poets already published in the magazine. A lifelong dream of NYQ's founding editor, William Packard, NYQ Books™ has been made possible by both growing foundation support and new technology that was not available during William Packard's lifetime. We are proud to present these books to you and hope that you will continue to support The New York Quarterly Foundation, Inc. and our poets and that you will enjoy these other titles from NYQ Books™:

Barbara Blatner	*The Still Position*
Amanda J. Bradley	*Hints and Allegations*
rd coleman	*beach tracks*
Joanna Crispi	*Soldier in the Grass*
Franz Douskey	*West of Midnight*
Ira Joe Fisher	*Songs from an Earlier Century*
Sanford Fraser	*Tourist*
Tony Gloeggler	*The Last Lie*
Adam Hughes	*Petrichor*
Ted Jonathan	*Bones & Jokes*
Luke Johnson	*After the Ark*
Richard Kostelanetz	*Recircuits*
Iris Lee	*Urban Bird Life*
Linda Lerner	*Takes Guts & Years Sometimes*
Tony Medina	*My Father Was Always on the Lam*
Michael Montlack	*Cool Limbo*
Kevin Pilkington	*In the Eyes of a Dog*
Jim Reese	*ghost on 3rd*
F. D. Reeve	*The Puzzle Master and Other Poems*
Jackie Sheeler	*Earthquake Came to Harlem*
Jayne Lyn Stahl	*Riding with Destiny*
Shelley Stenhouse	*Impunity*
Tim Suermondt	*Just Beautiful*
Douglas Treem	*Everything So Seriously*
Oren Wagner	*Voluptuous Gloom*
Joe Weil	*The Plumber's Apprentice*
Pui Ying Wong	*Yellow Plum Season*
Fred Yannantuono	*A Boilermaker for the Lady*
Grace Zabriskie	*Poems*

Please visit our website for these and other titles:

www.nyqbooks.org